Special Educational Needs and Disabilities in Schools

Also available from Bloomsbury

Reflective Teaching in Schools Andrew Pollard

Readings for Reflective Teaching in Schools edited by Andrew Pollard

Reflective Teaching in Early Education Jennifer Colwell

Readings for Reflective Teaching in Early Education edited by Jennifer Colwell and Andrew Pollard

Reflective Teaching in Further, Adult and Vocational Education Margaret Gregson and Yvonne Hillier

Readings for Reflective Teaching in Further, Adult and Vocational Education edited by Margaret Gregson, Lawrence Nixon, Andrew Pollard and Trish Spedding

Reflective Teaching in Higher Education Paul Ashwin

Pastoral Care 11–16: A Critical Introduction edited by Noel Purdy

Special Educational Needs and Disabilities in Schools

A Critical Introduction

Janice Wearmouth

Online resources to accompany this book are available at:
http://bloomsbury.com/cw/special-educational-needs-and-disabilities-in-schools/

Please type the URL into your web browser and follow the instructions to access the Companion Website. If you experience any problems, please contact Bloomsbury at: contact@bloomsbury.com

Wherever you see you can find accompanying resources on the companion website.

Bloomsbury Academic
An imprint of Bloomsbury Publishing Plc

B L O O M S B U R Y
LONDON · OXFORD · NEW YORK · NEW DELHI · SYDNEY

Bloomsbury Academic

An imprint of Bloomsbury Publishing Plc

50 Bedford Square   1385 Broadway
London   New York
WC1B 3DP   NY 10018
UK   USA

www.bloomsbury.com

BLOOMSBURY and the Diana logo are trademarks of Bloomsbury Publishing Plc

First published 2017
Reprinted 2017

© Janice Wearmouth, 2017

References to legislation related to special educational, or additional support, needs across the United Kingdom are correct at the time of writing, December, 2016. However, legislation is always open to modification and development and may be changed over time.

British Library Cataloguing-in-Publication Data
A catalogue record for this book is available from the British Library.

ISBN: HB: 978-1-4742-8763-0
PB: 978-1-4742-8762-3
ePDF: 978-1-4742-8761-6
ePub: 978-1-4742-8764-7

Library of Congress Cataloging-in-Publication Data
Names: Wearmouth, Janice, author.
Title: Special educational needs and disabilities in schools :
a critical introduction / Janice Wearmouth.
Description: London ; New York : Bloomsbury Academic, 2017. |
Includes bibliographical references and index.
Identifiers: LCCN 2016052064| ISBN 9781474287630 (hardback) |
ISBN 9781474287647 (epub)
Subjects: LCSH: Learning disabled children–Education–Great Britain. |
Special education teachers–Professional relationships–Great Britain. |
BISAC: EDUCATION / General. | EDUCATION /
Special Education / Learning Disabilities.
Classification: LCC LC4706.G7 W43 2017 | DDC 371.90941–dc23 LC record
available at https://lccn.loc.gov/2016052064

Cover image © ducu59us/Shutterstock

Typeset by Newgen Knowledge Works (P) Ltd., Chennai, India.
Printed and bound in Great Britain

Contents

List of Figures

List of Tables

Preface

This book has been designed as a key resource in supporting student teachers during and beyond their teaching training, as well as others interested in education, to begin to understand how, and to be able, to address the special educational, and/or additional support, needs of children and young people within schools and colleges. Legislation across the United Kingdom and in Northern Ireland has established the legal requirement to ensure the availability of provision for special educational, or additional support, needs and disabilities in schools and, as in England for the first time, in further education colleges. In England, for example, the Children and Families Act, introduced in September 2014, has strengthened and extended this legislation. Under the terms of Section 19(d) of Part 3 of this Act, simply to ensure that young people with special educational needs and disability (SEND) have access to an appropriate education is no longer sufficient. Instead, it specifies access that enables young people to 'achieve the best possible' educational and other outcomes. This reflects a new and higher level of outcome required by law. *Codes of Practice* to ensure that education law in this area is implemented in schools and colleges have been developed in each of the four countries. These *Codes* have the status of statutory guidance. Teachers in schools (and, in England, colleges) continue to be expected to provide effective learning opportunities for all their pupils, including those who have special educational needs and/or disabilities. Schools, colleges and other settings have clear duties under the statutory guidance of the *Code* that applies in their own geographical area.

Current legislation promotes the inclusion of (almost) all young people in mainstream schools and colleges. However this often has to be implemented within a national context of school and college 'improvement' and competition and market-oriented practices where, in some (but not all!) places, young people who experience difficulties may not be welcomed. Such challenges are not necessarily insurmountable however and the book discusses the debates and dilemmas and offers practical suggestions to address these. It is essential that all involved understand what 'having' a special educational, or additional support, need or disability means for the young person and his/her family, and what addressing such needs and/or disabilities entails in schools.

Chapter 1, 'Special educational, or additional support, needs and disability: General considerations', discusses issues related to the whole concept of special educational, or additional support, needs and disabilities in schools and colleges, and ways of meeting these needs. Included in this chapter is a discussion of theories of learning and behaviour that are commonly used to underpin the way programmes are designed to address young people's special educational, or additional support, needs and disabilities. The chapter concludes by setting out the principles of a successful problem-solving approach to including children with needs of this kind in learning activities.

For **Chapter 2**, 'A historical perspective and the current legal position', an overarching question is set: what should be, and has in the past been, done with children who make little or no progress and who were/are thought to be holding others back? This chapter first offers an overview of the history of provision for children seen as 'different' from peers on account of the learning or physical difficulties they experienced, or the behaviour they displayed, and the changes in thinking about learning, behaviour and children's rights over time. This begins from the inception of vocational education for those who experienced physical and/or sensory impairments and moves through to current approaches to inclusive education and its associated policy, practice and legal framework. It continues by outlining current legislative frameworks for special educational, or additional support, provision in schools and colleges in countries across the United Kingdom, England, Scotland and Wales, and Northern Ireland.

Chapter 3, 'Assessment of, and planning for, learning needs', opens by discussing ways to assess the degree to which classrooms are inclusive and teaching differentiated so that fewer individual learning or behaviour needs arise in the first place. It continues by explaining why the whole area of assessment is so controversial in schools, how some young people can be devalued by it, and others privileged, outlining ways to assess needs at the level of the individual student, and considers the place of, and appropriate tools to enable, assessment of learning, behaviour and sensory needs. This includes discussion of students' and families' perceptions of needs. Finally the chapter reflects on the formalities of statutory assessment in the various areas of the United Kingdom.

Chapter 4, 'Approaches to understanding and addressing four areas of need', acknowledges that need can be interpreted in different ways and that, in a sense, the definition of the four broad areas in the *Code of Practice* in England (DfE, 2015) is an administrative convenience. It then takes the four areas of need with examples of each, and discusses issues around addressing these needs in classrooms in ways that assume children are active agents in their own learning.

Chapter 5, 'Focus on literacy difficulties', acknowledges that, as in other curriculum areas, good quality teaching predisposes to fewer difficulties in literacy acquisition arising in the first place. We recognise that many of the approaches discussed here in relation to supporting the literacy development of all students may well be appropriate for use with those who experience specific difficulties in literacy learning, such as dyslexia. We begin this chapter by reflecting on the attributes of an effective teacher of literacy for a diverse range of students in a classroom and go on to consider a range of understandings of the literacy learning process, and approaches that reflect these understandings. We then discuss issues of reading comprehension, accuracy and written expression, with suggestions of 'tried and tested' ways to address these areas of literacy learning at different ages and stages. We conclude by examining the issue of difficulties of a dyslexic nature: theoretical explanations, policy implications and practical strategies for overcoming barriers to learning.

Chapter 6, 'Focus on numeracy difficulties', opens with a brief overview of the attributes of effective mathematics teachers and characteristics of inclusive mathematics classrooms. We outline the skills needed to be a good mathematician in school and reflect these against some of the cognitive difficulties experienced by students. We go on to consider, and then look in more detail at, areas of mathematics learning with which some students may struggle and some of the ways to begin to deal with these. We conclude by discussing the issue of specific numeracy difficulties and strategies to address these.

Chapter 7, 'Focus on behaviour in schools and colleges', begins with a discussion of the links between school failure, disaffection and challenging or otherwise socially inappropriate behaviour. In this discussion, we consider the importance of ensuring that the learning environment predisposes to positive learning and behaviour and thus reduce the probability of disaffection in the first place and reflect on frameworks to underpin this at school and classroom level. We offer an overview of the theories that we draw on to discuss understandings of behaviour experienced by peers and teachers as anti-social, and go on to discuss ways to address the issues, in particular as these relate to attention deficit/hyperactivity disorder (AD/HD), physical aggression and bullying.

Chapter 8, 'Uses of technology to support learning needs', poses the question: What, if anything, can be achieved by using technology to support young people's learning in situations that would not be achieved otherwise? It sets out a practical way of carrying out an audit of need to highlight whether the use of technology is appropriate in the first place for the student and the learning context. The chapter goes on to discuss the range of technology that is available in schools to support young people's special learning needs, with examples.

Chapter 9, 'Professional relationships with others', first outlines the range of people with whom teachers might be expected to work in support of children who experience some sort of difficulty, and their likely role: the special educational needs co-ordinator, teaching assistants, parents and families, outside agencies and so on. It goes on to discuss challenges in relation to this kind of partnership work, with examples of what can happen in practice. This discussion includes issues of planning as well as what might be considered examples of good practice.

The final chapter, **Chapter 10**, 'Including young people: Moving forward', discusses the importance of policy and practice in this area of education and the inherent challenges.

Chapter 1
Special educational, or additional support, needs and disability: General considerations

The major questions in this chapter are:

- What might be seen as the 'special educational' or 'additional support' needs of young people in school?
- How should we understand the learning of all young people?
- What issues should be taken into account in labelling these young people as 'needy' in some way: positives and negatives?
- What theories of learning and behaviour are commonly used to underpin the way that programmes are designed to address young people's special educational, or additional support, needs and disabilities?

Introduction

The way in which educational provision is currently organised is a product both of its own history and of the values, beliefs and political ideology of our society (Wearmouth, 2009; Broadfoot, 2011). Over the years, special, or additional, educational provision has been characterised by a number of recurring themes. For example, there is the question of whether to separate off children who experience difficulties of various kinds into a special segregated provision or integrate them into the mainstream. Then there is the issue of what kind of curriculum should be offered: whether it should be the same for all children or different for some groups. For many years there was debate about whether some young people are capable of being educated in any form that is recognisable as 'education' at all. Echoing down the years, too, has been discussion about whether, and how, to classify children into the various groupings of difficulties. As a corollary of this, if classification is seen as appropriate, the question is what characterises the differences both between the groupings themselves and between the children so classified and others, and what value can be deduced from the kind of provision that is deemed to be appropriate for which group.

Discourses associated with special educational, or additional support, needs and disability, learning and behaviour

Over time, a number of discourses (the frames of reference used to talk about and interpret what is around us) have become important in the world of special educational needs and disability (SEND), and additional support needs. We often use the terms 'special educational', or 'additional support', needs as if we all know what they mean, while at the same time we all know that we can define 'need' in different ways. It is important to recognise these frames of reference and have a grasp of how they are used in order to understand SEND policy, practice and provision.

 Reflective activity: Learning from personal experiences of difficulties in learning

We can only make sense of new ideas and information in terms of what we already know. It is hard to learn unless what we are reading about, listening to or looking at makes sense to us. In a conversation with the author, a number of colleagues reflected on what was the hardest thing they had ever tried to do:

- What it was that made it so hard?
- Did they succeed?
- If so, what helped them to do this?
- If not how did it make them feel?
- What might have helped them?

Try this activity for yourself.

Responses to what it was that made the task so hard seemed to fall into a number of categories:

- too big a gap between current level of understanding and/or skill and what was required to complete the task;

- poor level of teaching or support on offer;
- lack of confidence or belief that they would be successful;
- excessive anxiety that filled their heads and prevented them from thinking clearly;
- prior belief, gained from previous experience of failure, that they would fail again.

For the current author, the hardest text she ever tried to read was the text of Shakespeare's Macbeth in school at the age of 13. The teacher had given no introduction or explanation. She remembered feeling bemused, and then frustrated and stupid by turns, as a result of the unfamiliar language and vocabulary of the play. She certainly did not want to admit out loud to any of her classmates that she could not cope with the text. She became completely hostile to the suggestion of anything Shakespearean for years afterwards – until a very good live production and excellent acting made the plot clear and undid the damage.

Without a way of relating to the words and ideas in a text we are not likely to be interested in it. Learning happens in the same way for all students of any age. What would have helped the author to make more sense of Macbeth, and what she needed, was a clear introduction at the beginning, perhaps watching a film of the play (had it been available at the time) and teacher explanation of the vocabulary.

When you tried this activity, how did your experiences reflect those described above?

What is implied by 'special educational' or 'additional support' needs?

 ### Reflective activity: Defining 'needs' in educational terms

We all know that we can define 'needs' in different ways. For example, a need might be interpreted as rooted in:

- social factors, for example, family poverty and unemployment, or
- cultural differences in understanding and expectations between family and school, or
- the immediate learning environment, for example, inappropriate teaching methods or texts, or inadequate school resources, or
- attributes of the learner him/herself.

However, it is only when we have a clear definition that we can begin to answer questions about how those 'needs' can be addressed in the context of education.

> Take a few moments to note down how you would define 'need' in general terms and then either 'special educational needs' or 'additional support needs' in education.

Defining needs

'Need' can be understood in relation to a situation in which something must be supplied for a desired goal to be achieved. Needs can range from the necessities of life (food, drink, shelter, and so on), if the goal is basic survival, to literature, music, conversation with others, and so on, if the goal is to satisfy human intellectual and social needs. Apart from basic survival, needs will vary from one society or culture to another, from place to place and age group to age group because societal norms and goals vary.

Translated into the context of education, educational needs can therefore be seen in relation to what a young person requires in order to be able to achieve the goals of the education system within which s/he is a student. Who has, or should have, the power to decide what the goals of any national education system should be is, of course, a political question. The *Primary Review Research Survey 1/2 Aims and Values in Primary Education: England and other countries* (Shuayb & O'Donnell, 2008) carried out as part of Alexander's Primary Review makes particularly interesting reading in this regard. It notes (para 2) that 'in the last 40 years, primary education in […] countries of the study has witnessed considerable change and, in some cases, restructuring'. Two main influences shaped the aims of education and, within this, the goals of special education.

1.1

> The first, put forward by advocates of a child-centred and progressive education, calls for a flexible and autonomous system of primary education […] the second, driven more by a country's political and socio-economic goals, emphasises centralisation and standardisation. (Shuayb & O'Donnell, 2008, para 2)

Under the Labour government of the 1960s there was a child-centred approach strongly manifested in the (1967) Plowden Report Central Advisory Council for Education) which largely endorsed emphasis on individualisation (child-centredness) and learning by discovery. The most significant effect of this approach was, in terms of special education, 'changing attitudes towards […] pupils with special educational needs' (para 2.1). In England this resulted in a range of legislation and policy documents, published later in the 1970s, that related specifically to the needs of individual 'handicapped' children.

1.2

Most recently, in relation to special educational provision in England, for example, the increased focus on schools' accountability for the measured achievement of their students and the need to achieve targets set for all students has been reflected in a number of ways.

> By the end of each key stage, pupils are expected to know, apply and understand the matters, skills and processes specified in the relevant programme of study. (DfE, 2013a, p. 18)

Necessarily, therefore, students' needs should be seen in relation to what they require to meet these targets. The first *Code of Practice for the identification and assessment of special educational needs* (DfE, 1994) was introduced with its status of statutory guidance, to be used as a shared text at special educational needs tribunals that were established on the model of industrial tribunals to hear the appeals of families who were dissatisfied with the special provision that had been made to address their children's special educational needs. Many schools have become concerned to have the students whom they identified as under-achieving assessed for the purpose of accessing the special or additional resources, such as teaching assistants, that might assist them to achieve more highly. Between 1997 and 2003 there was a 99% increase in teaching assistants in English schools for this reason. 1.3

The aims of education are not framed in the same way in all countries of the United Kingdom, however. For example, in Scotland, where the term used is 'additional support' rather than 'special educational' needs:

> the development of a **Curriculum for Excellence** (Scottish Executive 2004) [. . .] focused on developing successful learners, confident individuals, responsible citizens, and effective contributors. It also emphasised values of wisdom, justice, compassion and integrity. (Shuayb & O'Donnell, 2008, para 2.4)

Formal definitions of 'special educational' and 'additional support' needs

Special educational needs

In England, Northern Ireland and, at the time of writing, in Wales also, legislation, government publications, regulations, official circulars, consultation, advice and guidance documents employ the expression 'children with special educational needs and/or disability' (SEND). Therefore, as we discuss more fully in the next chapter, schools are required to operate within the law which pertains to SEND.

Under the terms of the relevant legislation a child[1] has special educational needs if he or she has a learning difficulty[2] that calls for special educational provision to be made for him or her (Education Act, 1996, Part 1V, §312(1), Education Order (Northern Ireland), 1996, Part 11, §3(1); (Children and Families Act, 2014, Part 3, §20 (1)). That is, a young person only has 'special educational needs' when special provision is required to meet them. We discuss the issues involved with this definition in Chapter 2. Suffice it to say here that what is meant by 'learning difficulty' is not as straightforward as it sounds. 1.4 1.5 1.6

---

[1]child or young person in England
[2]or disability in England

1.7   The situation is different in Scotland. Here, the Education (Additional Support for Learning) (Scotland) Act (2004) (as amended – see Chapter 2 for discussion of this law) established the concept of 'additional support needs'. Under this Act, a child or young person has such needs if 'for whatever reason', s/he is not likely to be able 'to benefit from school education provided or to be provided' for him/her 'without the provision of additional support' (Scottish Government, p. 18, §1).

It is not simply the complexity of the term within the legal definition that is challenging, but also its associations, together with issues of power over decision-making.

Underpinning assumptions

There are a number of assumptions that underpin decision-making related to special or additional needs. Sometimes these may be pragmatic and relate to, for example, cost and/or availability of resources. Sometimes, however, they may relate to the values attributed to students who experience particular kinds of need or the way in which we understand the learning process or why we behave the way we do and, as a result, how we believe difficulties in learning and/or behaviour should be addressed.

Values and labels

Marginalising discourse: The example of Down's syndrome

We have only to look at some of the ways in which children with Down's syndrome were portrayed in the past to realise why it is so important to understand the influence of terms that are used to identify or describe young people who are different in some way. For example, owing to his perception that children with Down's syndrome shared facial similarities such as folds in the upper eyelids (epicanthal folds) with those of the Mongolian race as identified by the German physiologist and anthropologist, Johann Friedrich Blumenbach, John Langdon Down used the term mongoloid. He wrote in 1866:

1.8

'A very large number of congenital idiots are typical Mongols. So marked is this, that when placed side by side, it is difficult to believe that the specimens compared are not children of the same parents. The number of idiots who arrange themselves around the Mongolian type is so great, and they present such a close resemblance to one another in mental power, that I shall describe an idiot member of this racial division, selected from the large number that have fallen under my observation' (Down, 1866, p. 259).

With the rise of the eugenics movement in the first half of the twentieth century, a number of countries, including certain states in the United States, began programmes of forced sterilization of individuals with Down's syndrome. 'Action T4' was a programme of the systematic murder of individuals with Down's syndrome and other comparable disabilities in Nazi Germany, for example (Lifton, 2000). Since the Second World War, however, laws relating to such sterilization programmes have been repealed.

In 1961, a number of geneticists wrote to the editor of *The Lancet*, suggesting that the term 'Mongolian idiocy' had 'misleading connotations', had become 'an embarrassing term', and should therefore be changed (Gordon, 1961). *The Lancet* advocated using the term Down's syndrome. The World Health Organization (WHO) officially dropped references to mongolism in 1965 after a request by the Mongolian delegate (Howard-Jones, 1979).

Down's syndrome cannot be cured, but the learning and other difficulties associated with it can be addressed if people with the syndrome are offered appropriate help and if other people accept and include. Above all it is important to stress that children with Down's syndrome are individuals with their own abilities and achievements. (adapted from Wearmouth, 2009).

Discourses associated with needs

In schools, staff may react to children's difficulties in a variety of ways (Fulcher, 1989).

 Reflective activity: Discourses related to needs in schools

How do staff in your own school or college refer to young people who experience difficulties of various sorts?

Do the labels or descriptors say anything about the worth given to these students in your view?

Some might use a discourse or frame of reference concerned with what is 'wrong' with children and how this 'problem' can be dealt with. Focusing on what is wrong with a person means emphasising ways in which s/he is different or deficient, where 'deficiencies' can be 'treated' like an illness. Where use of the 'needs' label depends on the sense of deficiency in children, it is often seen as reflecting a 'medical' or 'deficit model' of difficulties in learning and/or behaviour. This model has a sense of being in some way inferior or distant from the norm, as is evident from the use of prefixes and terms such as *dis-, un-, challenged, difficulty*. This way of looking at students' difficulties may in itself prevent a positive approach to diversity and difference.

Other people's discourses might be more concerned with children's well-being and their own moral duty to help them. They may worry about the child and feel sympathy for the child's struggles. In some situations, the difficulties that children experience may be seen as a tragedy for the individual and/or the family, and the children treated like 'charity cases'.

Another discourse is associated with the social context in which learning takes place as a potential barrier. An examination of the physical environment, including the resources, teaching approaches, the difficulty and/or interest level of the task or activity, may show how they can act as facilitators for, or constraints on, learning. Social factors can turn some differences into disabilities. In a broader context, one might ask, for example, what part economic deprivation and poverty contribute to creating difficulties in learning experienced by children. We might add here that the National Archives for the Department for Education in England, Table A1 (http://webarchive.nationalarchives.gov.uk/20130123124929/http://www.education.gov.uk/researchandstatistics/statistics/a00196275/ – accessed 01.03.16) consistently indicate from 2006 to 2009 that there is a one-to-one correspondence between the decile level of schools, that is, the poverty–affluence levels of schools on a scale of 1 to 10, and the outcomes of 5+ A–C grades at GCSE. Schools in the lowest decile level have the smallest percentage of the highest grades. We might then think about the extent to which 'learning difficulties' might be seen as 'obstacles to learning' arising from the societal context in which those students live. It might be economic factors, government policy, institutional practices, broader social attitudes or inappropriate physical surroundings that stop people from doing things.

 Reflective activity: What was his problem?

Within school or college settings we often see some of the above views of the difficulties experienced by children. Have a look at the text below and note down whether you see any parallels among students with whom you are associated.

We might take the example of 'Melvin', aged 13, who was small, thin, frequently hungry and dirty. Whilst at his previous schools he had acquired the reputation of being an incurable kleptomaniac. He had stolen items from other students, staff, the local shops and an old lady queuing at the bus stop near the school, for which some of his peers had beaten him up. Aged only 12, he was caught driving a local bus along the high street. He was so small that he could only see through the spokes of the steering wheel and passers-by reported a bus travelling along with no driver. Interpretations of the root cause of his 'problem' varied.

The local educational psychologist thought he 'needed' hypnotherapy, to 'treat' and 'cure' him, as if he had a medical condition.

Some of his teachers saw him as intrinsically bad and wanted him to be excluded permanently because they thought he was a threat to his peers and to the school. They thought what he 'needed' was expulsion from mainstream and segregation in a special school.

Others took a more charitable view. His problem was not badness within himself, but neglect by his family. They felt that what he really 'needed' was food and clean clothes and that then he would be 'sorted out'.

> What actually happened to him was that, after a final act of theft, he was expelled from his school and admitted to a special school for students 'with emotional and behavioural difficulties'. Within a week, however, he had stolen money from the head teacher's office and was excluded from the special school as well.

Connotations of the 'need' label

Discourses associated with the 'need' label may carry positive or negative connotations in relation to individual children which often (but not always, of course) ignore 'crucial issues' of the lack of power that may be allowed to pupils and parents in the decision-making process (Armstrong, 1994). Sometimes, as discussed below, this is associated with a view that interventions should be planned by experts and 'done to' the child seen as having a 'need'.

> ### Discourses around challenging behaviour
>
> Sometimes personal experiences with students can open our eyes to some of the issues related to the labels we give to students. Eleven-year-old 'Jamie S' was a boy identified as 'having problems', but this time categorised as both disruptive and lazy. He was placed in the 'remedial' band, along with students who experienced difficulty in conceptual development: language, problem-solving, communication and abstract thinking. I taught his group Classical Studies which Jamie loved. He was the first with the answer to everything and was very articulate. At the end of one year, he corrected my version of a tale from Greek mythology that I had related many months before. He was right; I was wrong. There was a clear disjunction between the label 'remedial' and my observation of him as articulate, interested and engaged in his learning. He loudly resisted writing tasks because, as I later (but much too late for Jamie) realised, he was dyslexic. He was being educated in a local authority where dyslexia was not recognised. In some lessons he expressed his feelings of frustration with the lack of cognitive challenge and pressure to write with obviously hostile behaviour. In my lessons I was relying largely on narrative, so the pressure to cope with text did not apply. In the hierarchy of power and influence in schools, those with a professional responsibility for sustaining existing organisational structures may well experience the rejection of school provision by students such as Jamie as challenging to the existing order as well as to themselves. They may then go on to interpret the behaviour of these students, and the students themselves, as deviant and as 'needing' to be cured by a special intervention programme. (adapted from Wearmouth, 2009)

Positive aspects of labelling

Not all educators take a disparaging view of needs-related labels, however. The principle of equity assumes difference between individual students. Where some experience barriers of various kinds that prevent them from accessing the curriculum in the same way as their peers, and achieving what they otherwise might do, equity means making special provision available to enable students to overcome these barriers.

 Reflective activity: Issues of equity in identifying young people's needs

Cole (1990) suggests that a very important reason for identifying children's special educational, or additional support, needs is to provide additional resources, develop specialist methods to address particular difficulties in learning, or overcome the effects of a disability in order that children can benefit from their education and/ or achieve targets set by the school.

How far does the consideration of equity here override disadvantages of labelling young people in your view?

So far we have seen how important it is to recognise the discourse or frame of reference within which the special or additional educational needs of children are understood. Related to the issues of discourses and labels, there is a question about the appropriate expectations of children identified as 'having' a need in education. There is a strong relationship between teachers' expectations and student achievement, self-esteem and development that has been well documented since the seminal work of 1.9   Rosenthal and Jacobson (1968).

In my own experience of teaching in eight different schools, it is very clear that prevailing discourses and teacher expectations strongly affect how we treat these children and the kind of provision that is made. We might also ask ourselves whether the frame of reference we use to judge the learning and behaviour of children identified as having 'special educational' or 'additional support' needs and/or a disability enables us to understand these children in the same way as we do others. These days, with inclusion in schools and society in such high focus, the practical consequences of our answer to 1.10   this question are very important for us all.

Models of learning

How we understand learning and what lies at the root of a 'learning difficulty' in school has a very strong influence on how we respond. Over the years, different social or psychological understandings with the different frames of reference that are associated with these have given rise to different interventions to address needs in education.

There is a crucial, though in some ways simplistic, distinction that we can make between the view of the learner 'as a rather passive recipient of pre-packaged knowledge' (Kozulin, 2003, p. 16), a container that must be filled by teachers, and the view that the learner has active agency in learning in school, and is proactive in interpreting and constructing the world.

Understanding learning from a behaviourist view

It is particularly important to be familiar with the principles linked to behaviourist psychology because it is this approach that has often dominated thinking about how to intervene when things are seen to have gone wrong in terms of learning and behaviour in educational institutions (Dwivedi & Gupta, 2000). A passive view of the human mind is most commonly reflected in the behaviourist model. The behavioural model works on the principle that all behaviour is learned through a process of conditioning, and that behaviours are strengthened or weakened by their consequences. Underlying behavioural principles is a basic concern with observed events, that is, what people actually do, not with assumptions about intentions or feelings. It tends to a view that the psychology of learning should be scientific: the only acceptable evidence is that which is observable and measurable. Knowledge can be transmitted to learners, with the view of the teacher as the all-knowing 'sage'. This has been the predominant model of learning for many years, particularly in the world of special needs provision where individual education, learning or behaviour plans have often been drawn up with interventions designed to be 'done to' the child to shape learning and behaviour.

Principles of behaviourism

Almost all the principles of behaviourist approaches were derived from work with laboratory animals, for example Skinner (1938; 1953). In a famous sequence of tasks, rats learned through trial-and-error to press levers in order to find food (Skinner, 1938). Learning involved the formation of a stimulus–response association, that is, pressing the lever and finding food, in the rats' memory. A reinforcer, in this case 1.11 food, strengthened the association between stimulus and response. If the association between stimulus and response was broken by removing the reward, the rats' behaviour would gradually cease through 'extinction'. The opposite of positive reinforcement is negative reinforcement. Undesirable behaviour is discouraged through putting a stop to something unpleasant. Where something unpleasant occurs as a result of an action it is viewed as 'punishment'.

The same behavioural principles have been applied to attempts to modify interactions between teachers and pupils in school contexts.

Applications of behaviourist principles in educational contexts

When behavioural principles are applied to modify undesirable behaviour in school settings, such behaviour is interpreted as having been learned as a result of some kind of reinforcement. To address this, the consequences that reinforce the behaviour and/or the physical and social context in which the behaviour occurs can be systematically modified in order to bring about improvement. Operant conditioning – reinforcing what teachers want their students to do again and ignoring or punishing what they want students to stop doing – has been widely applied in teaching in UK classrooms. Most work using this model has been based 'on behavioural management approaches (which employ strategies such as positive reinforcement, response cost, extinction and so on) where the reinforcing conditions or consequences of a behaviour are adjusted in order to moderate its frequency' (Dwivedi & Gupta, 2000, p. 76). The key to all this is consistency on the part of teachers. One way to address undesirable behaviour is therefore to identify and alter the stimulus (the 'setting conditions') in which that behaviour occurs. Alternatively, it is to ensure that whatever is rewarding and reinforcing is removed so that the behaviour is extinguished. In addition, whenever individuals behave in ways that are seen as more appropriate, they should be rewarded in a way that clearly recognises the greater acceptability of the new behaviour within the relevant contexts.

Critiques of behavioural principles

A number of criticisms of the underlying principles of behaviourism and behaviourist techniques for controlling and changing behaviour have been commonly expressed. For example, whilst this approach might be able, to explain natural unthinking reflexes and responses to stimuli, it ignores what one might think of as the workings of the mind and precludes the study of inner states and consciousness because they cannot be observed directly. Behavioural approaches might also serve teachers' wishes to manage students rather than responding to individual needs (Hanko, 1994) and engaging students' interests. These approaches might also lead children into becoming overly dependent on praise. In any case, inappropriate use of praise can be damaging to some students for two reasons. If it is not sincere students may well see through it. Also, students who have learned from previous experiences that they are likely to find learning activities in school difficult will be very discouraged by teachers' obvious lack of understanding of their situation. Consequently, 'a praise-refusing student's determination not to be lured into the risks of failing yet again may be further reinforced' (Hanko, 1994, p. 166).

 Reflective activity: The needs of the hard-to-reach

Not all behaviour can be shaped, of course. Behavioural approaches often fail to take adequate account of the emotions. As Hanko (1994) comments, 'emotional factors affect learning, especially if we see only their provocative or withdrawn facade which usually hides children in constant misery, loneliness, self-loathing and fear ... teachers are frequently baffled by children who "don't respond even to praise", "spoil their work the moment I praise it", 'just shrug it off' and "don't seem to care"' (Hanko, 1994, p. 166). Sometimes it takes a much greater degree of understanding what is going on in a student's mind.

Read the text below and consider the extent to which students in your own experience have been 'hard to reach'.

What, in your view, might the author have done to reach the students she describes here?

In every school in which the current author taught, she met praise-refusing students who had, seemingly, shut themselves off from teachers. Many had been socially isolated and, to judge by body language, felt appalled at their own loneliness yet could not do anything about it. She well remembers the case of Paul, undernourished, dirty, smelly, and always alone, but hovering as close to the entrance of the school building as he could manage. No amount of attempts by her to 'shape' his behaviour through praise would have enabled him to socialise more with peers. An adult whom she interviewed in the education wing of a prison commented: 'I just wanted teachers to go away and leave me alone. Just leave me alone.'

Arnold was another student about whom she had many concerns. Over the two years she worked with him in a comprehensive upper (13–18) school his written work showed just how little progress he seemed to have made in literacy skills. He just did not seem to care. He came to school in a shirt that was always dirty. He smelled of body odour and nicotine. She never knew what Arnold was thinking. She never knew what he felt about his own lack of literacy. If she had known, it might have made a difference either to our approach or to the outcome educationally. Arnold left school functionally illiterate. (adapted from Wearmouth, 2009)

Behavioural approaches might also encourage students into unthinking conformity to authority (Milgram, 1974). Further, these approaches tend to ignore the significance of behaviour within cultural and community contexts, together with the traditional values, in which behaviour is defined and understood (Glynn & Bishop, 1995; Macfarlane, 1997; 2000a and b). Where teachers do not understand the cultural norms of their students, they may 'mis-cue' in their application of behaviour management strategies. Gee (2000) illustrates this point vividly with an example of a small girl who told a story at the class 'sharing time'. The story was full of rhythm, pattern and repetition and would have been highly valued in the child's family and local community where oral performance was prized according to its entertainment value. The teacher, however, was anticipating a different (unarticulated) style of oral performance, that of being informative, linear and succinct, and did not appreciate the child's form of story-telling. Subsequently this child was referred to the school psychologist for telling tall stories.

Cognitive-behavioural approaches

In recent years, there has been a move away from strict behaviourist approaches towards alternative views on learning that take greater account of how individuals construct reality. For example, cognitive-behavioural approaches that developed from behavioural psychology include a focus on the way individuals process information. Such approaches can incorporate the use of perception, language, problem solving, memory, decision-making and imagery, for example, in the school situation to enable students to begin to pay attention to 'the stream of automatic thoughts which accompany and guide their behaviour'. In doing so, 'they can learn to make choices about the appropriateness of these self-statements, and if necessary introduce new thoughts and ideas' (McLeod, 1998, p. 72).

Applications of cognitive-behavioural approaches

Interventions that deliberately focus on developing meta-cognitive awareness: awareness of one's own thinking, feelings and emotions, in order to be able to regulate emotions and/or cope with feelings such as violence, bullying, disaffection or isolation (Meichenbaum & Turk, 1976; Shapiro & Cole, 1994) can be categorised as cognitive-behavioural.

Constructivist approaches

In recent years there has been an increasing interest in constructivist views of learning, focusing on individuals' active construction of the reality in which they live or study. There is an assumption here that 'the emotional and behavioural difficulties which people experience in their lives are not caused directly by events but by the way they interpret and make sense of these events' (McLeod, 1998, pp. 71–2). How young people view themselves in school has an enormous impact on their learning and behaviour. Some might be 'highly anxious and continually under-value themselves', some can seem 'over-confident and extremely resilient', whilst others may know their own strengths and weaknesses. 'Students may be gregarious, or loners, or they may be lonely' (Pollard, 2002, pp. 97–8). Learning is highly dependent on both the context, what the learner makes of the situation, and the interaction between them (Lave & Wenger, 1998; Greeno, 1998).

It is important therefore for adults to understand how children make sense of their own circumstances and what impression is conveyed to students of others' views of them. This is not simply a question of human rights, that children have a right to be heard, important though this is. From a learning perspective adults in schools have to be concerned all the time with the sense that children are making of their worlds, their experiences, tasks in classrooms, and so on. Being open to this demands careful and sensitive listening, observation and reflection.

It seems blindingly obvious that children, like the rest of us, come to decisions about what activities are worth investing in, and whether the benefits of any given learning situation outweigh the time, effort and (in some classrooms) the risk of being wrong and exposing themselves to public humiliation in being thought stupid. Questions of value-to-oneself are at the heart of the learning process. Young people may not make the effort if they do not perceive it as worthwhile in relation to the effort that is required. All learners have views about their learning, no matter what the context. All have some power and control. They may enthusiastically comply with the demands set for them, outwardly comply but inwardly be resentful, be uncooperative or disruptive and resist the demands made on them. Allowing learners some degree of choice in, or power over, what they learn and how they learn invites them to take control over their learning. This is not always easy in busy classrooms. However, offering some choices that can be accommodated within the school day gives learners responsibility and acknowledges that they have preferences, dislikes and ideas.

Seminal theorists in constructivist approaches in education

Whilst Skinner's work was seminal to advances in understanding learning from a behaviourist perspective, a number of researchers have contributed to the way we often think about children's learning from a constructivist view. Two of the foremost theorists are Jean Piaget (1896–1980) and Lev Vygotsky (1896–1934). Other leading educationalists, for example Jerome Bruner, have picked up and developed Vygotsky's ideas.

Jean Piaget

Jean Piaget, a Swiss psychologist, was one of the theorists who contributed a lot to the thinking that children learn from the experience of doing something. From his work with his own children Piaget (1954, 1964, 1969) concluded that there were four universal stages of learning:

1.13

- Sensorimotor (0–2 years). The child is born with a set of reflex movements and perceptual systems; learning is, in general, through trial and error and there is quick development of direct knowledge of the world as the child relates physical actions to perceived results of those actions.
- Preoperational (2–7 years). The child develops the ability mentally to represent events and objects (the semiotic function) and to engage in symbolic play but is not yet able to see others' point of view which is characteristic of 'egocentrism'.
- Concrete operational (7–11 years). The child develops the ability to use logical thought or operations (rules) but can only apply logic to physical objects, hence the term concrete operational. The child also becomes less egocentric and begins

to be able to see things from the viewpoint of others. S/he starts to develop an understanding of conservation of number, area, volume, orientation and reversibility, but is not yet able to think abstractly or hypothetically.

- Formal operational (11+ years). The child acquires the ability to use abstract reasoning and manipulate ideas in his/her head, without being dependent on concrete objects to, for example, combine and classify items, do mathematical calculations, think creatively and imagine the outcome of particular actions.

Piaget's work has been criticised in a number of respects. His work implies that child development occurs in discrete stages, but actually, of course, it continues throughout adulthood. He also appears to have underestimated children's abilities at different ages (Wood, Smith & Grossniklaus, 2001). In addition, there is insufficient consideration of different social or cultural contexts in which children in general live and grow. Further, some of the methods for the research on which these conclusions were based have been questioned (Donaldson, 1984). However, despite the criticisms, Piaget's conclusions that learners construct knowledge by interacting with their environment and that they reconstruct their thoughts in the light of new experiences have made a strong contribution to practice in primary schools particularly. Thinking about learning as a continuum from the sensorimotor to the formal operational stage can be very helpful in conceptualising strategies to address cognitive difficulties, as we discuss in Chapter 4.

Lev Vygotsky

Akin to Piaget's model of constructivism but developed in a very different context, that of Soviet Russia, is the social constructivist model of Lev Vygotsky. The distinctiveness of Vygotsky's work (Vygotsky, 1978) lay in the importance he placed on the social context in which learning takes place. Vygotsky (1978, p. 57) proposed that there were two places, or 'planes', where the learning process takes place:

- the interpersonal, that is, the 'between the people' plane where learning mainly occurs through interacting with others, especially a more informed other;
- the intrapersonal, within the individual, as s/he thinks about and reflects on new concepts and learning and appropriates skills and knowledge.

In this view of learning, the development of thinking, reflection, problem-solving, reasoning, and so on, what Vygotsky called 'higher mental processes', depends on the presence of 'mediators' to mediate learning during interactions between the individual and the environment.

Mediators can be humans who mediate prompt, guide, reward, punish or model the use of, particularly, language, signs, texts, graphic organisers and so on. Once their use has been appropriated by the learner, such use itself mediates new learning. One might take the example of language which, as Vygotsky (1962) suggested, is very important to the sense-making process. It is through interacting with a more knowledgeable mediator that language is developed. The meaning of language has to be learnt in a social context. For example, once a beginning driver has learnt through a human mediator or from the *Highway Code* the meaning of a road sign, the sign itself should mediate (or, perhaps, regulate) that driver's behaviour.

Applications of social constructivist approaches in education

One of the most well-known concepts for which Vygotsky is famous is that of the zone of proximal development (ZPD) to explain the process of learning in a social context.   1.14

The ZPD constitutes the next steps in learning and the range of knowledge and skills that learners are not ready to learn on their own but can learn in interaction with more informed and experienced others. The role of the more informed other is central in this. As Kozulin (2003, p. 19) comments, in terms of a human mediator a central question tends to be 'What sort of involvement by a more informed/expert other can enhance a learner's performance?'

A more informed/expert other may 'scaffold', that is, provide structured support for, new learning (Wood, Bruner & Ross, 1976) through the ZPD based on his/her knowledge of the learner and the learner's current level of knowledge and understanding of the topic. Learners need scaffolding from more knowledgeable others, but not too much. Learning in the ZPD is also about participating, for example, having the chance to behave as a reader or writer alongside other readers and writers. This issue is really important in relation to young people with difficulties in learning. Learning is often highly charged with emotion. Feelings are very powerful in supporting, or preventing, learning. Feelings of success are often pleasant and/or exciting, but the sense of failure is often upsetting and/or disturbing, especially when it is a frequent occurrence (Wearmouth, Glynn & Berryman, 2005). Feelings are therefore very powerful in supporting, or preventing, learning. Getting the balance right is crucial. Without active participation and construction of the self as a contributing member of the classroom, students are not included. They fail to learn properly and are likely to be marginalised (Wearmouth & Berryman, 2009). Very importantly, students' learning and behaviour are mediated through the kind of relationship s/he has with a teacher. This relationship both develops over time and is influenced by the teacher's sense of a student's value and worth.

Obvious implications of this view of learning is that all learners, including those who experience difficulties, need

- space and time for discussion between
  - themselves as learners and the more informed other(s), most often the teacher(s) and
  - themselves as learners with peers to enable 'interthinking' (Littleton & Mercer, 2013), that is, focused talk around new learning to clarify and consolidate their understanding of new concepts and knowledge;
- time for reflecting on what they make of what they have just learnt and the opportunity to raise questions with the more informed other(s);

- respectful relationships among learners and between learners and adults in the learning environment. In relation to young people with particular needs in education it is absolutely essential that they, along with all other students, feel safe in talking about themselves as well as asking and answering questions (Bishop, Berryman & Wearmouth, 2014) and are not humiliated by the teacher's, or peers', reactions.

We discuss the very important issue of scaffolding further in Chapter 4 where we consider appropriate support for young people who experience difficulties in cognition and learning.

Jerome Bruner

A different, but in some ways related, way to conceptualise progress is through Bruner's (1966) three modes of representation of reality used by humans: enactive, iconic and symbolic, as they develop their conceptual understanding of the world. Like Piaget's model above, these modes move from the concrete 'learn by doing' to the abstract:

- The 'enactive' mode of representation works through action. We 'do' and then we understand and know. In their very early years, young children rely on enactive modes to learn. As they learn to move, they learn to do so through their own actions without the need for verbal and/or written and/or physical symbols. Children unable to experience their world by sight, hearing, taste, touch or smell, or unable to move easily will be less able to understand and know through 'doing' unless special efforts are made to enable them to access their world otherwise.
- The 'iconic' mode is a visual representation of the real object. Images therefore stand for the physical object. Using this mode of representation, children learn to understand what pictures and diagrams are and how to do mathematical calculations using numbers and without counting objects.
- The 'symbolic' mode is an abstract representation of something else. Abstract symbols are 'arbitrary', meaning that they do not necessarily bear any resemblance to whatever it is that they represent. For example, commonly in spoken language the sound of a word bears no resemblance to reality, unless it is onomatopoeic.

Children's learning involves becoming proficient in each of these increasingly more complex modes, but they may experience difficulty at any point in their development.

 Reflective activity: Basing strategies on Bruner's (1966) modes of representation

As we will see in Chapter 4, a common feature in children who experience cognitive difficulties is weakness in understanding and remembering that a symbol can 'stand for' something else, for example, something concrete or an action.

In your experience, what kind of strategies, based on Bruner's modes of representation, can teachers and others incorporate into their teaching to facilitate access to the curriculum in ways that address these difficulties? For example, you might consider that some students require much more time to acquire concepts through experience of using and manipulating concrete objects.

Summary

How we understand learning and how we see what lies at the root of a 'learning difficulty' in school has a very strong influence on how we respond. Over the years, different social or psychological understandings about the root of the difficulty have given rise to different approaches. For example, some people might focus on 'what is wrong with a child' and refer to ways in which this 'problem with the child' can be dealt with. Focusing on what is wrong with a person means emphasising ways in which s/he is different or deficient, where 'deficiencies' can be 'treated' like an illness. Another way of looking at difficulties, and one that potentially gives agency to teachers and others in supporting the young person, is by examining the social context in which learning takes place. In other words, if they think they can control the cause of a difficulty, they believe 'that they can also sufficiently treat it. In addition, they perceived themselves in such cases as even more responsible for finding an effective solution for the child's problem' (Poulou & Norwich, 2002, p. 112).

Across time a range of social or psychological understandings of learning and behaviour has underpinned interventions. Among these it is possible to distinguish between the view of the learner rather as a container to be filled by teachers and the view that the learner is proactive in interpreting and constructing the world.

Asking for guidance is a very good way for beginning teachers to learn and to build confidence (Peacey & Wearmouth, 2007):

- In schools, mentors can be an important route to support.
- Students themselves who experience difficulties may tell teachers what works best for them.
- Parents and carers can often give valuable insights.
- The Special Educational Needs Co-ordinator (SENCo) and other teachers can advise and help those new to the profession to learn from outside experts like educational psychologists and therapists.

There is no golden formula for addressing the special learning needs of all students who experience difficulties in schools. There are some general principles, however. Every student is different and every situation is different. Addressing difficulties is a question of problem-solving. Firstly, find out about the learner and the difficulties s/he experiences. Then think about the requirements of the particular curriculum area and barriers to learning in the classroom environment and in the particular curriculum area. Finally, reflect on and implement what will best address those barriers to help the learner achieve in the classroom.

The extent to which young people qualify for special or additional resources to address their learning physical and/or behaviour needs depends to a large extent on the policies and resources within their Local Authorities (LAs) and educational settings as well as the wording of particular Education Acts. In Chapter 2 we look first at the way in which special provision developed within its historical context, and then move on to considering teachers' current legal responsibilities and young people's and families' rights in the areas of special educational, or additional support, provision in schools across the United Kingdom.

Chapter 2
A historical perspective and the current legal position

The major questions in this chapter are:

- How did special educational, and additional support, provision develop in the United Kingdom, and what purpose did it serve?
- What was the nature of the national context that supported this development?
- What are the current legislative frameworks across the United Kingdom that govern the area of special educational, or additional support, needs and disabilities?

Introduction

In Chapter 1 we saw how our own experiences and values as human beings and professional educators influence the way in which we interpret difficulties experienced by students in schools (Fulcher, 1989; Wearmouth, 2009). Chapter 2 begins with an overview of the history of provision for children seen as 'different' from peers on account of the learning or physical difficulties they experienced, or the behaviour they displayed, and continues with a discussion of the way that schools' thinking about learning, behaviour and children's rights has changed over time. It culminates by comparing the law in the different countries of the United Kingdom. These differences serve to illustrate that there is nothing 'set in stone' about the terms 'special educational needs' or 'additional support needs'. These terms are constructions that some might think of as an administrative convenience that is useful for identifying differences against the expected framework of progression in schools. Once these differences have been identified then decisions can be taken about what additional resources might be needed to support young people to make formally acceptable progress.

A historical perspective on the development of the 'special' education sector

 Reflective activity: Understanding the historical context of the special education sector

Take a few moments to reflect on:

- what you know about the historical development of the 'special' education sector;
- why it may be important to be aware of the historical origins to understand current provision.

School curricula 'and even schools themselves are seen to be products of the social system in which they exist' (Broadfoot, 2011, p. 9). This system includes society's values, beliefs and political ideology (Wearmouth, 2009) and the question about what purpose the special education sector was developed to serve. There are a number of different ways of looking at this. For example some consider it was developed to:

- serve the economic and commercial interests of society, so that as many people as possible with difficulties should be productive and contribute to an industrial society. Certainly businessmen 'played a part in the founding of pioneer establishments for the deaf and for the blind, and […] throughout the 19th century trade training took up much of the lives of the handicapped attending them' (Cole, 1990, p. 101); and/or
- address the needs of children in difficulty more effectively from an essentially benevolent position (Cole, 1989); and/or
- provide a deliberate means to exclude troublesome pupils, or pupils who required a lot of the teacher's time, from mainstream classes (Loxley & Thomas, 2007). For example, when a new national system of secondary schools was designed following the 1944 Education Act, it might be argued that the smooth running of those schools demanded the exclusion of some pupils, for instance those categorised as 'educationally subnormal'; and/or
- serve the vested interest of, for example, the medical profession and psychologists who benefit from the continued existence of special provision (Tomlinson, 1988).

Early years of special education provision: Training for employment

In the United Kingdom, the development of early special education provision, beginning at the end of the eighteenth century, should be seen in a national context where industry was rapidly developing and expanding. This was an age of child labour in, for example, factories in towns and cities, and on the land in the countryside. 'There could be no question of establishing a system of compulsory popular education when the new factory system was insistently demanding child labour' (Simon, 1974, p. 152). As recorded by the National Archives in Kew, London, a Factory Act of 1833 had mandated that children under 9 years of age should not be employed, but that those between 9 and 13 could work no more than 9 hours a day (http://www.nationalarchives.gov.uk/education/resources/1833-factory-act/ – accessed 21.06.16). The minimum age of employment was not raised to 10 years until 1876, and to 11 in 1893. Until the later part of the nineteenth century, education was largely for the children of the wealthy. For all those children whose parents were unable to afford fees, education was minimal, and largely religious. Children of poor and lower-middle-class parents might attend a network of Sunday Schools, 'voluntary' (mostly church) schools, and informal neighbourhood schools with low fees, but a significant proportion of the poorest children had no access to education at all.

In a societal context where child labour was the norm, the earliest institutions for children who experienced difficulties of any kind, learning, sensory or physical, were established to provide training rather than education. Firstly came schools for blind and deaf children founded by individuals or by charities, not by government (Warnock, DES, 1978, ch. 2). Subsequently, central government intervened, initially to support and supplement what voluntary agencies provided, and later to create a national framework for special education provision. Even so, it was not until the 1970s that all children, however severe the difficulties they experienced, were deemed entitled to an appropriate education.

Early private foundations such as the School of Instruction for the Indigent[1] Blind, established in 1791 in Liverpool, the School for the Indigent Blind in London founded in 1800 and the Asylum and School for the Indigent Blind at Norwich in 1805 were designed to focus on training in work skills, moral improvement and the Christian religion (Oliphant, 2006). The founding plan of the School of Industry in Liverpool included 'to furnish the blind with employment that may prevent them from being burdens to their family and community [...]'. As recipients of public charity, the inmates should form 'habits of industry', with men making baskets, tablecloths and whips while the women spun yarn, made sail-cloths and picked oakum. The penalty for misdemeanours could be harsh. As the Liverpool School Visitors' Books record, in 1825, two boys were flogged for insolence and another for 'making away with his yarns' (Oliphant, 2006, p. 58). Educational aspects were not introduced into the curriculum until other schools were founded thirty years later, for example, in the London Society for Teaching the Blind to Read in 1838.

Other charitable institutions were similarly limited in what they offered and most children's prospects were grim. Attempts were made to teach a trade to girls with physical disabilities from poor homes in the Cripples' Home and Industrial School for Girls established in Marylebone in 1851, and to boys in the Training Home for Crippled Boys founded in Kensington in 1865. However, as the Warnock Report (DES, 1978,

---

[1] i.e. poor/destitute

p. 9) notes in relation to institutions for the deaf, ironically, although the curriculum was predominantly training, 'many of their inmates failed to find employment on leaving and had recourse to begging'.

Until the end of the nineteenth century there was little provision for those children who experienced serious difficulties in learning, apart from workhouses and infirmaries with secure care. The first specific provision made for them was the Earlswood Asylum for Idiots established at Highgate in 1847, the first philanthropic asylum for 'idiot' children in Britain. The aim of this asylum, as recorded in the National Archives, was

> not merely to take the Idiot and Imbecile under its care, but especially, by the skilful and earnest application of the best means in his education, to prepare him, as far as possible, for the duties and enjoyments of life [Bye-laws 1857].
>
> (http://discovery.nationalarchives.gov.uk/details/rd/ed87972d-14f1-4b0c-ab59-d72bcdbee573, accessed 18.06.16)

However, as Hall (2008, p. 1006) notes, the philanthropic optimism accompanying the founding of the Earlswood Asylum, that those with difficulties in learning could be educated, faded and

> was replaced by a eugenicist preoccupation with fears of national decline, because of what was seen to be a link between mental defectiveness and criminality (Thomson, 1998; Wright & Digby, 1996). Mental defectives were seen as genetically tainted; they should be both separated from society, and prevented from reproducing.

By 1870 there were five asylums. For children to be admitted parents had to agree to them being certified as 'idiots', a label that attracted much odium (Cole, 1989, p. 22).

In summary, during this period, there were very few attempts to challenge the general attitude to the way in which young people with sensory or physical difficulties, or difficulties in learning should be treated. One exception was the foundation of the 'College for the Blind Sons of Gentlemen' in 1866 in Worcester. (In its 1872 report, 'gentlemen' were described as 'belonging by birth or kinship to upper, the professional or the middle classes of society' [Bell, 1967, p. 16].) Worcester College remained the only route for blind boys to achieve higher qualifications and entry into the professions until after the Second World War. (The equivalent for girls was not established until 1921, by the National Institute for the Blind [NIB] in Chorleywood.)

2.1

Education for (almost) all

For a whole variety of reasons pressure grew in the second half of the nineteenth century for a nationally-organised system of universal elementary education that was to have a consequent effect on the organisation of special education provision. For example, the expansion of industry during the industrial revolution led some manufacturers to call for a greater pool of educated individuals from which to 'select the higher grades of workers, foremen and managers' (Simon, 1974, p. 360). A Reform Act of 1867 enfranchised the lower middle class and better off workers. The extension of voting rights under this Act led some politicians to argue that the lower classes must now be educated 'to qualify them for the power that has passed … into their hands', as a Liberal Party parliamentarian, Robert Lowe, (1867, pp. 31–2) cited in Simon (1974, p. 356), commented at the time. Then there was the question of the social control of children in cities and towns. Those under 9 years of age could not legally be employed under the terms of the 1833 Factory Act, as noted above and, in any case, fewer children were needed to work in factories once machinery became more complex. Deliberate moves were therefore made towards universal elementary education under the terms of the 1870 Forster Education Act in England and Wales, and the 1872 Education (Scotland) Act. School boards were charged with ensuring provision of elementary education in locations where there were insufficient places through voluntary enterprise. In 1880 a further Act finally made school attendance compulsory in England between the ages of five and ten, although attendance until the age of 13 was compulsory for those who had not achieved the standard of education that was 'fixed by a byelaw in force in the district' (§4, p. 143).

2.2

Development of special education post-1870

The introduction of compulsory schooling meant that large numbers of children who seemed to have poor intellectual ability came to school for the first time. The question was what to do with these children. Now that they were compelled to attend, their presence was felt to be holding others back in the large classes that existed in public elementary schools. Besides, national level funding for individual schools, including teachers' salaries, depended in part on the outcomes of examinations of pupils conducted by school inspectors. For example, the policy of payment by results was introduced into schools in England in 1863. It lasted until 1890 when it was abandoned.

In 1889 a Royal Commission recommended compulsory education for the blind from age 5 to 16, and for the deaf from age 7 to 16. Deaf children, generally considered slower to learn on account of difficulties in communication, were to be taught separately by teachers who should be specially qualified to do so.[2] Legislation in Scotland followed in 1890 with the Education of the Blind and Deaf Mute Children (Scotland) Act, and in England and Wales in 1893 with the Elementary Education (Blind and Deaf Children) Act.

The same 1889 Royal Commission distinguished between three groups of children seen as experiencing varying degrees of learning difficulties: 'feeble-minded',

---

[2] It is interesting to note that teachers in special schools for children with visual and auditory impairments still require specialist qualifications but those in some other kinds of special educational institutions do not.

'imbeciles' and 'idiots'. Feeble-minded should be educated in 'auxiliary' schools away from other children, imbeciles should be sent to institutions where education should concentrate on sensory and physical development and improved speech. 'Idiots' were not thought to be educable. These days we would consider the use of these labels for children unacceptable. However, in the nineteenth century there was a big difference in status and respect given to those groups of students who had been identified as 'different' from the rest.

 Reflective activity: Hiding the evidence

Cole (1989, p. 40) outlines evidence presented to the Sharpe Report (Education Department, 1898) of what might happen to children identified in mainstream schools as 'feeble-minded'. 'In London, before 1892, the feeble-minded over 11 years old had been mixed with 5-year-olds in Standard 1'. However, teachers were 'so concerned with getting their average children through the Standards and so conscious of HMI's [inspectors'] expectations that they would send the feeble-minded to play in a corner with a slate'.

Cole is describing practice in some schools at the end of the nineteenth century. Do you have any experience of instances where particular children have been removed from mainstream classrooms to hide them away? If so

- what purpose was their removal intended to serve?
- what are some of the issues involved here, do you think?
- what do you think of this practice yourself?

Formalising categories of difference

The new discipline of psychology made formal identification and assessment of 'deficiencies' in children seem more legitimate in the context of the time. A Mental Deficiency Act was passed in 1913 with only three MPs voting against it. One of them, Josiah Wedgwood, is cited in Woodhouse (1982, p. 13) as saying: 'It is a spirit of the Horrible Eugenic Society which is setting out to breed up the working class as though they were cattle.' The 1913 Mental Deficiency Act defined four grades of Mental Defective. In each case the condition had to be present 'from birth or from an early age'. The archive of the National Association for the Feebleminded (Kirby, 1914) reads as follows in relation to this Act:

 2.3

> It would be well for every public official and social worker to commit the wording of these definitions to memory, in order that the mentally defective may not pass unrecognized, and be, in consequence, committed to unsuitable institutions, submitted to inappropriate treatment, and discharged; his mental abnormality still remaining undiscovered and ignored.

Definition.

The four classes of mental defectives within the meaning of the Act are described as follows:

(1) Idiots; that is to say, persons so deeply defective in mind from birth or from an early age as to be unable to guard themselves against common physical dangers.
(2) Imbeciles; that is to say, persons in whose case there exists from birth or from an early age mental defectiveness not amounting to idiocy, yet so pronounced that they are incapable of managing themselves or their affairs, or, in the case of children, of being taught to do so.
(3) Feeble-minded Persons; that is to say, persons in whose case there exists from birth or from an early age mental defectiveness not amounting to imbecility, yet so pronounced that they require care, supervision, and control for their own protection, or for the protection of others, or, in the case of children, that they by reason of such defectiveness appear to be permanently incapable of receiving proper benefit from the instruction in ordinary schools.
(4) Moral Imbeciles; that is to say, persons who from an early age display some permanent mental defect coupled with strong vicious, or criminal propensities, on which punishment has had little or no deterrent effect.

The scheme of provision under the Mental Deficiency Act is based upon the assumption that a defective person is one who remains mentally immature, and in need, therefore, of the permanent care and protection which should be the natural right of every child during immature years.

(http://www.archive.org/stream/legislationforfe00kirbrich/
legislationforfe00kirbrich_djvu.txt accessed 19.02.16)

The 1913 Act required local education authorities (LEAs) in England and Wales to ascertain and certify which children aged 7 to 16 in their area were defective. Those judged by the authority to be incapable of being taught in special schools were to pass to the care of local mental deficiency committees. Interestingly, Cyril Burt, later Sir Cyril, was appointed to a part-time position of school psychologist for the London County Council in 1913, with the responsibility of picking out the 'feeble-minded' children, in accordance with the 1913 Act. In Scotland, the Mental Deficiency (Scotland) Act of 1913 required school boards to identify children in their area who were 'defective'. Those children who were considered ineducable became the responsibility of parish councils for placement in an institution.

2.4

In 1921 in England an Education Act consolidated previous legislation, requiring children in the four categories of blind, deaf, mentally and physically defective (but not 'idiots' or 'imbeciles') and epileptic to be educated. 'Defective' and epileptic children should be certified by LEAs and then educated in special provision of which there was a whole range made by both voluntary bodies and LEAs. As Warnock (DES, 1978) comments, the statutory foundation of special provision continued broadly until the 1944 Act. The parents of children in any of the four categories were required to see that their child attended a suitable special school from the age of five in the case of blind or deaf children, or seven for other children, until the age of 16. LEAs had the duty to ensure the provision of such schools.

Reflective activity: The case of open-air schools

To understand the current form and organisation of special provision we have to be aware of the social, political and ideological context in which that provision develops (Wearmouth, 2009) so that we can properly understand the function served by the provision.

Read through the description of the development and demise of open-air schools for 'delicate' children. As you do so, reflect on how this particular category of child and form of special provision reflects the national societal context of the time.

The foundation of open-air schools in Britain at the beginning of the twentieth century has to be seen in relation to concerns that had arisen around the physical well-being of large numbers of children, particularly in the cities where the air was often heavily polluted and living conditions for most people were wretched. Recruitment of soldiers to fight in the Boer War had highlighted the large proportion who were medically unfit to fight, and as a result of this concern the government passed the 1906 Education (Provision of School Meals) Act to enable LEAs to provide school lunches (Cole, 1989). In 1907, the Education (Administrative Provisions) Act required LEAs to carry out medical checks on all their pupils.

Open-air schools were modelled on a German example (Gamlin, 1935). A school doctor examining children in Berlin observed that many were anaemic and debilitated and strongly recommended open-air treatment, suitable surroundings, careful supervision, good feeding, and exercise. In consequence, the first open-air school was founded in 1904 in pine woods in Charlottenburg, followed by the first British open-air school, Bostall Woods, in Woolwich, in 1907. Others followed, where 'pupils with weak hearts, bronchial complaints or suffering from malnutrition were subjected to a somewhat Spartan regime'. Lessons were 'spent out of doors or in three-sided rooms, with meals provided and a compulsory rest period in the middle of the day' (Cole, 1989, p. 51).

Classrooms in Aspen House open-air school in Streatham, London, had floors and roofs but no walls. A personal recollection reported in an article 'School's Out' in the Independent newspaper (23 January 2005) describes how, when it rained, children might get wet and, if it snowed in winter, children might have to clear it away before they could start lessons. There was no heating but, however cold it became, lessons continued and pupils just had their clothes and blankets with which to keep warm. A medical official in Leicester noted that among the characteristics of children admitted to these schools were 'Stunted growth, loss of muscular tone and dryness of hair [and] rings around the eyes, long silky eyelashes, inflammation of the eyelids, enlarged glands, anaemia, feeble circulation and shallow breathing' (Cathcart, *Independent on Sunday*, 23 January 2005). Thousands of children in Britain matched this description, particularly in city slum areas. This, combined with the cheapness of schools that were effectively three-sided sheds with corrugated iron roofs, led to an expansion of their numbers. By the 1930s there were 4000 children a year from London who were sent to open-air boarding schools. They might be funded by LEAs, charities or private philanthropists, for example, the Cadbury family in Birmingham.

Gradually, however, the value of being out of doors in all weathers began to be questioned. In 1955, 12,000 'delicate' children were still being educated in open-air schools in England and Wales, but medical opinion was moving away from favouring this provision for 'such' children. Improved standards of living, slum clearances, the after-effects of the introduction of the National Health Service by the Labour government in 1948, the arrival of antibiotics, notably streptomycin that reduced the incidence of tuberculosis, and the provision of milk and meals in schools meant that the open-air movement gradually became redundant.

Developments in differentiated curricula for different learners after 1944

Between the introduction of compulsory elementary education and the Second World War there were a number of developments in the education system. In particular, after 1870, further legislation extended the age of compulsory attendance: to 11 in 1893, to 12 in 1899, to 14 in 1918 and to 15 in 1936. The expansion of secondary education consequent on this legislation was fragmented, with considerable variation across the country.

Towards the end of the Second World War, a coalition government therefore reorganised the education system through the 1944 Education Act in England and Wales and sought to develop a common national framework for the education of a diverse student population. The statutory system of education was to be organised

> in three progressive stages to be known as primary education, secondary education, and further education. (1944 Education Act, Part 11, § 7)

Reorganisation of mainstream secondary schools

A report by Sir William Spens in 1938, *Secondary Education with Special Reference to Grammar Schools and Technical High Schools*, had recommended that there should be three types of secondary school:

- grammar schools for the academically able;
- technical schools for those with a practical bent; and
- new 'modern' secondary schools for the rest.

Central government therefore advised LEAs to 'think in terms of three types' of state secondary schools in circular No. 73 (12 December 1945). A booklet, *The Nation's Schools*, explained that the new 'modern' schools would be for working-class children 'whose future employment will not demand any measure of technical skill or knowledge' (MoE 1945, quoted in Benn and Chitty, 1996, p. 5). Although this booklet was withdrawn, the policy remained the same and was restated in *The New Secondary Education* two years later (Wilkinson, 1947).

The tripartite system of secondary education, as had been recommended in the 1938 Spens Report, was quickly adopted by many LEAs, with grammar schools for the most able, secondary modern schools for the majority, and secondary technical schools for those with a technical or scientific aptitude. In fact, the Act itself never mentioned the words 'tripartite', 'grammar schools' or 'secondary modern schools'. It simply required that education should be provided at three levels: primary, secondary and further. Indeed, the Parliamentary Secretary to the Board of Education, J. Chuter Ede, commented in a speech reported in *The Times* of 14 April 1944:

> I do not know where people get the idea about three types of school, because I have gone through the Bill with a small toothcomb, and I can find only one school for senior pupils – and that is a secondary school. (quoted in Chitty and Dunford, 1999, p. 20)

Nevertheless a system of selection was introduced based on the results of an examination at the age of 11 that, it was believed, could differentiate different 'types' of learners who should be educated in different types of secondary schools: grammar, technical and secondary modern. Within individual mainstream schools students were selected into ability 'streams'. Students might be directed into academic or work-related programmes according to measured 'ability'. It seemed to many that the educational hierarchy that developed was fair, as it was based on psychometric testing which, at that time, was thought by many educators to be reliable and valid.[3]

Reorganisation of special education

Assessment by category in mainstream might be seen reflected in the way special education was organised also. In the area of special education, the 1944 Education Act, Sections 33 and 34, and associated Regulations also assume that clearly categorising young people is both possible and appropriate. The duty of LEAs to ascertain which children required special educational treatment, hitherto confined to 'defective' and epileptic children, was extended to children with all types of disability, generally described in the Act as 'pupils who suffer from any disability of mind or body'. These days we might call this way of viewing difficulties in learning as the 'medical' or 'deficit model'. Certification of defective children within the education system was abolished. Any child considered educable would have access to schooling. Children seen as ineducable in school were to be reported to the local authority for the purposes of the

---

[3]In Scotland the system was different. The 1918 Education (Scotland) Act had introduced the principle of universal free secondary education. Unlike the Education Act 1944 in England and Wales, following which the tripartite system was established, the Education (Scotland) Act 1945 consolidated what had already been established.

Mental Deficiency Act 1913. Local authorities were empowered to require parents to submit their children for medical examination. In Scotland, the Education (Scotland) Act (1945) repeated much of the content of the Education Act 1944. 2.5

The Handicapped Students and School Health Service Regulations (1945) in England and Wales developed a new framework of eleven categories of students: blind, partially sighted, deaf, partially deaf, delicate, diabetic, educationally subnormal, epileptic, maladjusted, physically handicapped and those with speech defects. Maladjustment and speech defects were included for the first time. The regulations required blind, deaf, epileptic, physically handicapped and aphasic children to be educated in special schools. Children with other disabilities could attend mainstream if there was adequate provision (Warnock, 1978, 2.46). Official guidance (Ministry of Education, 1946) estimated that the number of children who might be expected to require special educational treatment, not necessarily in special schools, would range from between 14 per cent and 17 per cent of the school population.

Table 2.1 summarises development in special education provision between 1760 and 1945, and outlines the context within which these developments occurred.

Expansion of numbers of students in special education

During the years which followed, the two groups which continually expanded in numbers were those students considered 'educationally sub-normal' (ESN) and those identified as 'maladjusted' (Warnock, 1978):

> The category of educationally sub-normal children was seen as consisting of children of limited ability and children retarded by 'other conditions' such as irregular attendance, ill-health, lack of continuity in their education or unsatisfactory school conditions. These children would be those who for any reason were retarded by more than 20 per cent for their age and who were not so low-graded as to be ineducable or to be detrimental to the education of other children. They would amount to approximately 10 per cent of the school population. (Warnock, 1978, 2.48)

? Reflective activity: The case of 'maladjustment'

'Maladjustment' is an interesting category. It had its origins in the 1913 Mental Deficiency Act that, as noted above, created a category of moral imbeciles or defectives.

You might wish to look back at the terms of this Act as outlined above, and the reactions to the passing of the Bill in parliament at the time.

The 'maladjusted' label is one 'which has a powerful history of stigma, being associated with undesirable personal and social characteristics' (Galloway, Armstrong & Tomlinson, 1994). After 1945 all LEAs had a responsibility to establish special educational treatment in special or ordinary schools for pupils defined as maladjusted. However, there was a lot of uncertainty around what constitutes 'maladjustment', and the Underwood Committee was set up in 1950 to enquire into 'maladjusted' students' medical, educational and social problems. The (1955) Underwood Report (Chapter IV, para 96) lists six symptoms of maladjustment:

● nervous disorders, e.g., fears, depression, apathy, excitability;
● habit disorders, e.g., speech defects, sleep-walking, twitching and incontinence;
● behaviour disorders, e.g., defiance, aggression, jealousy and stealing;
● organic disorders, e.g., cerebral tumours;
● psychotic behaviour, e.g., delusions, bizarre behaviour;
● educational and vocational difficulties, e.g., inability to concentrate or keep jobs.

 2.6

The overall definition read as follows: 'In our view, a child may be regarded as maladjusted who is developing in ways that have a bad effect on himself or his fellows and cannot, without help, be remedied by his parents, teachers and other adults in ordinary contact with him.' (Chapter IV, p. 22)

There has never been a consensus on what defines 'problem behaviour', of the sort categorised by the term 'maladjusted'. It was 'a ragbag term describing any kind of behaviour that teachers and parents find disturbing (Galloway & Goodwin, 1987, p. 32) and could use to justify special provision. Between 1945 and 1960, the numbers of pupils classified as maladjusted rose from 0 to 1742. By 1975, there were 13,000 pupils labelled as maladjusted (Furlong, 1985) – but now there are none. The term 'maladjusted' has been replaced by ill-defined terms such as 'emotional and behavioural difficulties', first formally used by Warnock (DES, 1978) and which enabled pupils to be removed from the mainstream, or, as now in England, 'social, emotional and mental health' difficulties.

Table 2.1 Special education timeline, 1760–1944. Overview

Time period	National context	Special education provision
1760–1870	'new factory system insistently demanding child labour' (Simon, 1974, p.152). Minimum age of employment not raised to 10 years until 1876.	1791: School of Instruction for Indigent Blind, Liverpool. 1799: London School for Indigent Blind to instruct blind in a trade. 1809–1870: Charitable institutions for those with sensory impairment established: • Asylums and Schools for the Deaf: Margate, Manchester, Liverpool, Exeter, Doncaster, Aberystwyth, Bristol, Whitechapel; • Schools for the Blind: York, London, Manchester, Liverpool, Birmingham; • Schools for the Blind and Deaf: Newcastle, Brighton; • Asylums for 'Idiots': Bath, Highgate, Colchester, Starcross (Devon), Lancaster. 1851/1865: 'Cripples' Homes and Industrial Schools in London. 1867: Metropolitan Poor Act: first state run 'idiot' and 'imbecile' asylums in Surrey and Hertfordshire 1868: Founding of British and Foreign Association for Promoting Education and Employment of Blind (now RNIB).

1870–1944	Extension of enfranchisement and increased complexity of working contexts led to pressure to open up education for all.	Pressure to cater for all children: More schools for the blind and for the deaf were established.
		1889 Edgerton Commission: 'The blind, deaf, dumb and the educable class of imbecile ... if left uneducated become not only a burden to themselves but a weighty burden to the state. It is in the interests of the state to educate them, so as to dry up, as far as possible, the minor streams which must ultimately swell to a great torrent of pauperism.'
	Focus on social control as well as future employment.	By 1913, 12,000 'defective' children in 177 special schools, plus voluntary provision.
	Universal primary education introduced in 1870 and made compulsory for most children in 1880.	1913: Mental Deficiency Act. Education authorities have duty to identify which children are defective.
		1914: Elementary Education (Defective and Epileptic Children) Act. Local authorities required to provide for 'mentally defective' children.
	School leaving age extended.	1918: Education Act. Local authorities required to provide for 'physically defective'.
	New discipline of psychology supported assessment of child 'deficiencies' and categorisation.	1921: Education Act. Enables local authorities to compel families of 'certified' children to send them to special schools.
		1939: 17,000 children in state special schools.
1944–5	Reorganisation of education after World War II.	1944 Education Act: Local education authorities required to identify children with 'a disability of body or mind' and provide 'special educational treatment' in special schools or elsewhere.
		1945 Regulations: Defined 11 categories of handicap.

Post-war planners assumed that ordinary schools would have the major share in making provision for those young people with difficulties in learning and/or behaviour:

> Detailed suggestions were made for provision. In large urban areas about 1–2 per cent of the school population would need to be educated in special schools (including 0.2 per cent in boarding schools); the remaining 8–9 per cent of the school population would be provided for in ordinary schools. (Warnock, 1978, 2.48)

However, during the war a lot of accommodation in schools had been destroyed or were in a bad state, and raising the school leaving age meant that additional building was needed. Secondary modern schools in particular often had large classes, and suitably trained teachers were in short supply (Warnock, 1978, 33–40). The outcome was that the planners' intentions were not wholly fulfilled, provision in ordinary schools failed to develop as expected and special education came to be interpreted much more narrowly than official guidance anticipated.

Politicians increasingly looked to medicine and the growing profession of psychology for solutions to behaviour in schools that was construed as deviant (Ford, Mongon & Whelan, 1982). The number of children in ESN special schools nearly doubled between 1947 and 1955 from 12,060 to 22,639, with a further 12,000 children awaiting placement. Warnock (1978) notes that education authorities in Scotland were empowered in 1945 to provide a child guidance service which would advise teachers and parents on appropriate methods of education and training for these children. By 1966, 25 of the 35 education authorities had a child guidance service. In England, the number of child guidance clinics increased from 162 in 1950 to 367 twenty years later. To keep pace with this kind of expansion in numbers, the Summerfield Working Party (1968) recommended new and expanded arrangements for training of educational psychologists and a doubling of numbers.

Changes in the system in the latter part of the twentieth century

The system established after 1944 was not as stable as it first appeared. In special education, there was obvious overlap between the learning needs of students in mainstream and special schools (Wearmouth, 1986) that cast doubt on the validity of the process of identification and assessment, but movement between school types was very difficult indeed, regardless of the amount of progress made by individual students. In addition, some educators began to be concerned about the 32,000 children in institutions of various sorts together with an unknown number at home who were deemed ineducable. In mainstream, many commentators began to see that the system of selection into grammar, technical and secondary modern schools was not as fair as had been assumed (Clark, Dyson, Millward & Skidmore, 1997). Research had shown that differing proportions of students were selected for each of the three types of school in different areas of the country. Considerable doubt was increasingly thrown on the reliability and validity of the psychometric tests that were used to discriminate between children. Further, a growing concern for equality of opportunity in society at large led some researchers in education to comment that the system was divisive and functioned to sustain the position of some already advantaged societal groups. For example, a disproportionate number of middle-class children were to be found in grammar schools (Douglas, 1967; Hargreaves, 1967). The majority of children – up to 86% in some LEAs – failed the 11+ examination and were assigned to secondary schools where the quality of the education on offer might be substandard. The 1963 Newsom Report, *Half Our Future* (Central Advisory Council for Education), investigating the education of secondary modern students, recognised the high quality of some secondary modern schools, but also provided severe criticisms. Richmond (1978, p. 75), commenting on the findings, wrote:

> It revealed that nearly 80% of Secondary Modern school buildings were seriously deficient, that the qualifications of Secondary Modern school teachers were often as "below average" as their pupils were said to be, that the rapid turnover of staff vitiated the work of schools in the poorer districts–in short that more than half the nation's children were getting a raw deal. […] it urged the need for more intellectually demanding courses to counteract the aimless drift and low morale which characterised the work of many schools particularly among older pupils […] the Newsom message

amounted to saying that the abilities of the broad mass of children had been grossly underestimated and that, given the chance, they were capable of better things.

As a result, beginning in the 1960s and increasingly in the 1970s, a growing number of comprehensive schools were opened, increasingly special classes and 'remedial' provision were established in mainstream, and some children were integrated from special into mainstream schools.   🖱2.7

In terms of special provision, the Education (Handicapped Children) Act 1970 removed the power of health authorities to provide training for children who experienced the most serious difficulties in learning (deemed 'mentally handicapped') and required the staff and buildings of junior training centres to be transferred to the education service. In future they were to be regarded as 'severely educationally subnormal' (ESN(S)), and entitled to education. In Scotland the 1974 Act also gave education authorities responsibility for the education of children who previously had been viewed as 'ineducable and untrainable'.

Introduction of the concept of special educational needs

In November 1973 Margaret Thatcher, then education secretary in the Conservative government, announced that she proposed, in conjunction with the secretaries of state for Scotland and Wales, to appoint a committee of enquiry into education in the special sector chaired by Mary Warnock. The wording of the aim of this enquiry very clearly reflects the greater emphasis on the purpose of education as preparation for employment, driven, at least in part, 'by a country's socio-economic goals' (Shuayb & O'Donnell, 2008, para 2):

> To review educational provision in England, Scotland and Wales for children and young people handicapped by disabilities of body or mind, taking account of the medical aspects of their needs, together with arrangements to prepare them for entry into employment; to consider the most effective use of resources for these purposes; and to make recommendations. (DES, 1978, p. 1)

The very influential 1978 Warnock report of special educational provision in Great Britain introduced a new concept of 'special educational needs' to replace the previous categorisation 'by disabilities of body or mind'. A study in 1970 by Rutter, Tizard   🖱2.8
and Whitmore had enquired into the incidence of difficulties in learning in the school population. The study reported teachers' perceptions that, on average, 20 per cent of their students were experiencing difficulty of some kind. Following Warnock teachers were advised to plan on the assumption that one in five children would have 'special educational needs' at some time in their school career. It is noteworthy that, since that time, the figure of 20 per cent has been used to estimate the number of children

nationally who might experience difficulties at some point in their educational career. Of the total number of students, approximately 2 per cent were seen by policy makers as likely to have difficulties which require additional or extra resources to be provided. This figure of 2 per cent is an arbitrary one, drawn from a count of students in special schools in 1944 (Warnock, 1978). Legally there are no official figures for the incidence of children likely to need statutory assessment. However, it is clearly useful to resource-providers, for example LAs, to estimate what proportion of their resources they are likely to have to set aside for individual students' educational needs.

Learning difficulties, disabilities and the law across the United Kingdom

In the United Kingdom, until recently there have been strong similarities in England, Wales and Northern Ireland in terms of education law, including the definition of what constitutes a special learning or behavioural need as well as the assessment of the need and the kind of provision that is made. Proposals by the National Assembly for Wales for revisions to legislation in Wales and by the Department for Education, for revisions in Northern Ireland, and new legislation that was introduced in England in 2014, may increase the differences between them, however. Education law in Scotland is regulated by the Scottish Government in Edinburgh and continues to be different.

In relation to disability law that applies to education as well as to other aspects of public life, most recently the Equality Act, 2010, the same legislation operates across all the countries of the United Kingdom. It does not, however, apply to Northern Ireland where the relevant disability equality legislation is the Disability Discrimination (Northern Ireland) Order 2006.

Definitions of special educational needs in England, Wales and Northern Ireland

The 1981 Education Act in England and Wales was based to a large extent on the 1978 Warnock Report's recommendations to replace the eleven categories of handicap with a new umbrella category of 'special educational needs' and an understanding that students' difficulties occur on a continuum. LEAs were given responsibilities to identify needs that required provision in addition to what was normally available in schools. Parents were to be consulted about provision for their child, and could appeal against a local authority's decisions. All children were to be educated in mainstream schools but with certain provisos:

- their needs should be met there, and
- it was compatible with the education of other children and with the 'efficient use of resources'.

In England, Wales and Northern Ireland, the definition of 'special educational needs' has remained largely constant since Warnock. Under the terms of the relevant legislation a child[4] has special educational needs if he or she has a learning difficulty[5] which calls for special educational provision to be made for him or her (Education Act, 1996, Part 1V, §312(1); Education Order (Northern Ireland) 1996, Part 11, §3(1); Children and Families Act, 2014, Part 3, §20 (1)). That is, a young person only has 'special educational needs' when special provision is required to meet them: learning difficulties do not in themselves constitute such a need.

To understand the definition of SEN, we first need to know what is meant by 'learning difficulty'. Similar definitions apply in England, Wales and Northern Ireland. That is, a child or young person may be seen as having such a difficulty if s/he experiences

a)   significantly greater difficulty in learning than the majority of same-age peers, or

b)   s/he has a disability which prevents him (or her) from making use of (educational) facilities 'of a kind generally provided for' same-age peers in mainstream educational institutions.

(Education Act 1996, Part 1V, §312 (2); Education Order (Northern Ireland) 1996, Part 11, §3(1); Children and Families Act 2014, Part 3, §20 (2))

In education law, a learning difficulty creates a need which is 'special 'only if the provision required to address it is 'special'. A specific literacy difficulty which makes it hard for a student to engage in the same learning activities as others might mean that s/he might have a 'learning difficulty', for example. This much is fairly obvious. However, a student might also have a 'learning difficulty' if s/he has a physical disability that creates a barrier to moving around the school or classroom to participate in those activities with peers.

 Reflective activity: Implications of legal definitions

How straightforward do you find this way of defining learning difficulties?
Note down any questions this definition raises for you.

This way of defining a learning difficulty raises major questions, for example:

- how to measure 'significantly greater difficulty in learning';

- how to compare one student to the majority. If we compare individuals against a mean average of the rest of the child population of the same age, it is bound to lead to mistakes, leaving some children with, and others without, support that might be needed;

---

[4]child or young person in England
[5]or disability in England

- how to gauge the contexts in which a difficulty becomes significant;
- what is meant by a general level of provision. Some schools have space for particular music, art, drama or sporting activities, others do not, for example.

Whether students are identified as needing additional support is very variable across the country. Inevitably, however needs are identified, the professional, resource and policy judgments involved in the decision-making process will always leave room for inequality. In England, for example, it is not unusual for schools to identify children with learning difficulties or disabilities in relation to expected progress in the National Curriculum. The danger here is that this allows assessment designed for a different purpose to validate decisions which affect provision and children's learning.

The second part of the definition refers to a 'disability' as causing learning difficulties. By law, then, a person with a visual impairment has a learning difficulty if the individual cannot access the same facilities as peers. The implication is that, if LAs and schools generally provide appropriate learning opportunities, then no student would be prevented 'from making use of educational facilities generally provided' (Education Act 1996, S. 312, DENI, 1998, para 1.4; Children and Families Act 2014, Part 3, §20 (2)(b)), and therefore no child would have special educational needs.

Definition of additional support needs in Scotland

The situation is different in Scotland. Here, the Education (Additional Support for Learning) (Scotland) Act (2004) (as amended – see below for discussion of this law) established the concept of 'additional support needs'. Under this Act, a child or young person has such needs if 'for whatever reason', s/he is not likely to be able 'to benefit from school education provided or to be provided' for him/her 'without the provision of additional support' (Scottish Government, p. 18, §1). 'School education' here includes, in particular, 'such education that is directed to the development of the personality, talents and mental and physical abilities of the child or young person to their fullest potential' (ibid., §3).

'Additional support' is defined as:

> provision which is additional to, or otherwise different from, the educational provision made generally for children or, as the case may be, young persons of the same age in schools (other than special schools) under the management of the education authority for the area to which the child or young person belongs. (ibid., p. 206)

A 'co-ordinated support plan' is seen as needed if the child or young person has additional support needs arising from

(i) one or more complex factors, or

(ii) multiple factors,

and if the needs 'are likely to continue for more than a year' (p. 74, §3), with the proviso that 'significant additional support' is required to address the needs. In this situation, a factor is defined as 'complex' if 'it has, or is likely to have, a significant adverse effect on the school education of the child or young person'.

Special educational needs legislation in England, Wales and Northern Ireland

In England and Wales the 1981 Act is seen by many as the key piece of legislation concerned with children and young people who experience difficulties or have disabilities in education. It introduced 'statements of special educational need', which set out an analysis of the difficulties students experience in schools and the curricular and human and material resources needed to address them.

The 1993 Education Act replaced the 1981 Education Act in all but a few minor details, although it covered much the same ground. This Act gave the responsibility for co-ordinating special education provision solely to LAs irrespective of the type of school attended by the pupils concerned. It introduced a *Code of Practice for the identification and assessment of special educational needs* (DfE, 1994), new procedures for assessing 'needs' and specifying resources in 'statements of special educational needs' and a new tribunal system to hear appeals against these formal assessment procedures. As noted in Chapter 1, parents were given legal remedies against decisions about their children in assessment and statementing. 'Independent' tribunals chaired by lawyers were introduced, following the model of industrial tribunals. The introduction of the *Code of Practice*, with its status of statutory guidance, gave the tribunals a shared text to guide their practice in hearing appeals about formal assessments.

🖉 1.3

The 1993 Act was repealed and replaced by the 1996 Act in November 1996, with Part IV of the new Act incorporating all the provisions of Part III of the 1993 Act. The 1996 Act remains the basis for education-related law in Wales, but the law in England changed substantially in 2014 with the Children and Families Act.

Legislation in England

Since 1996 a further Act, the Children and Families Act (2014) has brought about a number of changes in the law in England. Much of the new law is still the same as in 1996. However, the new system of supporting children and young people with SEN now applies to young people from birth to 25 years as long as they stay in education or training. This issue of age is important. In law a child becomes a young person when s/he is no longer of compulsory school age (that is, s/he became 16 before the last day of the summer term (Section 83(2)). Once a child becomes a young person s/he can take decisions in relation to the Act on his/her own behalf, rather than the parents, subject to a young person 'having capacity' to take a decision under the Mental Capacity Act (2005). If young people do not have the mental capacity to make a decision on their own, their parents will automatically be assumed to be making the decision on their behalf unless the Court of Protection has appointed a Deputy.

A child or young person with special educational needs and disability (SEND) is entitled to support that enables him/her to achieve the 'best possible educational and other outcomes', and it is the LA's duty to ensure they identify all children and young people who have or may have SEN and/or disabilities in their geographical area. Under this Act, statements of special education need[6] are being replaced by Education, Health and Care plans (EHCs). If an EHC plan is issued, the LA has the legal duty to ensure that the educational provision is made. The school or college that a child or young person attends should put support in place to make sure this is happening, but, if it does not, the LA has the responsibility to ensure it does.

A young person in further education is now legally entitled to the special educational provision specified in their EHC plan, but EHC plans do not apply to higher education. Where there is health provision in an EHC plan, the local health commissioning body – usually the Clinical Commissioning Group – has the duty to provide.

Every LA must develop and publish a 'Local Offer' (§30) that sets out the services and provision it expects to be available both inside and outside the LA's area for children and young people with SEN and/or a disability. The Local Offer should make clear what special educational provision it expects the schools and colleges in its area to make from their existing budgets. LAs have a duty to publish comments about the Local Offer from children, young people and their parents, and the action they intend to take in response (§30(6)).

The LA is obliged to consider identifying a personal budget (§48) for educational provision for a young person if the parent requests it when they are carrying out an EHC needs assessment or reviewing an EHC plan. This is the notional amount of money that is needed to cover the cost of making the special provision specified in the EHC plan. Head teachers or principals have a veto if they do not agree to a direct payment being made for special educational provision needed in their institution.

Legislation in Wales

Unlike in England, education-related law in Wales is still based on the 1996 Act. However, the National Assembly of Wales set out a proposal to amend legislation related to SEND policy and provision in 2012 in a consultation document *Forward in partnership for children and young people with additional needs*. In summary, the proposal in this consultation document was to:

- introduce the concept of 'additional needs' (AN), rather than 'special educational needs';

[6]See below for an explanation of statutory assessment of special educational needs that previously might result in a Statement of SEN, but now may result in an EHC plan.

- replace statements of SEN with new integrated 'Individual Development Plans' (IDPs) that:
  ○ include assessment and provision involving agencies beyond education where appropriate for young people aged 0–25 years with the highest levels of need, and
  ○ require multi-agency panels, called 'Support Panels', to assess and agree the support services from education, social and health services that should be recorded in the IDP.
- require relevant bodies to collaborate in respect of provision for additional needs;
- set out the duties to be required of relevant bodies (such as LAs and health services);
- set out the resolution process for any disputes;
- require the Welsh Ministers to issue a code of practice related to the new statutory framework for AN.

At the time of writing the new legislation has not yet been approved by the National Assembly of Wales.

Legislation in Northern Ireland

In Northern Ireland Part 11 of the Education Order (Northern Ireland) (1996) which remains the basis of legislation related to special educational needs in the province bears a close similarity to the 1996 Act in England and Wales. The 1996 Education Order was amended by the Special Educational Needs and Disability (Northern Ireland) Order (SENDO), (2005) Part II, Articles 3 to 12 and Schedule 1 to take account, specifically, of disability legislation that had been introduced across the United Kingdom in 2001. Recently a proposition to amend the law related to SEND was introduced in the Northern Ireland Assembly on 2nd March 2015 through the Special Educational Needs and Disability Bill (Bill 46/11–16). Among the proposals in the Bill:

Clause 1 places a new duty on the Education Authority to have regard to the views of the child in relation to decisions affecting them;
Clause 3 extends the existing duties of Boards of Governors in relation to SEN, including a requirement to maintain a personal learning plan (PLP) for each pupil with SEN and ensuring that a teacher is designated as a learning support coordinator (LSC)
[. . .]
Clause 9 gives children with SEN who are over compulsory school age rights previously exercisable by parents, including the right to appeal and to request a statutory assessment
(http://www.niassembly.gov.uk/globalassets/documents/raise/publications/2015/education/3815.pdf, accessed 20.02.16)

Additional support needs legislation in Scotland

The Education (Additional Support for Learning) (Scotland) Act 2004 provides the legal framework for provision of additional support for learning. The Act places duties on education authorities (and in certain circumstances health, social work and Skills Development Scotland) to make joint provision for all children and young people with additional support needs, including those with complex or multiple additional support needs. Where needs are significant and would last more than one year, they may require a statutory co-ordinated support plan to meet their learning needs. This Act also sets out rights for parents, establishes mechanisms for resolving differences for families and authorities through mediation and dispute resolution, and has established the Additional Support Needs Tribunals (Scotland).

The legislation was amended by the Education (Additional Support for Learning) (Scotland) Act 2009. The amendments related, among other issues, to the provision of a new national advocacy service for parents and young people. In addition the 2009 Act automatically deemed that all looked after children and young people have additional support needs unless the education authority determines that they do not require this support.

Definitions of areas of need across the United Kingdom

Reasons why students might experience special or additional needs are conceptualised somewhat differently in the different countries of the United Kingdom. The *Special Educational Needs Code of Practice for Wales* (2004, §7.52), just as the previous *Code of Practice* in England (DfES, 2001, para 7:52) recommends that assessment and provision should focus on four broad 'areas of need': communication and interaction; cognition and learning; behaviour, emotional and social development; and sensory and/or physical. More recently, the *SEN and Disability Code of Practice 0 to 25 Years* (DfE, 2015, §5.32) in England has amended the conceptualisation of the third 'broad' area of need from 'behaviour, emotional and social development' to 'social, emotional and mental health'.

Clearly there is a lot of overlap between these areas, For example, in terms of communication and interaction, lack of facility with receptive and expressive language has important implications for cognition and learning. As the *Code* in Wales, cautions:

> Although needs and requirements can usefully be organised into areas, individual
> pupils may well have needs which span two or more areas. For example, a pupil

with general learning difficulties may also have behavioural difficulties or a sensory impairment. Where needs are complex in this sense it is important to carry out a detailed assessment of individual pupils and their situations. (NAW, 2004, (§7:53).

Teaching approaches suggested in the *Code* in Wales as appropriate for addressing the learning needs of students who experience difficulties in communication and inter-action may also be appropriate to those who experience difficulties in cognition and learning. 2.9

In Scotland the approach is rather different, however. The revised *Supporting Children's Learning Code of Practice* (2010, p. 13) offers a (non-exhaustive) list of children or young people who may require additional support for a variety of reasons. This includes those who: 2.10

- have motor or sensory impairments
- are being bullied
- are particularly able or talented
- have experienced a bereavement
- are interrupted learners
- have a learning disability
- are looked after by a local authority
- have a learning difficulty, such as dyslexia
- are living with parents who are abusing substances
- are living with parents who have mental health problems
- have English as an additional language
- are not attending school regularly
- have emotional or social difficulties
- are on the child protection register
- are young carers.

A wide range of factors broadly grouped into four overlapping areas are identified as potentially creating barriers that may lead to the need for additional support:

- learning environment
- family circumstances
- disability or health need
- social and emotional factors.

The definition of additional support provided in the Act is broad and inclusive to reflect the rather broader concept of who might require additional provision. Forms of additional support identified in the *Code* in Scotland are categorised under three broad headings (p. 21):

- approaches to learning and teaching
- support from personnel
- provision of resources.

Codes of Practice across the United Kingdom

When a teacher is seriously concerned about the progress made by a child in a classroom, it is very important to be aware of the legal process that should be followed to maintain the child's access to education. In the years following the 1981 Education Act in England and Wales a number of issues relating to the procedures for assessing pupils thought to 'have special educational needs' became apparent. The Audit Commission and Her Majesty's Inspectorate identified three key problems:

- lack of clarity about what constitutes special educational need and about the respective responsibilities of schools and LEAs;
- lack of systems to ensure that schools and LEAs are accountable for their work in the area of special needs;
- lack of incentives for LEAs to implement the 1981 Act. (Audit Commission/ HMI, 1992, para 126).

In 1994, as noted already, the government published a *Code of Practice for the identification and assessment of special educational needs* (DfE, 1994) with the status of 'statutory guidance' to schools in England and Wales on how to interpret the law to provide appropriate support to those with learning difficulties. A similar publication was produced later in Northern Ireland (DENI, 1998). In Scotland the *Code* reflects a somewhat different legal framework.

Since that time two further Codes have been published reflecting changes in the law, firstly in relation to the 1996 Education Act and, most recently, to the Children and Families Act 2014 (DfES 2001; National Assembly of Wales, 2004; DfE, 2015). Their statutory nature is reflected in Part 1V of the 1996 Education Act, §313, in England and Wales:

> (1) The Secretary of State shall issue, and may from time to time revise, a code of practice giving practical guidance in respect of the discharge by [local authorities] and the governing bodies of [maintained schools] [and maintained nursery schools] of their functions under this Part.
>
> [. . .]
>
> On any appeal under this Part to the Tribunal, the Tribunal shall have regard to any provision of the code which appears to the Tribunal to be relevant to any question arising on the appeal.

In the section below the content and implications of the most recent *Codes*[7] in operation in the United Kingdom are reviewed in chronological order of their publication.

Code of Practice in Northern Ireland

The Department of Education, Northern Ireland (DENI) provided statutory guidance for Education and Library Boards and schools in a *Code of Practice on the
Identification and Assessment of Special Educational Needs* (DENI, 1998) and also
a *Supplement to the Code of Practice* (DENI, 2005). The statutory guidance in these
two documents reflects the Education (Northern Ireland) Order 1996 as amended
by The Special Educational Needs and Disability (Northern Ireland) Order 2005
(SENDO).

2.11

A principal element in the Northern Ireland Code (DENI, 1998) that reflects what
was in the original Code in England and Wales (DfE, 1994) was the introduction of a
five-stage model of assessment. This staged model reflects that set out in the Warnock
Report (DES, 1978, pp. 60–63). The first three stages are based in the school, with the
assistance of external specialists where needed; at Stages 4 and 5 the Library Board
shares responsibility with schools.

- Stage 1: teachers identify and register a child's special educational needs and,
  consulting the school's SEN co-ordinator, take initial action.
- Stage 2: the SEN co-ordinator takes lead responsibility for collecting and
  recording information and for co-ordinating the child's special educational
  provision, working with the child's teachers.
- Stage 3: teachers and the SEN co-ordinator are supported by specialists from
  outside the school.
- Stage 4: the Board considers the need for a statutory assessment and, if
  appropriate, makes a multi-disciplinary assessment.
- Stage 5: the Board considers the need for a statement of special educational
  needs; if appropriate, it makes a statement and arranges, monitors and reviews
  provision. (DENI, 1998, §1.7)

In this *Code of Practice*, an 'individual education plan' (IEP) is introduced at Stage
2. This term 'individual education plan' follows the American model outlined in the
1975 special education law in the United States, Public Law 94–142, where a plan
for a child perceived as having difficulties had to be drawn up in order to attract
additional federal funds. The IEP summarises action to be taken at home and at
school to address difficulties in learning. It focuses on the nature of the child's
learning difficulties rather than other elements of the school context which impact
on learning.

---

[7] i.e., most recent at the time of writing (April 2016)

If the Special Educational Needs and Disability Bill mentioned above is passed into law, it seems likely that a revised Code of Practice will be published for Northern Ireland. Updates will be uploaded on the website associated with the current book as they occur.

Code of Practice in Wales

The fundamental principles of the *Special Educational Needs Code of Practice for Wales* (NAW, 2004) are linked to the 1996 Education Act that applied in both England and Wales when the *Code* was published. Strong similarities can be seen here with the principles of the *Code* in operation in Northern Ireland in relation to a young person's entitlement to having his/her needs met 'normally' in a mainstream setting with access to a broad balanced curriculum, and a focus on the need to listen to the views of the young person and his/her family (NAW, 2004, §1.5).

The 2004 *Code* in Wales also acknowledges the idea of a continuum of needs but, like the (2001) *Code* in England,[8] moves away from the five-staged approach to recommend a graduated approach to individualised interventions through provision at 'School Action' or 'School Action Plus'. Class teachers should know which children have been identified at School Action and School Action Plus, contribute information about children's progress at each stage and be aware of the content of children's IEPs. They are also expected to take a leading role in monitoring and recording of children's progress and work with the school's special educational needs co-ordinator (SENCo) and with professionals from outside the school.

School Action begins when a class teacher, SENCo or teaching assistant identifies a child as having special educational needs that require individual provision additional to, or different from, a differentiated curriculum and strategies that are usually provided in the class. The school receives no additional funding for the child. 'School Action' is likely to involve consultation between the class teacher, the school's SENCo and the parents, collation of information already available about the child's progress, and closer attention to the child's programme of work in the classroom, and closer monitoring of progress. The individual education plan for the young person

> should only record that which is additional to or different from the differentiated curriculum plan that is in place as part of normal provision. The IEP should be crisply written and may focus on three or four key targets. IEPs should be written in Welsh, English or bilingually if appropriate. IEPs, and the ways in which they can help, should be discussed with parents and the child. (NAW, 2004, §4.27)

School Action Plus is for children who are likely to need support from specialists outside the school: a teacher from the LA's special needs support service or an educational psychologist, for example: or therapists of various kinds: speech, physio- and/or occupational, health professionals: nurses, health visitors, doctors, education welfare officers

---

[8]The 2001 *Code* has now been superseded as a result of the change in legislation in England in 2014.

and social workers, member of the local child guidance or family guidance team, and specialist teachers for children with physical or visual disabilities or hearing impairments.

If insufficient progress is made at School Action Plus, a request for a statutory assessment might be made. If so, the process is handled by the school and the LA, and may result in a Statement of Special Educational Needs that outlines special educational provision determined by the LA.

Code of Practice in England

In England, schools, further education colleges and other settings have clear duties under the *SEN and Disability Code of Practice 0 to 25 Years* (DfE, 2015) One of the significant changes in the Code in England is the advice given to class and subject teachers, supported by the senior leadership team, to identify pupils who make less than expected progress by making regular assessments of the progress of all pupils (§6.17). Gathering of information about pupils should include discussion early on with both the pupil and their parents so that all can be clear about the pupil's areas of strength and difficulty, any concerns the parent(s) might have, the outcomes agreed for the child and the next steps.

If a pupil is identified as having SEN, schools are exhorted to remove barriers to learning and put effective special provision, to be known as 'SEN provision', in place through a graduated approach in the form of a four-part cycle of assessment, planning, intervention and review (assess→plan→do→review) where previous decisions and actions are revisited, refined and revised as staff and parents understand more about what supports the pupil in making good progress. This approach should utilise more frequent review and more specialist expertise in successive cycles as required to match interventions to the educational needs of children and young people.

Where, despite appropriate interventions a pupil continues to make less than expected progress, the school should consider involving specialists, including from outside agencies. Together, the SENCo, class teacher, specialists, and parents/family, should consider a range of approaches to support the child's progress and agree the outcomes and a date by which progress will be reviewed.

If the child or young person still does not make the progress that is expected, the school or parents should consider requesting an Education, Health and Care needs assessment and provide evidence of the action taken by the school as part of its SEN support.

Guidance given in the 2014 *Code* about EHC plans is discussed in the section on statutory assessment below.

Code of Practice in Scotland

In Scotland, a revised *Supporting Children's Learning Code of Practice* was published in 2010 to reflect changes in the law in Scotland that had taken place in 2009. Within this document (p. 9) the purpose of this *Code* is defined as explaining

> the duties on education authorities and other agencies to support children's and
> young people's learning. It provides guidance on the Act's provisions as well as on the

supporting framework of secondary legislation. [...] It also sets out arrangements for avoiding and resolving differences between families and education authorities.

The *Code* (§ 81) sets out a phased approach to addressing individual needs. A process of 'personal learning planning' is considered appropriate to address many needs:

All children with additional support needs should be engaged in personal learning planning and for many this process will be sufficient to address their additional support needs.

Personal learning planning (PLP) that should be manageable, realistic and reflect strengths as well as needs is intended to result in aims and goals that relate to the young person's own circumstances. The child should be given the opportunity regularly to discuss his/her progress with a member of staff. The parent(s), child and school should be fully involved in the PLP process.

The Code (§ 82) goes on to note how, if required, a PLP can be supported by an individualised educational programme. In Scotland, if children or young people require more detailed planning for their learning than can be made through PLP, they may have an individualised educational programme (IEP). This details the nature of a child's or young person's additional support needs, the ways these are to be met, the learning outcomes to be achieved and specifies what additional support is needed. At this point support from other agencies such as health, social work, or voluntary agencies may be required. If so, the relevant agencies should be involved in developing the child's IEP so that the work is properly co-ordinated. Again, the parent(s) and the child should be fully involved in the process.

 Reflective activity: Usefulness of Codes of Practice

Like a number of others areas in the context of special educational, or additional support, provision, the publication of Codes of Practice and the establishment of tribunals to hear parental appeals can be viewed in different ways:

- On the one hand they can be interpreted as divisive in setting families against schools and LAs.
- On the other they may be seen as protecting young people's entitlements to having their individual needs identified and assessed, and appropriate provision guaranteed.

What is your own view on this?

Statutory assessment of needs across the United Kingdom

In all four countries there is provision for statutory assessment of young people's educational needs. The processes for this, and the requirements of the final legal document of entitlement to the identified resources, are included in Chapter 3.

Disability equality legislation across the United Kingdom

Since 2000 a number of pieces of legislation relating to disability equality have been passed across the United Kingdom.[9] Most recently, the Equality Act, 2010, stresses planned approaches to eliminating discrimination and improving access and is nation-wide (including private education), imposing duties on schools and LAs. This means that organisations such as schools and colleges are expected to be proactive in antici-pating and responding to the needs of disabled students.

Definition of 'disabled'

 Reflective activity: Considering how to define 'disabled'

'Disabled' and 'disability' are terms that may, or may not, provoke strong reactions for reasons that may be similar to those discussed above in relation to connotations of the terms 'special educational' or 'additional support' needs.

In law, a child or young person is disabled under the Equality Act 2010 (section 6) if s/he has a physical or mental impairment which has a substantial and long-term adverse effect on his/her ability to carry out normal day-to-day activities.

How clear do you find that definition?

Can you see any overlap between the definition of 'disabled' and that of 'special educational needs'?

Under the terms of the 2010 Act, 'substantial' means more than minor or trivial and 'long term" means lasting more than one year or likely to last more than one year. Not all children or young people with special educational, or additional support, needs will be disabled and not all disabled children or young people will have special educa-tional, or additional support, needs. The vast majority, however, will fall under both legal definitions.

Early years settings, schools, colleges and LAs have clear legal duties to act to pre-vent unlawful discrimination, whether directly or indirectly. For example, Paragraph 85 of the Equality Act 2010 states that there must be no discrimination by a school, for example

(2) (a) in the way it provides education for the pupil;

  (b) in the way it affords the pupil access to a benefit, facility or service;

  (c) by not providing education for the pupil;

  (d) by not affording the pupil access to a benefit, facility or service.

---

[9]This does not apply in Northern Ireland where policy related to disability is devolved to the Northern Ireland Assembly.

Educational institutions must therefore ensure that they do not treat children and young people with disabilities less favourably than others. Since the original 1981 Act in England and Wales the law has changed to increase children's rights to be educated in mainstream. Stronger rights to a place in a mainstream school have made it unlawful for schools and LAs to discriminate against disabled students, particularly in relation to admission arrangements and the educational provision in school. Paragraph 85 of the 2010 Equality Act, for example, also states that there must be no discrimination by a school against a young person:

(1) (a) in the arrangements it makes for deciding who is offered admission as a pupil;

(b) as to the terms on which it offers to admit the person as a pupil;

(c) by not admitting the person as a pupil.

Schools and colleges also have a duty to make reasonable adjustments – to change what they do or were proposing to do – to ensure a child or young person is not disadvantaged. This includes the provision of aids and services to support a child or young person.

The 2010 Equality Act gives parents (and/or young people of a responsible age in Scotland) the right of appeal to a Tribunal, if they feel their child has suffered discrimination. The Tribunal in England is the First-tier Tribunal, in Wales the Special Educational Needs Tribunal for Wales, and in Scotland an Additional Support Needs Tribunal for Scotland.

2.13

In Northern Ireland the relevant disability equality legislation is the Disability Discrimination (Northern Ireland) Order 2006. This Order extends previous legislation, the Disability Discrimination Act, 1995, to bring the functions of public authorities within the scope of disability legislation and imposes a new duty to promote positive attitudes towards disabled people and encourage participation in public life (§49A).

Summary

Over the years, the conceptualisations of differences between people, the development of notions of entitlements and human rights, and the change in focus of, and on, education itself, have all contributed to the complexity and changing nature of the field of special educational needs. Whatever an individual's view, parents, teachers and other professionals in education have to conform to aspects of the official definitions when engaged on formal processes under the Act, such as assessment and statementing.

In England, the aspect of law currently relating to special educational needs and disabilities is the 2014 Children and Families Act, Part 3; in Wales (at the time of writing) it is the 1996 Education Act, Part 1V; in Northern Ireland it is Part 11 of the

Education Order (Northern Ireland) 1996 with revisions and additions made in the Special Educational Needs and Disability (Northern Ireland) Order 2005, together with their associated Regulations and statutory guidance documents. In Scotland it is the Education (Additional Support for Learning) (Scotland) Act (2004), subsequently amended by the Education (Additional Support for Learning) (Scotland) Act (2009). In addition, aspects of legislation related to disability equality also apply to education provision. The Equality Act 2010 consolidates previous discrimination legislation and is nationwide, operating across all the United Kingdom, but not in Northern Ireland.

Chapter 3
Assessment of, and planning for, learning needs

The major questions in this chapter are:

- How can we assess the inclusivity of the learning environment for all students?
- How and why is the whole area of assessment in schools and colleges controversial?
- What is the process of an 'assess → plan → do → review' framework, for example, in the new Code of Practice (DfE, 2015) in England?
- What are the principles of different kinds of assessment: formative, criterion-referenced, summative and standardised?
- How can behaviour be assessed?
- How can we plan effectively to meet individual needs?
- What are the statutory requirements of plans designed to meet extreme needs?

Introduction

By definition, a child or young person has special or additional needs if he or she has a difficulty within learning or behaviour, or an emotional issue or a disability that calls for special or additional educational provision to be made for him or her of a kind that is not normally available in schools and colleges. Whether special or additional provision is required must be seen within the learning context of the individual child. It is obvious that in classrooms where the work is tailored to the needs of individual students, fewer students will experience difficulties of the kind that require special or additional provision to be made to address them. As the *Code of Practice* in England (DfE, 2015, §1.14) notes:

> High quality teaching that is differentiated and personalised will meet the individual
> needs of the majority of children and young people. Some children and young people

need educational provision that is additional to or different from this. This is special educational provision under Section 21 of the Children and Families Act 2014. Schools and colleges must use their best endeavours to ensure that such provision is made for those who need it.

A few students may experience serious difficulties despite efforts to ensure the classroom pedagogy is inclusive and differentiated. All students have a statutory right to having their special educational needs, or their additional learning needs, and disabilities identified and met. However, it is really important to acknowledge that particular approaches to identification and assessment have an important influence on how a school constructs its special needs policies and provision. There are a number of different approaches to this process. Sometimes this can mean using a form of assessment, often very formal, summative by nature and standardised against national norms, that enables comparison with the learning achievement and behaviour patterns of peers, or norms for sight, hearing, movement and so on. There are some obvious questions raised here, however, for example:

- how to gauge whether what is already provided in the learning context is insufficient so that 'special' provision is therefore required, and
- how to ensure that a child whose attainment levels are demonstrated to be very poor in comparison with peers does not feel so demoralised that s/he will not try any more. (Murphy, 2002)

Young people can be supported to make huge learning gains and, consequently, will feel much more positively about themselves as learners if teachers, families and others clearly understand the power of some forms of assessment, monitoring and focused feedback, and also how some forms can have negative effects on students.

This chapter opens with a discussion of ways to assess the degree to which classrooms are inclusive and teaching differentiated. It continues by outlining ways to assess needs at the level of the individual student and considers the place of, and appropriate tools to enable, assessment of learning, behaviour and sensory needs. This includes discussion of students' and families' perceptions of needs. Finally the chapter reflects on the formalities of statutory assessment in the various areas of the United Kingdom and Northern Ireland.

Ensuring inclusive classrooms

We begin here by looking first at ways to evaluate the degree to which learning environments might contribute to students' difficulties.

Reflective activity: Effective differentiation in classrooms

Note down what, in your own experience, are the characteristics of effective differentiation in classrooms.
What would you be looking for in an inclusive classroom?

It is very clear from the various Codes of Practice across the United Kingdom that additional intervention and support for individuals in schools/colleges should not be expected to compensate for lack of good teaching.

High-quality teaching, appropriately differentiated for individuals, is the first step in responding to possible special or additional needs. In England, for example, the new system of special educational needs (SEN) support that is recommended for schools/colleges should be designed to ensure support is focused on individual need and outcomes, not on the amount of support that is available or classifications of difficulties.

Differentiation of lesson activities, tasks and resources needs to take account of the full range of learning needs among children in the classroom and any requirements on individual education plans. This includes current reading levels, taking into account possible visual and auditory difficulties, interest level of the materials that are used, consideration of student grouping in the classroom, prior experiences of students, the potential range of applications of technology that might support learning, and so on. Resources include the human as well as the material. Discussion and preparation with teaching assistants and any other adults prior to the sequence of lessons is vital. If a student cannot work on the same objectives as the class as a whole, the teacher might want to choose learning objectives that are linked to the topic on which the whole class is working, but earlier in a learning progression. It will often be possible to 'track back' to locate earlier learning objectives.

 3.1

Auditing the learning environment

There is a variety of ways through which to assess the degree to which the learning environment predisposes to positive learning and behaviour. One way to do this is to carry out an audit of teaching in the classroom.

 Reflective activity: Auditing the degree to which teaching is inclusive

The authors of the Primary Strategy (DCSF, 2005; DfES, 2006) developed an inclusive teaching checklist to evaluate the extent to which pedagogy in classrooms can be evaluated as inclusive of all learners. This checklist has proved to be really useful to

many class teachers. It has been archived and is now available at http://webarchive.
nationalarchives.gov.uk/20110202171650/http:/nationalstrategies.standards.dcsf.
gov.uk/node/317753 – accessed 02.03.16.

You might choose to download a copy of this checklist to

- audit the degree to which the teaching in a classroom with which you are familiar is inclusive;
- reflect on what changes might be made to ensure that the teaching approach is more inclusive, if relevant.

Auditing support for positive behaviour in classrooms

Birmingham (England) Local Education Authority's three-level approach outlined in its strategy document *Behaviour in schools: framework for intervention* (Williams & Birmingham City Council Education Department, 1998) offers a very useful initial audit of the learning environment in which a student's unacceptable behaviour occurs. This is followed by reflection on how to alter that environment to make a positive impact on behaviour and learning.

The teacher first takes a baseline of behaviour by recording:

- frequency
- place
- time
- social situation
- setting events
- description of problem behaviour
- duration of problem behaviour
- severity of behaviour (if appropriate)
- consequences to exhibiting child
- consequences to others.

(Williams & Birmingham City Council Education Department, 2004, p. 285)

The teacher then audits changeable factors in the general learning environment that may influence the learner's behaviour:

- classroom physical environment, organisation and equipment;
- classroom management;
- classroom rules and routines;
- environment, routines and rules outside class;

- whole school policies and support for staff;
- roles of parents and governors.

(Williams & Birmingham City Council Education Department, 2004, pp. 285–6)

Next, s/he considers information relating to the individual student:

- possible sensory difficulty – particularly with hearing;
- significant medical factors affecting the child;
- significant life events which may affect the child.

(Williams & Birmingham City Council Education Department, 2004, p. 285)

We might add to this list other difficulties in learning, for example, in reading, writing and spelling, that might influence behaviour.

The next step is to think about what changes in the environment and teaching approaches might influence behaviour in a positive way, and then implement these changes and monitor the consequences. After this has been done, responses continue if necessary with a greater focus on the individual student within the learning environment. Reference to external agencies for support and advice should occur only after the above steps have been taken.

The place of assessment in supporting learning and behaviour needs

Assessment of need should start with a whole school/college approach to monitoring all students' progress that can quickly identify where a young person is not making adequate progress. Schools should assess each pupil's current skills and levels of attainment on entry. The *Code of Practice* in England (DfE, 2015, §6.16) notes, for example, that 'Schools should assess each pupil's current skills and levels of attainment on entry, building on information from previous settings and key stages where appropriate'.

Class and subject teachers, supported by the senior leadership team, should make regular assessments of progress for all students. Where individuals are falling behind or making inadequate progress, given their age and starting point, they should be given extra support. Support that is organised for individuals should be evaluated by its focus and success in achieving specified outcomes and not on the amount that has been made available, as a number of reports have noted, for example Lamb (2009). Adequate progress, as implied for example in England in the *Code of Practice* (DfE, 2015, §6.17), might be seen as including that which

- is similar to that of peers starting from the same baseline;
- matches or betters the child's previous rate of progress;

- closes the attainment gap between the child and their peers;
- prevents the attainment gap from growing wider.

'Assess → plan → do → review' cycle

Assessment of individual needs is the starting point for developing appropriate individual intervention plans to meet learning or behavioural needs. The recommended assess→plan→do→review cycle in the *Code of Practice* (DfE, 2015) outlines what many outside England may also view as good practice in identifying, assessing and addressing needs. It assumes that a clear understanding of a student's or child's needs is a critical precondition to planning effective provision and adjustments to teaching that will in turn lead to good progress and improved outcomes. This process begins by ensuring that students receive appropriate learning goals related to the appropriate stage of learning with the National Curriculum guidelines; and that they are engaged in interactive learning conversations throughout their learning activities within a well-informed understanding of what constitutes an appropriate curriculum for the age group and the students' peers in the first place. Learning conversations are based on evidence from assessments and observations carried out in authentic learning contexts. Learning conversations include responsive feedback that connects to the student's own experience of difficulties in learning and feed forward to help the student identify their next most appropriate learning steps.

Where pupils continue to make inadequate progress, despite high-quality teaching targeted at their areas of weakness, the class or subject teacher, working with the co-ordinator, should assess whether the child has a significant need. Assessment should draw on:

- teachers' assessments/experience of the student;
- information from school's core approach to student progress, attainment and behaviour;
- the individual's development in comparison to peers;
- the views and experience of parents, the child's own views and, if relevant, advice from external support services.

Information gathering should include the use of high-quality formative assessment, effective tools and early assessment materials. For higher levels of need, schools should have arrangements in place to draw on more specialised assessments from external agencies and professionals.

Where there has been an individual assessment of need, there should be agreement about the particular support that is required for the young person. Any concern raised by a parent should be recorded. Assessment should be regularly reviewed. Necessarily differentiation must take account of those students who experience difficulties of various sorts, and this will be dependent on the exchange of information regarding individual needs. In some schools this has been achieved through the use of 'pupil passports'.

Teacher assessments

We do not always wish to compare one child with others. It is always important to have a sense of children's ongoing progress in learning through continuous formative assessment that can provide teachers and others with opportunities to notice what is happening during learning activities, recognise the level and direction of the learning of individuals and see how they can help to take that learning further.

Formative assessment

Assessment can be a powerful educational tool for promoting learning, 'but there is no evidence that increasing the amount of testing will enhance learning' on its own (Assessment Reform Group, 1999, p. 2). In a seminal piece of work Black and Wiliam (1998) demonstrated clearly that student achievement can be raised through formative assessment in the classroom. Improving learning through assessment depends on five, 'deceptively simple', factors: providing effective feedback; actively involving students in their own learning; modifying teaching in response to the results of assessment; recognising the influence of assessment on students' motivation and self-esteem; and enabling students to assess themselves and understand that they need to do to improve (Assessment Reform Group, 1999, p. 5). The shift in emphasis in the purpose of day-to-day assessment in classrooms has resulted in a focus, in many places, on 'Assessment for Learning' (AfL): ongoing day-to-day assessments that include questioning and discussions with children, observations of children while they are working, analysing children's work and giving quick feedback.

 Reflective activity: Link between assessment for learning and scaffolding by more informed others

Look back at the discussion of sociocultural views of learning in Chapter 1 and as you do so reflect on the significance of scaffolding in new learning.

It is easy to see why it is important in the learning process for students to have the opportunity for discussion with a more expert other who can scaffold new learning through the zone of proximal development (ZPD). Assessment that supports learning must therefore enable students to see how well they are doing to guide subsequent learning in a constructive way that shows them what they need to do, and can do, to make progress.

Sometimes also we need to know whether a child has reached a particular threshold or level in his/her learning through so-called criterion referencing.

Criterion-referencing

Criterion-referencing is different from norm-referencing. It is designed to compare a learner's performance against identified criteria and standards that illustrate key features of learning, achievement and quality at different stages of children's development (Dunn, Parry & Morgan, 2002) and clear descriptors of particular levels of performance within them. Setting out criteria for an assessment clarifies both what is required of learners but also assists teachers or others in deciding what they need to teach. Schools often use authentic examples of students' work that illustrate what these criteria look like so that teachers can compare a student's work sample with the exemplars to identify specific strengths and weaknesses, identify individual teaching and learning needs and prioritise new learning goals. Criterion-referencing can also improve the quality of feedback offered to learners as the descriptors of levels of performance and the overall criteria should be clear enough to serve as indicators of what learners have to do to succeed (Wearmouth, 2016a, b). Parents and caregivers can also be better informed about what work at a particular curriculum level looks like and how they too can better support the next learning steps.

Formal, norm-referenced (standardised) tests

As we have already discussed in Chapter 2, deciding whether a child's need is 'special' or 'additional' raises some obvious questions about the assessment of difference. Identification of differences between young people in education may depend on the results of norm-referenced assessment that is designed to compare one student's achievement with that of others of the same age across a whole population.

 Reflective activity: Prior understandings of norm-referenced tests

Before reading the section below on norm-referenced (standardised) test procedures and their uses, you might wish to reflect on what you already know and understand about this particular topic.

Whatever is assessed in a norm-referenced test has to be measurable. For example, it is very common to use norm-referenced tests in the area of literacy. These might be in the areas of comprehension or reading accuracy, or spelling, for example, or in some aspects of mathematics. Are you familiar with standardised tests in any other area of the curriculum?

Rationale underpinning norm-referencing

There are occasions when we wish to compare young people's scores on different tests. For example, we might wish to compare a child's test score in reading comprehension with that in mathematics to have an understanding of his/her overall achievement. Or, we might wish to compare a young person's achievement with the national cohort of peers. One way to make test scores such as 23 out of 36 more readily understandable and comparable with another test score such as 13 out of 30 would be to convert both to percentages (64 per cent and 43 per cent, to the nearest whole number). However, these percentages do not tell us the average score of all children against which we can judge how well or badly children are doing in comparison with peers, or how spread out the scores are.

Standardisation process

Standardising a test score involves assessing a large, nationally representative sample using a particular test and then adjusting the mean (average) to a score of 100. It is then easy to compare a child's result with this score of 100. A glance at Figure 3.1 is an example of what the normal distribution of scores in a norm-referenced test might look like on a graph.

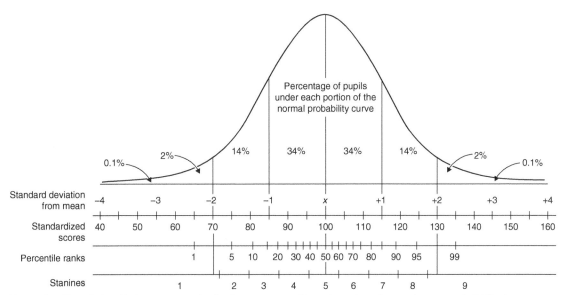

Figure 3.1 The relationship between standardised scores, percentile ranks and stanines under a normal distribution curve

To understand the use of standardised testing it is important to be aware of a number of important concepts: 'measure of spread' (the so-called standard deviation of scores), validity and reliability, the usefulness of standardised scores and interpretations of percentile ranks, confidence bands and reading ages.

Measure of spread/standard deviation

An important concept associated with standardised tests is that of the measure of spread or standard deviation of scores. This is usually set to 15 for educational attainment and ability tests. Irrespective of the difficulty of the test, about 68 per cent of students in a national sample will have a standardised score within one standard deviation (15 points) of the average (that is, between 85 and 115) and about 95 per cent will have a standardised score within two standard deviations (30 points) of the average (between 70 and 130). These examples come from a frequency distribution, known as the 'normal distribution', which is shown in Figure 3.1. Just to recap, you will see that the biggest proportion of scores lies between a score of 85 and 115.

Validity and reliability

The terms 'validity' and 'reliability' are often used in relation to both formal and informal tests. In general, the 'validity' of a test is the degree to which that test assesses what it is intended to test. We might ask, for example, whether a test of cognitive ability or reading that has been developed and standardised in Britain would be valid for young people from a completely different culture and new to the United Kingdom, or how valid is the concept of 'reading age' and whether and/or how this might relate to adults. We might also ask whether the test tests what we expect it to test in the context in which it is being used, in other words whether a test has 'context validity'.

'Reliability', on the other hand, generally means whether we would obtain the same result on the same test with the same cohort of individuals if we did the test procedure again.

Percentile ranks

There is a constant relationship between percentile ranks and standardised scores when the same average score and standard deviation are used. The percentile rank is the percentage of students in the sample of the same age who gained a score at the same level or below that of the child's score. So performance at the 50th percentile indicates that the child performed as well as or better than 50 per cent of the sample when age is taken into account.

Confidence Bands

'Confidence bands' indicate the range of scores within which the accurate assessment of attainment is likely to fall. It is not possible to obtain the 'true score', that is, the hypothetically perfect measurement of the individual's ability. Tests of the sort discussed here measure attainment, that is, the outcome of the student's work at any particular time, not 'ability'. In addition, however carefully educational tests are put together and administered, errors can result from factors such as the child's state of health, tiredness, lack of familiarity with formal assessments, and so on.

The concept of 'reading age'

'Reading age' is a very commonly used concept in relation to norm-referenced assessments of literacy learning, for example, in standardised assessments such as the Neale Analysis of Reading Ability (Neale, 1999). Reading age indicates the age at which a given raw score was the average. It is obtained by working out for each age group the average raw score of all of the children in the sample of that age and then smoothing out any irregularities in the resulting graph. Increases in performance with age are smaller for older age groups. This raises issues for using this measurement with older students because accuracy and rate of reading would show no improvement beyond a certain point.

Reading ages represent snapshots of a progression in literacy development. They are not fixed and exact measures of reading attainment. Reading is a learned behaviour that is closely aligned with development and age. Thus a low reading score does not necessarily suggest general low ability, slow developmental growth, and so on. However, if we use these normative scores while taking into account the confidence bands attributed to the known score, we can then view reading ages as estimates of reading ability at the time of testing.

Usefulness of standardised scores

Standardised scores are often thought to be useful for a number of reasons. Firstly, standardisation produces a scale that enables a comparison of results so that we can see whether a child is above or below the national average. The date when the test was standardised is important here because an old test might well be out of date in terms of comparisons of individuals with national norms. Re-standardisation of an old test might well give different national norms in relation to the current generation of children. Secondly, scores are standardised so that the ages of the children are taken into account. When looking at a child's score on a standardised assessment against national norms, we will be able to tell whether that child is above or below other children of the same age. Thirdly, using standardised scores allows us to compare a child's performance on a test in one area of the curriculum, for example reading, with another, for example mathematics. Or, we might compare a child's performance in two different aspects of the same area, for example, reading comprehension and reading accuracy, which might be important in assessing whether a child is dyslexic.

Reflective activity: Understanding the theory underpinning, and applications of, norm-referenced/ standardised tests

Anyone considering assessing a child needs to be fully conversant with test procedures, their aims and rationale as well as wider cultural and social factors, the school, the area of the curriculum concerned, and also attributes of the individual child and above all, of course, what useful information the assessment can give.

If you have access to such a test, now that you have finished reading the section above, have a look at the manual to check your understanding both of the terminology used, the test procedures themselves and also how to interpret the results.

Issues associated with norm-referencing

Standardised tests alone are not designed to diagnose the root of difficulties in learning experienced by a learner. Besides this, there are a number of issues associated with normative assessment that imply the use of such test procedures cannot be considered neutral.

 Reflective activity: Consideration of concerns related to the use of norm-referenced assessment

A number of concerns have been raised by various researchers in relation to the use of standardised assessment related to equity and the link between achievement norms and teacher expectations of particular learners. There is plenty of evidence to indicate that assessment itself can serve to reinforce or undermine the motivation to strive for future achievement in schools (Murphy, 2002).

As you read the discussion below, reflect on the extent to which you agree with the points that are made.

Results from externally imposed summative tests, especially where there are very high stakes attached to these results in countries such as England, can have very negative effects on students (Wearmouth, 2008).

First, in relation to the question of equity, some students may be allocated additional resources after achieving only very low scores on norm-referenced tests. However, there is a very grey area around the cut-off point above which other students will receive no additional provision.

Then there is the issue that when an individual student's test score lies within the bottom 'tail' of a normal distribution curve there is often an assumption that the student's innate ability is very low. Using standardised forms of tests means that we can pinpoint those students whose scores fall into the lowest 2 per cent or so. However, poor scores on normative tests can also mean that students' failure to achieve in school is automatically 'blamed' on poor ability, or the family, or the ethnic group. Sometimes this is known as the 'deficit' view of children who experience difficulties. This view can limit teachers' expectations of what to expect of certain students and, therefore, lead to continued poor achievement (Rosenthal & Jacobson, 1968). It may also absolve schools from responsibility for that learner's progress in school. 'Success' and 'failure' in norm-referenced tests are not just the result of children's natural ability, however (Tomlinson, 1988). Some families cannot support their own children adequately as a result of the circumstances in which they find themselves and the way that the school curriculum functions.

Assessment of behaviour

Difficult behaviour which seems to relate to a particular student may be indicative of a range of contextual issues associated with society, the family, ethnic or community group, school, classroom, peer group or teacher, as well as the individual student (Wearmouth, Glynn & Berryman, 2005).

 Reflective activity: Assessing the severity of individual behaviour

Students' behaviour may be very different from one context to another. How do you think we might begin to conceptualise:

● the root cause of an individual student's difficult behaviour;

● the degree of severity of behaviour;

● the difference between the severity of different students' behaviour?

Observation of behaviour

Assessment of behaviour is bound to include some form of observation by teachers or others. Observing children and young people in the environment of the classroom or school is something that is a part of teachers' everyday practice. For the purposes of assessment of individual students' behaviour, the process of observation might need to be formalised. If so, it should be systematic and there should be an effective means of recording and interpreting what is seen.

There are a number of tools or frameworks that can be used in classroom observations. Below we describe, first, two frameworks based on behaviourist psychology that are designed to identify the trigger(s) for the behaviour seen as problematic and the consequences of this behaviour.

Using behaviourist principles

 Reflective activity: Assessment tools based on a behaviourist model

Before reading the section below, go back to Chapter 1 and re-read the sections on the principles and applications of behaviourism. As you do so reflect on:

● what is meant by 'setting conditions', 'consequences' and 'reinforcers' of behaviour;
● the significance of consistency in implementing interventions based on a behaviourist approach;
● how you might apply an understanding of this approach to supporting one or more students you know to improve their behaviour;
● whether you feel there are any ethical issues implicit in this approach.

In any assessment involving observation of behaviour the first step is to make decisions about exactly *what* will be the focus of the observation: people, activities or events, or a combination of these. It might be important to observe an individual, a group, or a whole class in particular lessons or playground activities.

Framework 1: Watkins and Wagner (1995)

The protocol recommended by Watkins and Wagner (1995) below implies that observations may take place in specific, preselected lessons or locations where individual students' behaviour has been identified as particularly problematic.

 Reflective activity: Considering the use of a behaviourist framework

In order to identify when the challenges presented by an individual student's behaviour require special consideration, Watkins and Wagner (1995, p. 59), as cited by Wearmouth (2009, pp. 70–1), pose a number of questions. As you read these, consider:

● how they reflect a behaviourist understanding of behaviour;
● whether and how you might use this framework in a classroom or setting with which you are familiar.

These questions are:

● What specific behaviour is causing concern?
● In what situations does the behaviour occur/not occur?

- What, specifically, happens before and after the behaviour (i.e., what triggers it and what maintains it?)
- What skills does the person demonstrate/not demonstrate?
- What does the person's behaviour mean to him/her?
- What does the person think of him/herself, and what do others think?
- Who is most affected by this behaviour?

The last question often turns attention from the behaviour causing concern to the way the concern is being handled by others.

Interventions designed to improve student behaviour that are based on the outcomes of this assessment can be centred on changing aspects of the environment(s) that appear to be provoking, or maintaining the behaviour that is of concern, on developing the child's skills where appropriate and/or his/her sense of worth, or on the interface between the child and their environment.

Framework 2: Functional assessment of individual behaviour

Functional assessment is also based on a behaviourist understanding of learning. It relates to analysing the function that is served by the individual young person behaving in a particular way (Moore, 2004). It aims to discover the antecedents, setting events (contexts) and consequences that cause or maintain challenging behaviours. The analysis can then be used as a means for identifying the functional relationships between a particular behaviour and what provokes or reinforces it.

 Reflective activity: Carrying out functional analysis

Read the text below associated with functional assessment of behaviour, reflect on the behaviourist principles underpinning this and compare the protocol for the assessment with that recommended by Watkins and Wagner above.

What are the similarities and differences between them?

The first requirement of functional analysis is a clear definition of the target behaviour, that is, what the young person does that needs to be changed. Once the behaviour has been defined, there should be systematic observational sampling across times of day, situations, nature of activity, person in charge and so on. Such observations need to be taken over a period of about five days to establish a baseline level of behaviour. Once this has been established, the following three stages should be carried out:

A the antecedent event(s), that is, whatever starts off or prompts
B the behaviour, which is followed in turn by
C the consequence(s). (Merrett, 1985, p. 8)

Merrett advises that where a consequence of a behaviour 'is shown to be maintaining [the] behaviour at a high level then that consequence is, by definition, and regardless of its nature, reinforcing it positively'. Telling children off can temporarily inhibit certain behaviours, but these may recur after a very short time. However, by definition, ''ticking off' is positively reinforcing the child's 'attention-seeking' behaviour. If that positive reinforcement is removed then the rate of occurrence of the behaviour will be reduced. It will eventually become extinguished' (Merrett, 1985, p. 9).

Recording the specifics of behaviour

There are a number of different formats that can be adopted to observe behaviour in classrooms which attempt to be objective and record what is seen rather than making any interpretation of it. The kind of systematic observation methods that are implied here are also characteristic of assessments based on behaviourist understandings. These methods include time sampling and checklists.

Time and interval sampling

Time and interval sampling can be used as an attempt to gain an understanding of a student's learning and behaviour that might be viewed as typical of him/her. If, as often happens, the observer is looking for particular events or behaviours which can be easily categorised, s/he could devise an 'observation schedule'. Systematic observation procedures might involve the construction of an open grid in which instances of specified learner, peer and adult behaviours can be recorded as they occur. Then, as Fisher, Richmond & Wearmouth (2004) note, there is the question about the time frames to be used: whether to sample what goes on at one point at the end of predetermined short time periods or to record any of the behaviours that occurred during the preceding time interval. Then there is the question of whether an individual student will be 'shadowed' for a longer period of time. The answers to these questions will, to a large extent, be dictated by the kinds of concerns raised in relation to the behaviour of individual students, the kinds of reflection that have already taken place in relation to the evidence already collected, and the extent to which there has been an audit of the learning environment.

In brief,

- time sampling means observing for a set number of seconds. At the end of this the observer records whether or not, at that particular moment in time, the student is engaging in any of the behaviours that have been defined. The assumption here is that, if a recording is made regularly and systematically, it will represent what the student's behaviour generally is like.
- depending upon the particular purpose, event sampling means that, within a predetermined interval such as every twenty or thirty seconds, the teacher records the number of times a behaviour has been observed during that time period.

Both time and interval sampling can be carried out across different lessons and in different contexts.

Using checklists

On occasions it might be appropriate for classroom teachers to use a preset list of behaviours as a checklist against which the seriousness of particular kinds of behaviour can be assessed across different contexts. Sometimes a checklist might have a range of scores next to each behaviour so that a score can be given against each as a baseline. Teachers' scores of the behaviour of the same student might be compared to analyse whether the behaviour is different or the same in different contexts. Alternatively, the same student's behaviour can be scored at a later date to see whether the teacher's perception is that the behaviour has improved or deteriorated. It has to be said, however, that the reliability of any kind of checklist is open to personal interpretation or the influence of the learning environment, and so on.

? Reflective activity: Using checklists of behaviour

Have a look at the examples of behaviour checklists on the companion web site.   3.2
How might you use one of these in your own context?
How might you amend this to suit your own purpose and context more appropriately?

When conducting observations, it is usually helpful to make notes at the time, even if systematic time sampling or event recording procedures are being implemented. These notes might be open-ended, where general points of interest are recorded, or can be focussed on targeted events as and when they happen. A useful format is to write down what happened, and then to add a brief comment or interpretation later.

Assessment of visual impairment

Visual impairment (VI) is a general term indicating a continuum of sight loss (Mason, 2001). Total blindness is extremely rare. The vision of each eye is recorded separately, as well as both eyes together. The most common chart used to test visual acuity is the Snellen eye chart, originally devised by a Dutch Ophthalmologist, Dr. Hermann Snellen, in 1862. This has a series of letters or letters and numbers, with the largest at the top. As the person being tested reads down the chart, the letters gradually become smaller. Other versions can be used for people who cannot read the alphabet.

In the Snellen fraction 20/20, the top number represents the test distance, 20 feet. The lower number represents the distance at which the average eye can see the letters on a particular line of the eye chart. So, 20/20 means that the eye being tested can read a certain size letter when it is 20 feet away. If a person sees 20/40, at 20 feet from the chart s/he can read letters that a person with 20/20 vision could read from 40 feet away. Originally Snellen worked in feet but later (in 1875) he changed from usingfeet to metres (from 20/20 to 6/6 respectively). Currently, the 20-foot distance continues to be used in the United States, but 6 metres is used in Britain.

The Snellen fractions are measures of sharpness of sight in relation to identifying letters or symbols with high contrast, but tell us nothing about the quality of vision, for example, seeing larger objects and objects with poor contrast, or whether vision is more or less efficient when using both eyes together (Strouse Watt, 2003).

A clinical assessment of vision usually focuses on four aspects: distance, near, field and colour vision (Mason, 2001). However, students with the same eye condition may have very different strengths and needs from each other, with different interests, background experiences and so on, as well as differing degrees of useful vision (Miller & Ockleford, 2005). A whole range of information is therefore needed to ensure that support for an individual is appropriate (Miller & Ockleford, 2005). This includes the views of the child and the parents/family, medical and school records as well as the clinical assessment of vision.

Many children who are classed as blind have some 'functional' vision, and it is important to teach the child how to make best use of this (Davis, 2003). Where a distinction is necessary for any reason, the term blind is used to refer to pupils who rely on tactile methods in their learning, for example, Braille or Tactile diagrams, and the term low vision is used with reference to children and young people who are taught through methods which rely on sight (Mason, McCall, Arter, McLinden, & Stone, 1997).

Auditory impairment

A decibel (dB) is a measure of sound pressure level. Normal voice measures 60 dB at a distance of one metre, a raised voice 70 dB at one metre, and shouting 80 dB at one metre. The severity of a hearing impairment is measured in decibels of hearing loss and is ranked according to the additional intensity above a nominal threshold that a sound must be before being detected by an individual.

Assessment of hearing

There is a variety of tests of hearing loss. The tests used depend on the child's age and stage of development. It is possible to test the hearing of all children from birth onwards.

Since 2006, babies have been screened to test their hearing within a few days of their birth. Babies 'begin to develop language and communication from their earliest months', so early screening means that 'much can be done to positively support and encourage that development [...] when early identification of deafness is combined with effective early intervention, with parents and professionals working together, language outcomes for deaf children can be similar to those for hearing children.
(NDCS, 2010, p. 6)

For children of school age, hearing is usually measured with behavioural tests using pure tones. The sounds come through headphones and each time a child hears a sound they respond by moving an object, pressing a button or saying 'yes'.

Quantification of hearing loss

Hearing sensitivity varies according to the frequency of sounds. It is indicated by the 'hearing threshold', the quietest sound to which a person responds. The test is carried out for sounds of different frequencies, and, in humans, the term 'hearing impairment' is usually reserved for people who have relative insensitivity to sound in the frequencies of speech.

Four categories of hearing impairment are generally used: mild, moderate, severe and profound. As noted by NHS Choices (2015) (http://www.nhs.uk/Conditions/Hearing-impairment/Pages/Diagnosis.aspx – accessed 02.03.16):

- with 'mild deafness: 20–40 dB' a child could hear a baby crying but may be unable to hear whispered conversation. Mild deafness can sometimes make hearing speech difficult, particularly in noisy situations.

- with 'moderate deafness: 41–70 dB', a child could hear a dog barking but not a baby crying. A young person may have difficulty following speech without using a hearing aid.

- with 'severe deafness: 71–90 dB', a child would hear drums being played but not a dog barking. S/he would usually need to lip-read or use sign language, even with the use of a hearing aid.

- with 'profound deafness: >90 dB', a child might hear a large lorry but not drums being played. People who are profoundly deaf can often benefit from a cochlear implant. Other forms of communication include lip-reading and sign language.

About 20 per cent of primary children suffer from conductive hearing loss caused by middle-ear problems, reducing to 2 per cent by secondary age. In some instances there is a serious difference of opinion between those who believe that deaf children can be taught to speak using auditory-oral approaches, that is, assisted by hearing aids, cochlear implants, radio aids, and so on, and be integrated into mainstream society, and those who believe they should be taught through sign language. What suits the child best may depend on the degree of hearing loss, the extent of the delay in language acquisition and, of course, what the child him/herself and the family feel about his/her situation.

Listening to students' views

Legislation across the United Kingdom requires young people's views to be taken into account when assessing needs and planning learning or behaviour interventions. Young people have a right to be heard. However, it is also really important to reflect why we need to listen to what they have to say in terms of the way we understand the learning process.

 Reflective activity: Links between listening to students' views and the process of learning

We can understand students' learning in a number of ways, as discussed in Chapter 1. Look back at the section titled 'Constructivist approaches' and reflect on what the applications of these approaches mean in practice.

In that section we make the point that, if we assume that students are active agents in their own learning, we have to try to understand how they feel about difficulties in learning, behaviour, motor skills or in any other area and what they know will support them most effectively. From a learning perspective it is important for adults to understand how children make sense of their own circumstances and what impression is conveyed to students of others' views of them, in other words, how young people understand their worlds, their experiences, tasks in classrooms, and so on. This is not simply a question of human rights, that children have a right to be heard, important though it is. Young people will not engage in classroom activities if they see no value in this for themselves. Besides this, it is difficult to see how teachers can support learning through the zone of proximal development if they do not pay close attention to what young people say, how they react to things and what they do. Eliciting students' views depends on very finely tuned listening skills as well as suspension of judgmental responses on the part of professionals. It is important to recognise that 'children will make decisions about people they can talk to and trust, and those they cannot' (Gersch, 1995, p. 48).

 Reflective activity: 'Talking Stones'

Wearmouth (2004) describes a projective interview technique, 'Talking Stones', which is an interesting assessment strategy to help students represent problematic relationships and situations as they see them. Read the following paraphrase of this technique. As you do so, consider whether, how, with whom and why you might use this, and the issues you would have to take into careful account in doing so.

'Talking Stones' was originally based on personal construct psychology and developed from Crosby's therapeutic work with adults (Crosby, S., unpublished report, 1993, Centre for Personal Construct Education). This technique is designed to address the challenge of engaging with a student's perspective meaningfully in order to work through what are often difficult situations in schools, and matching provision to real needs. The assumption underpinning this technique is that, for the individual learner, everything is perceived and mediated by what is salient, socially and personally. This view of behaviour implies that it is possible for a person acting in support to enter the student's reality and hold dialogue.

During an individual interview, a student is given a pile of stones of varying shapes, sizes, colours and textures and encouraged to explore thoughts and feelings about school and him/herself in relation to it by projection on to them. The individual selects one stone to represent him/herself in school and discusses his/her choice. Subsequently s/he selects more stones to represent significant others in the context about which there is current concern, describes why they have been chosen, and then places them on a rectangular white cloth or large sheet of paper. The edges of this set a boundary to the positioning of the stones and their distance from each other. Stones, their attributes and their positions in relation to each other can be understood as a student's representation of individually constructed meanings.

One way in which a procedure such as 'Talking Stones' can contribute to the process of assessment in schools is in the manner in which it can open up problematic relationships between, typically, teenagers and staff members, and facilitate dialogue or conversation. The student is not seen as 'mad' and therefore unintelligible and threatening, but engaging with life in an alternative mode.

'Talking Stones' is a powerful procedure. The ethics surrounding its use should therefore be taken into careful consideration. It should be used only where there is positive benefit to the student. Its use is ethically questionable unless there is a clear benefit for the student. Teachers using 'Talking Stones' should be aware of ethical principles associated with techniques of a counselling nature, for example, those of 'non-maleficence' and 'beneficence'. As McLeod (1998, pp. 272–3) notes, 'non-maleficence' refers to the principle of not doing any harm, and 'beneficence' to promoting human welfare. Asking personal questions may be construed as prying into a student's privacy. It raises the question about what teachers and schools should do with sensitive information of this sort that is very important to understanding individuals, but may be used by some to belittle or stereotype students.

Raising self-esteem is frequently set as a target for students seen as having a low self-image. However, attempting to raise self-esteem may have little point if teachers are not aware of major factors driving students' behaviour. It also raises the question of who should decide whether the risks of using a technique such as this outweigh the benefits.

There are many instances in schools where students disclose very sensitive information about themselves to teachers. Before engaging in any activity where this is likely to happen, including using 'Talking Stones', teachers need to familiarise themselves very well with any guidelines that may exist in their own schools about handling information that may emerge from student self disclosure, for example information relating to sexual abuse.

The assessment of students' perceptions of, and feelings about, their own behaviour depends on very finely tuned listening skills as well as suspension of judgmental responses on the part of professionals.

'Talking Stones' is a technique not to be used lightly. Once a student has begun to disclose personal information, it may be difficult for an inexperienced teacher-interviewer to bring about closure in a way that leaves the student in a frame of mind sufficiently comfortable to return to regular classroom activities.

Assessment of students who experience communication difficulties

Some students, of course, find it much more difficult to communicate than others. Difficulties in accessing information, communication, sensory impairment, mobility and relationship-building might make meaningful discussion with some young people problematic. For example, the communication of students with profound and multiple learning disabilities and involving reflexes, actions, sounds and facial expression needs to be carefully observed and interpreted by the various people who know those pupils the best (Porter, Ouvry, Morgan & Downs (2001). Preece (2002), working with autistic children, discusses how inflexible thought processes, lack of personal insight and dislike of change inhibit some children from participating in meaningful discussion of their ideas. For those young people who cannot express themselves verbally, but for whom pictures and symbols are meaningful and who can understand what is going on, a variety of powerful and useful tools have been developed to attempt to elicit their views. These include the use of cue cards (Lewis, 2002, p. 114) that can act 'as prompts for ideas about […] people, talk, setting (indoor/outdoor variants), feelings and consequences about the particular event under discussion […] that can convey meaning in a neutral way. In a similar way, 'Talking Mats' (Cameron & Murphy, 2002) can enable children who experience difficulties in verbal expression to express their views by moving symbols about on mats.

3.4

Engaging with parents' or carers' perspectives

In a number of countries across the world there is a formal acceptance that parents and carers have the right to know about decisions taken in schools in relation to their children, and that they themselves are, potentially, an important source of additional support in addressing difficulties in learning and/or behaviour experienced by young people. The right of parents and/or carers to be consulted at every stage of decision-making about their children is enshrined in law across the United Kingdom (Special Educational Needs and Disability (Northern Ireland) Order, 2005; Children and Families Act, 2014 in England; 1996 Education Act, Part 1V in Wales; Education (Additional Support for Learning) (Scotland) Acts, 2004 and 2009). A number of guides for parents and carers have been issued to support families to understand their entitlements also, for example, *The parents' guide to additional support for learning* (Enquire, 2014) that is funded by the Scottish government, and the *Special Educational Needs and Disability (SEND) – A guide for parents and carers* (DfE, 2014a) published in England.

Parental/family engagement with the assessment process

 Reflective activity: Principles enabling effective home–school partnerships

Not all families feel comfortable in formal school/college settings particularly if, for example, their own educational experiences were difficult. From your own experience what would you say are the most important issues to take into consideration when working in partnership with families?

In a recent discussion with a group of SENCos from schools and colleges across the sectors, the following principles were agreed as important in establishing effective partnership-working with parents and families:

- building trust and rapport
- keeping parents up to date
- transparency – under promise and over deliver
- communication with all involved that enables everyone to be heard
- NB differences between primary and secondary
- mutual respect – ground rules
- listening without talking
- establish understanding of the three-way partnership
- the meeting must be 'going somewhere'
- consistent approach between home and school
- consistent personnel – single point of contact for families
- clear channel of communication and process within the school and with other agencies
- child needs led
- clear communication
- openness in a safe environment

- trust and shared realistic expectations
- accessibility of information
- positive and collaborative working relationship
- resourcing
- consistency.

To what extent do you feel these principles are important? Do you have any to add?

Planning to meet pupils' special educational, or additional support, needs and disabilities

Planning a curriculum to meet particular special learning needs of individual students should take place within the context of the same decision-making processes that relate to teaching and learning for all students in a school, otherwise there is the danger that individual plans will lack coherence in relation to the whole school system. In addition, planning to address individuals' learning needs effectively means setting out to working from strengths and interests with due account taken of any formal and informal individual assessment of student learning that has taken place. This should address any statutory requirements.

Planning will also need to be informed by the individual priorities for students. Normally, it will be appropriate for them to work on objectives that are similar and related to the whole class topic. However, at other times teachers will also have to consider whether the students have other priority needs that are central to their learning, for example, a need to concentrate on some key skills such as communication, problem solving, working with others, managing their own emotions and so on. These needs may be detailed in the student's individual plan. They can often be met within the whole class learning; for example, relating physiotherapy objectives to the PE curriculum, communication to literacy lessons, problem solving to mathematics, history or geography.

Some students may have additional therapeutic or other needs which cannot easily be met through class activities. For these students alternative objectives may be needed to meet specific needs for identified periods of time as long as they are in the context of ensuring that, over time, all students receive a broad and balanced curriculum.

Making effective use of individual plans

The term 'Individual Education Plan' (IEP) follows the American model outlined in the 1975 special education law in the United States (Public Law 94–142) where a plan for a child perceived as having difficulties had to be drawn up in order to attract federal funds (Wearmouth, 2000). In the countries across the United Kingdom and a number of other countries also, for example New Zealand, the individual education and/or learning plan, in some form or another, has become a major tool for planning programmes of study for individual students (NAW, 2004; DENI, 1998; Scottish Government, 2010; DfE, 2015). The *Code* in Scotland (2010, p. 208), for example, describes an 'Individualised Educational Programme' (IEP) as a 'written document which outline the steps to be taken to help children and young people who have additional support needs to achieve specified learning outcomes'. Although the details, and title of the document, may vary slightly from one country to another, overall these records are expected to contain information about the nature of the child/young person's learning difficulties, the special or additional educational provision to be made and strategies to be used, specific programmes, activities, materials, and/or equipment, targets to be achieved in a specified time, monitoring and assessment arrangements and review arrangements and date. We might also add that effective planning, as exemplified in the *Code of Practice* (DfE, 2015), is that which

- focuses on the child or young person as an individual, not the SEN label;
- uses clear ordinary language and images, not professional jargon, so is easy for children, young people and their parents to understand;
- highlights the young person's strengths;
- enables the young person, and his/her family to say what they have done, what they are interested in and what outcomes they are seeking in the future;
- tailors support to the needs of the individual;
- organises assessments to minimise demands on families;
- brings together professionals to agree the overall approach.

Complying with the procedures relating to individual plans can be very time-intensive. It is important therefore for schools to develop ways of working that keep this pressure to a minimum while developing systems for ensuring that the learning programme is carried out, monitored and evaluated. These days in England some SENCos have dispensed with individual plans for some children and use group plans instead. Some may rely on 'provision maps' which can be either documents that identify provision for individual children with the targets, progress and review dates, or whole-school provision with analyses of student outcomes and value for money, or both.

'Pupil passports'

 Reflective activity: Ensuring individual plans are integrated into classroom activities

Ever since the system for identifying, assessing and providing for students with special educational, or additional support, needs was introduced into mainstream schools/colleges to promote the inclusion of students who experience difficulties of various sorts, there has been this question of how to manage and disseminate information relating to individual students.

Mainstream class teachers are expected to take responsibility for the progress of all the young people in their classrooms. Do you have any experience of, or suggestions to make about, ways in which information about the needs of individual students and possible ways to address these needs might be shared effectively across the staff in a school/college to make a difference for those students?

 3.3 In order to ensure that all staff are aware of students'/ individual needs, some schools have adopted 'pupil/student passports' which the young person carries with him/her to each lesson. These comprise a one-page summary document that is often compiled with the student and written in the first person. There is no formal requirement or set format, but as a general guide they contain the student's name and photograph together with the following, written in the first person:

- 'I would like you to know that . . .'
- 'This means that . . .'
- 'I find it difficult to . . .'
- 'It would help me if you could . . .'
- 'I will help myself by . . .' (self-help strategies agreed with the student)
- Additional support, for example, interventions in place
- Important data, for example, reading age. (www.pupilpassport.co.uk – accessed 28.05.15)

Target-setting

> **? Reflective activity: Effective target-setting**
>
> Individual plans, profiles or records can only be as effective as the rigour of the thinking underlying their design.
>
> Note down what you consider to be the hallmarks of effective target-setting.
> Is it always important, or possible, to set SMART targets?

Targets can provide a focus for the combined efforts of all those concerned to support a learner's progress and highlight the need to link planning and provision. However, there are specific areas of the curriculum where it may be problematic to conceptualise measurable targets, for example, those involving behaviour, the emotions and creativity.

Setting measurable targets is closely associated with behavioural approaches. A school and a national curriculum can be seen as a ladder of progression which children are expected to climb, with specific assessment learning goals at each rung. An inherent difficulty in this view, however, is that not all children learn the same way, so setting targets which follow in a similar sequence for all students is not necessarily appropriate (Dockrell & McShane, 1993). There is also a possibility that too much reliance on task components can lead to a rigid and prescriptive teaching, which takes no account of specific strategies that the learner brings to any particular task (ibid.).

Statutory assessment of educational needs and disability across the United Kingdom

We have outlined the assess→plan→do→review cycle above. If however a child fails to make 'adequate progress' then additional or different action should be taken. What constitutes 'adequate progress' might be defined in a number of ways. It might, for instance, be progress which, under the law in Northern Ireland:

- closes the attainment gap between the child and the child's peers;
- prevents the attainment gap growing wider;
- is similar to that of peers starting from the same attainment baseline, but less than that of the majority of peers;
- matches or betters the child's previous rate of progress;
- ensures access to the full curriculum;
- demonstrates an improvement in self-help, social or personal skills;
- demonstrates improvements in the pupil's behaviour;
- prevents the attainment gap growing wider. (NAW, 2004, § 4.14)

Of the children that schools identify as experiencing particular difficulties, those who have longer term or more severe disabilities or needs may be the subject of statutory assessment.

Education, Health and Care Plans in England

In England, schools and colleges should identify and support young people with SEN and/or a disability either from within their own resources under what is now to be called 'SEN Support' or, where the degree of need is such that it requires a higher level of resourcing than is available from these resources, through an Education, Health and Care (EHC) Plan. LAs, not schools, colleges or parents, have the legal duty to carry out an EHC needs assessment, issue an EHC plan and ensure the special educational provision that has been specified in an EHC plan. An LA has a clear duty to assess a child or young person's education, health and care needs where s/he may have SEN and may need special educational provision to be made at a level or of a kind which requires an EHC plan. An EHC needs assessment can only be requested if the young person has or may have educational needs, NOT where there are only health and/or care needs, no matter how severe.

The statutory assessment process and development and review of EHC plans require co-operation between schools and LAs. Where a child or young person has not made expected progress despite a school having taken appropriate action to identify, assess and meet the SEN, an EHC needs assessment might be requested. During the course of an assessment, the LA must gather advice from relevant professionals about the young person's education, health and care needs and special educational, health and care provision that may be required to achieve the desired outcomes. The child's parent or the young person has the right to request a particular school to be named in their EHC plan. The LA must consult the governing body of that school about admitting the child or young person and to name the school in the EHC plan, unless it would be unsuitable for the age, ability, aptitude or SEN of the child or young person, or the attendance of the child or young person would be incompatible with the efficient education of peers or efficient use of resources. The school is involved in the development or review of the EHC plan to determine what can be provided from within the school's own resources and what will require additional external expertise or further funding from the LA which must then make sure the support identified in the plan is provided.

Some of the provisions specified may be procured by the child's parent or the young person using a Personal Budget. Where a direct payment is to be used to deliver provision on the school premises, the LA must seek the written agreement of the school for this arrangement. Local authorities have a duty to review EHC plans as a minimum every twelve months, and can require schools or other educational institutions to convene and hold the review meeting on their behalf. In most cases, reviews are held at, and led by, the young person's educational institution. The child's parents or the young person, a representative of the school or other institution, a local authority SEN officer, a health service representative and a local authority social care representative must be invited and given at least two weeks' notice of the date of the meeting. Other individuals relevant to the review should also be invited.

The school should seek information about the child or young person prior to the meeting from all participants, and send any information gathered to all those invited at least two weeks before the meeting. Subsequently, and within two weeks of the meeting, the school should send a report to everyone invited with recommendations on any amendments required to the EHC plan, and should refer to any difference between the school or other institution's recommendations and those of others.

The test which local authorities must apply in coming to a decision about an EHC plan is set out in the Children and Families Act 2014 (§37 (1)). Based on the evidence gathered:

(1) Where, in the light of an EHC needs assessment, it is necessary for special educational provision to be made for a child or young person in accordance with an EHC plan -

(a) the local authority *must* secure that an EHC plan is prepared for the child or young person, and

(b) once an EHC plan has been prepared, it must maintain the plan.

There are specific requirements for the contents of an EHC Plan. An EHC plan specifies:

- the child's or young person's special educational needs;
- the outcomes sought for him or her;
- the special educational provision required by him or her;
- any health care provision reasonably required by the learning difficulties and disabilities which result in him or her having special educational needs;
- social care provision which is being made for the child/young person under the Chronically Sick and Disabled Persons Act 1970 and any social care provision reasonably required by the learning difficulties and disabilities which result in the child or young person having special educational needs, to the extent that the provision is not already specified in the plan.

If an EHC plan does not contain all of the sections which are needed, it will not be legally compliant.

 Reflective activity: Considering the whole EHC process

It can be very useful to look carefully at diagrammatic representations of a complex process such as that involved in the development and implementation of an Education, Health and Care Plan. Access the representation of the timeline for the EHC process that is published in the Code of Practice (DfE, 2015, p. 154). This is available at:
    https://www.gov.uk/government/uploads/system/uploads/attachment_data/file/398815/SEND_Code_of_Practice_January_2015.pdf – accessed 19.06.16.
    You can then see the whole of what is involved in summary, and reflect on what this means in terms of:

- information that is required at each stage, and from whom;
- the significance of the timescales that are given for each stage;
- what kind of support you feel that families in particular might need to be able to engage actively in this process.

Statementing in Northern Ireland and Wales

In Northern Ireland and Wales such assessment may result in the issuing of a Statement of Special Educational Need for which the specified provision is mandatory. Statements are usually drawn up for one of two reasons:

- the young person needs guaranteed access to special resources and expertise, a special curriculum, or an environment with higher than normal staff support, or
- parents, or professionals, want the young person to attend a special school, or some other form of special provision.

By law a Statement has to describe the child's special educational needs, and the special educational provision that is required, the objectives of the requisite provision, the resourcing, how progress will be monitored, the name of the school, and any 'non–educational' needs and provision that have been identified. The special provision listed must be provided by law, and the school named must admit the child. The Library Board in Northern Ireland, or LA in Wales, has to involve parents at many points, and parents have a number of legal rights. The Library Board or LA must also collect evidence and advice from several professionals, including the child's head teacher, a doctor and an educational psychologist.

Co-ordinated support plans (Scotland)

In Scotland, provision for children and young people with additional support needs associated with complex or multiple factors which require a high degree of support from education authorities and other agencies is organised through the provision of a statutory document called a 'co-ordinated support plan'. The *Code* in Scotland (§2, p. 74) lists the criteria required for a plan:

(a) an education authority is responsible for the school education of the child or young person,

(b) the child or young person has additional support needs arising from-
   (i) one or more complex factors,[1] or
   (ii) multiple factors,

(c) those needs are likely to continue for more than a year, and

(d) those needs require significant additional support to be provided-
   (i) by the education authority in the exercise of any of their other functions as well as in the exercise of their functions relating to education, or
   (ii) by one or more appropriate agencies (within the meaning of section 23(2)) as well as by the education authority themselves.

---

[1]Factors are interpreted as 'complex' if they have, or are likely to have, 'a significant adverse effect on the school education of the child or young person' (Code, p. 77, §13). Examples given in the *Code* of the source of such factors are the learning environment, family circumstances, disability of health and social and emotional factors.

During the preparation of the plan the views of the following should be sought and recorded: the parents, the young person, representatives of relevant agencies and any others who provide support. If the decision of the local authority is to issue a plan, there are statutory requirements[2] related to its contents:

- the education authority's conclusions about:
  - the factor(s) from which the additional support needs arise;
  - the intended educational objectives;
  - the additional support required to achieve the objectives.
- details of who should provide this support;
- the name of the school the young person is to attend;
- the details of the person who will co-ordinate the additional support;
- the details of a contact person within the local authority who can offer advice and further information.

It should include a focus on positive aspects of the young person's life, and include a review timetable.

Parents and young people have the right to refer particular matters, for example statutory parts of the plan and prescribed decisions, to the Additional Support Needs Tribunals for Scotland.

Summary

Assessment should be viewed as a tool that supports learning and not simply as a politically expedient solution to perceived concerns about standards and ways to make schools accountable to parents, families and society as a whole (Assessment Reform Group, 1999). A constructive and positive approach to assessment begins with an evaluation of the learning environment and considerations of how to modify to enhance behaviour and learning. The approach then continues, if necessary, with a greater focus on understanding the individual student as behaving 'normally' and actively engaged in making sense of the situation in which s/he finds him/herself. Such an approach is more likely to empower students to take an active part in the management of their own behaviour.

The awareness of learning and the ability of learners to direct it for themselves is of increasing importance in the context of encouraging lifelong learning. Assessment can therefore serve to either reinforce or undermine the motivation to strive for future achievement. Students' sense of themselves as having the potential to be effective in the community of practice of learners may be constructed and/or constrained by

---

[2]See the Additional Support for Learning (Co-ordinated Support Plan) (Scotland) Amendment Regulations 2005 (SSI 2005/518).

the forms of assessment that are used with them. Assessment therefore must aim to build on students' experiences and identities and not marginalise or destroy them (Wearmouth, 2009). Assessment that is ongoing, continuous and formative and provides teachers with formal and informal opportunities to notice what is happening during learning activities, recognise where the learning of individuals and groups of students is going and how they as the teacher can help take that learning further is likely to lead to positive learning gains (Assessment Reform Group, 1999). This process begins by ensuring students receive appropriate learning goals and are engaged in interactive conversations throughout their learning activities.

Chapter 4
Approaches to understanding and addressing four areas of need

The major questions in this chapter are:

- What is known about difficulties in learning and behaviour associated with the four areas of need as conceptualised in the Code of Practice (DfE, 2015) in England?
- What might be the practical implications of including young people who experience these needs in classrooms?

Introduction

The 'need' which assessment and subsequent provision should address can be conceptualised in a variety of ways. For example, in England, the new *Code of Practice* (DfE, 2015, §5.32), outlines the following four broad areas of need and support:

- communication and interaction
- cognition and learning
- social, emotional and mental health
- sensory and/or physical needs.

It is obvious that there can be a lot of overlap between these areas. Statutory advice in the current *Code* (DfE, 2015, §5.33) clearly acknowledges that individual needs may not be confined to one discrete area but can span them. One implication of this may be that conceptualising four areas of need is an administrative convenience. In any case, as we have already noted, 'need' can be conceptualised in a number of ways. In

England, Wales and Northern Ireland the term at the time of writing is 'special edu-cational needs'. In Scotland the term is 'additional support needs'. Nevertheless this chapter discusses research and practice related to understanding and making effective provision for needs as conceptualised in the four areas listed in the *Code of Practice* (DfE, 2015) in England, with examples in each of them.

Communication and interaction

Most people would probably agree that the need to communicate with others is a part of the human condition and is vital to our learning, particularly if we adopt a sociocultural model.

 Reflective activity: The importance of language acquisition

Take a few moments to note down what contribution you feel language makes to the development of thinking and learning.

What difference might language impairment make to a young person's learning and progress?

If we accept the views of Vygotsky, 1962, p. 51), 'thought development is deter-mined by language', it is important to recognise and respond to difficulties in this area for the sake of a young person's learning as well as for his/her well-being so that s/he can form positive relationships with peers and others.

Communication and language are closely linked, but are not synonymous. 'Communication is really more the means by which we convey language, both to get our meaning across and to understand the meaning of others'. It involves not only language, but also 'other things like eye contact, gesture, tone of voice, facial expres-sions and body language'. Language is 'the words (vocabulary), phrases, grammar and expressions we use and how we organise them to communicate' (National Deaf Children's Society, 2010, p. 8). Difficulties in this area may be associated with a num-ber of 'barriers to learning', for example, profound and multiple learning difficulties and pragmatic language impairment.

We look first at the needs of those for whom English is an additional language, however, before examining these 'barriers'.

English as an additional language

The identification and assessment of the special educational needs of young people whose first language is not English requires particular care, as the various Codes of

Practice across the United Kingdom note. The 2014 *Code* in England (§5:30), for example, advises that

> practitioners should look carefully at all aspects of a child's learning and development to establish whether any delay is related to learning English as an additional language or if it arises from SEN or disability. Difficulties related solely to learning English as an additional language are not SEN.

Unfamiliar language or expectations may not be the only reason for students who learn English as an additional language to make slow progress. They may also experience general cognitive difficulties. If cognitively demanding tasks can be accomplished by providing support in context the needs may well be linguistic; if not, they may be educational. Standardised tests in English are often culturally or linguistically biased so it is important always to try to obtain a first language assessment.

Language impairment

Difficulties in language acquisition may lie at the receptive (comprehending what is said and/or written) or expressive (putting thoughts coherently into words, verbal or written) level. The degree of difficulty that is experienced may be at a mild, or more severe, level. Below, we discuss ways to promote oral language through activities that can involve the whole class. We then turn to more serious difficulties.

Ways to support the development of oral language

Students who experience difficulty in listening to and understanding others and/or expressing themselves need frequent opportunities for exploratory talk in every area of the curriculum in order to put new information and ideas into their own words and link subject matter to what they already know.

 Reflective activity: Facilitating oral language development

Strategies that facilitate oral language development might include exploratory talk in small groups, problem-solving aloud, explanations of how something is made, or how and why things happen, dramatisation and role-play, interviews (live or taped), and group discussion.

What kind of activities might you devise in a classroom situation that would include some of these suggestions?

'Circle time'

One initiative, mostly used at primary school level in UK schools, that depends on listening and responding to the views of the student community in classrooms is that of 'Circle Time' (Mosley, 1996). It is a meeting that follows strict protocols of involving all participants in discussion where both teachers and students are bound by rules that stipulate no one may put anyone down, no one may use any name negatively (creating 'safety' for all individuals including teachers and parents), and when individuals speak, everyone must listen (Wearmouth, 2016b). 'Everyone has a turn and a chance to speak, all views are taken seriously, members of the class team suggest ways of solving problems and individuals can accept the help or politely refuse it' (Wearmouth, Glynn & Berryman, 2005, p. 184).

The author of Circle Time advises that the rules must be followed strictly. If a student breaks a rule a visual warning is given. If this persists, time away from the circle follows.

In a group situation such as this, how would you ensure that a student who experiences difficulties in expressive and/or receptive language can participate fully in an activity such as this?

Ways to overcome barriers to communication through the use of Alternative and Augmentative Communication

Some young people with very serious difficulties in communication may benefit from Alternative and Augmentative Communication (AAC), any kind of communication that replaces standard means of communication such as speech. This is often used where young people experience particular difficulties in verbal communication to complement and/or enhance standard means of communication (Research Autism, 2016) (http://researchautism.net/autism-interventions/types/alternative-and-augmentative-communication – accessed 25.02.16). One form of AAC is the Picture Exchange Communication System (PECS) in which an adult teaches a child to exchange a picture of something for an item s/he wants, for example, to exchange a picture of a drink for a drink. As we discuss below in the case of autism, pictures can be used to express preferences and, progressively, make whole sentences. It may take a long time to reach this stage of development in communication.

Objects of reference and symbol systems

Objects of reference and electronic banks of pictograms are forms of AAC that are often used to assist children with varying degrees of difficulties in communicating. 'Objects of reference' refer to physical objects used to represent those things about which humans communicate: activities, events, people, ideas and so on. These objects can be used as a 'bridge' to more abstract forms of communication such as sign, symbol or word. Objects of reference are often chosen because of their multi-sensory properties to give the individual a clue about what is about to happen, for example, a piece of soap to signify that washing is about to take place, or a seat buckle to signify a car journey. It is essential that the same item is always used to signify the same event (Park, 1997). The contexts in which various objects gain significance and meaning are obviously different for different people.

There are also other pictorial means of supporting communication. Symbol-based language programs have been developed over many years, for example. Widgit Software is one organisation that has produced an array of software that uses pictorial symbols to support the development of communication skills. Widgit describes its Symbol Set as 'comprehensive collections of images' designed to 'support text, making the meaning clearer and easier to understand' by providing a 'visual representation of a concept'. The Symbol Set often 'follows a schematic structure, or set of design "rules"', that enables the reader to develop his/her own receptive and expressive language skills (Widgit, 2016) (http://www.widgit.com/symbols/index.htm, accessed 25.02.16). The use of Widgit's Symbol Set is discussed further in Chapter 8.

In the section below we consider issues related to difficulties in cognition and learning, and some of the ways in which these might be addressed. Given the overlap between communication, cognition and learning, there is overlap also in the ways in which difficulties in these areas might be addressed.

Pragmatic language impairment

Some students may experience special barriers to using language appropriately in social situations and/or with semantic aspects of language, that is, understanding the meaning of what is said and/or written. These days this difficulty is called pragmatic language impairment (PLI), previously called 'semantic-pragmatic disorder'. PLI can create challenges in the classroom, given that so much of the teaching depends on spoken and written forms of language (Adams & Lloyd, 2007).

 Reflective activity: Including young people with PLI in classroom activities

Children with PLI commonly experience a number of barriers to their learning:

- difficulty in developing conversational skills: turn taking and maintaining the topic of the conversation (Bishop & Norbury, 2002);
- insensitivity to their listeners, and a propensity to talk endlessly about their own preoccupations;
- problems understanding discourse and telling stories in a logical order (Norbury & Bishop, 2003);

- over-literal interpretation of language (Leinonen, Letts & Smith, 2000);
- difficulties in understanding despite competent use of the formal structure of spoken or written language (Rapin & Allen, 1998).

Have a look at each of these areas of difficulty. What activities might be developed to support young people to begin to overcome these?

Programmes to address pragmatic language impairment

Adams and Lloyd (2007, pp. 229–30) describe a highly structured classroom intervention to address PLI, using 'modelling and individual practice; role-play; practising specific pragmatic skills in conversations; … promoting self-monitoring and coping strategies … to make both immediate and hidden meanings of language and communication explicit', as well as the pragmatics of grammatical structure:

- First, good practice 'in interacting at an appropriate social and language level with the child' was established. The complexity of the language in the classroom was modified, typically by 'having an assistant translate language into short meaningful utterances' accompanied by a visual demonstration.
- Next, the children were taught 'the vocabulary of social situations and insight' into others' emotions. Small incremental changes to routines were added and discussed before they were implemented. Children were supported to understand 'social and verbal inferences, metaphors and hidden meaning in language'.
- Finally, work on the pragmatics of language focused on 'explicit exercises and classroom support in exchange structure, turn-taking, topic management, conversational skills, building sequences, cohesion and coherence in narrative and discourse'.

PLI is one of the difficulties often experienced by autistic children as we discuss in the section 'Cognition and learning' next.

Cognition and learning

'Cognition' comes from the Latin 'cognoscere', 'to get to know', or 'to recognise'. As used in the *Code of practice* (DfE, 2015), it relates largely to information-processing associated with problem-solving, language, perception and memory and the development of concepts, thus overlapping with the area of language acquisition (Wearmouth, 2016a). Next we consider barriers to students' progress related to moderate difficulties in learning and ways to address these, autism, and profound and multiple difficulties in learning exemplified by Down's syndrome.

Moderate difficulties in learning

Much teaching and assessment take place in the context of a symbolic representation of ideas, that is, through written text and pictures (Rogers, 2007, p. 2). Learning to use number symbols, for example, is likely to occur simultaneously with acquiring the alphabetic principle and sound-symbol correspondence in literacy acquisition. Learners' ability to understand symbolic representation depends on understanding of the first-hand experience to which the symbolic representation refers.

Pictorial symbols or icons are clearly different from abstract symbols used at the formal operational (Piaget, 1964; Piaget & Inhelder, 2016) or symbolic representational stage (Bruner, 1966). Many children appear to adopt mathematical symbols and algorithms without having grasped the concepts that underpin them (Borthwick & Harcourt-Heath, 2007). It requires a lot of concrete activities in a variety of different contexts before a child with cognitive difficulties understands the concept of 'numberness' (Grauberg, 2002).

We discuss the issue of difficulties in mathematics acquisition in Chapter 6, 'Focus on numeracy difficulties'.

Strategies to address moderate difficulties in cognition and learning

 ? Reflective activity: Stages of learning and modes of representation

Before reading the text below, re-read the sections on Piaget's four universal stages of learning and Bruner's (1966) model of three modes of representation of reality in Chapter 1 (see pages 15–16 and 18–19).

To what extent do you feel these models are useful frameworks within which to think about young people's developing conceptual understanding of the world?

How might you begin to conceptualise a plan for addressing cognitive difficulties based on either the young person's stage of learning (Piaget, 1969) or the mode of representation habitually used (Bruner, 1966)?

Children who experience difficulty in understanding abstract concepts might learn effectively from the experience of doing first. Some also need a longer time than others. Whenever possible, young people should have direct experience of a concept before it is used (Primary National Strategy, 2005, ref 1235/2005). To ensure that all students understand what is said, as Wearmouth (2009) notes, it is important to ensure that students realise they are being spoken to, and when they are being asked a question. Teachers should check that they speak calmly and evenly, and that their faces are clearly visible. They might use visual aids related to the topics being discussed, and explain the topics in several different ways if they have not been understood the first time. For some children, in mathematics, it might be important to use concrete aids to establish number learning, for example, Cuisenaire rods and/or an abacus, for much longer than for other children. A major question is how to move from the act of adding, taking away or balancing to competent use of the abstract symbols. One way to do this might be to encourage children to devise their own symbols for the actions first so that the icon visibly represents their own understandings.

Scaffolding learning

As we discussed in Chapter 1, one of the ideas that has been developed from a socio-cultural view is that of 'scaffolding' to support learning (Wood, Bruner & Ross, 1976). 'Scaffolding' can be very important in supporting the learning of students who experience difficulties. To be successful, the interaction must be collaborative between student and the more knowledgeable other. The scaffolding must operate within the learner's zone of proximal development. The scaffolder must access the learner's current level of understanding and then work at slightly beyond that level, drawing the learner into new areas of learning. The scaffold should be withdrawn in stages as the learner becomes more competent. In schools, the final goal is for the learner to become autonomous, secure enough in the knowledge required to complete the task.

Task analysis and precision teaching

Behavioural approaches have often been used in the educational needs area for precision teaching consequent on task analysis. Here the skills underpinning particular tasks or component elements of a new concept are broken down into small precisely defined stages in a hierarchy of learning. This information is then taught stage by stage. Students learn and/or practise each stage to mastery level. This often requires repetitive practice, like learning multiplication tables, spelling, phonic work and word recognition. Correct responses are rewarded and reinforced. Good performance in the lesson, in other words the desired behaviour of effort and achievement, is reinforced

 4.1   by verbal praise, prizes and good grades.

 Reflective activity: Task analysis in preparation for precision teaching

Think of a particular task that you wish to teach to young people who experience some kind of cognitive difficulty.
  How would you break down that task into small achievable steps?
  How might you reward the achievement of each step?

Behaviourist approaches to learning in what we might call the basic skills can be identified in many software programmes intended, for example, to encourage awareness of the four rules of number in mathematics, phonics in decoding text and reading, and designed to provide immediate feedback and reinforcement of learning. However, these approaches cannot apply to all new learning as the requirement for information to be broken down into small steps and for each response to be reinforced immediately restricts what can be learned. Not everything can be broken down into a clear sequence of stages that are the same for all learners. Further, it is not possible, or desirable, that all new learning should be pre-programmed and that the outcomes should be known in advance because that would deny the importance of, for example, individual critical thinking, personal research and analysis and individual responses to art, drama, music and so on. Thus, behavioural approaches may fail to address students' ability to reflect on their own learning and achievement adequately (Hanko, 1994).

Autism

Reflective activity: What is known about autism?

Take a few moments to note down what you already know about autism:

- how it is identified;
- difficulties associated with it;
- approaches to addressing difficulties;
- how, in your experience, the general public tends to regard autistic individuals.

One 'condition', autism, spans two areas: communication and interaction and also cognition and learning. In 1943, Leo Kanner (Kanner, 1943) identified a difficulty marked by the inability to relate to people and social situations, profound 'aloneness', failure to use language competently to communicate, obsessive desire to maintain sameness, fascination for objects which are handled with skill in fine motor movements, a good rote memory, oversensitivity to stimuli and, often, difficulties in learning, some at a severe level. He called it 'early infantile autism' from the Greek αυτος (autos) to denote excessive focus on the self.

Around the same time, in 1944, Hans Asperger noted traits that bore some similarity to the early infantile autism commented on by Kanner (Wing, 1996). Additional features identified by Asperger were unusual responses to some sensory experiences: auditory, visual, olfactory (smell), taste and touch, an uneven developmental profile, good rote memory, circumscribed special interests and motor co-ordination difficulties. People with Asperger syndrome tend not to experience similar levels of learning difficulties that are associated with autism, and often have measured levels of intelligence that are average or above (National Autistic Society

(2016) http://www.autism.org.uk/About-autism/Autism-and-Asperger-syndrome-an-introduction/What-is-Asperger-syndrome.aspx – accessed 25.02.16).

Building on previous work, Wing and Gould (1979) identified a 'triad of impairments' in a broad group of 'autistic' children:

- *Difficulty in social interaction and social relationships*, for example, appearing indifferent to other people, difficulty in understanding unwritten social rules, recognising other's feelings, or seeking comfort from others. Temple Grandin (1996) is a very well-known author who is autistic herself. She recalls pulling away when others tried to give her a hug because being touched overwhelmed her senses. She remembers always wanting to participate in activities with other children but not knowing how and never fitting in.

- *Verbal and non-verbal social communication*, including difficulty in understanding the meaning of gestures, facial expressions or tone of voice.

- *Social imagination*, meaning inability to think and behave flexibly, restricted, obsessional or repetitive activities, difficulty in developing the skills of playing with others. Children often find it hard to understand and interpret other people's thoughts, feelings and actions, engage in imaginative play, predict what will or could happen next, understand the concept of danger and cope in new or unfamiliar situations.

In addition to this triad, repetitive behaviour patterns are often a notable feature, as well as a resistance to change in routine.

More recently the diagnostic manual, DSM-V, of the American Psychiatric Association (APA, 2013) has combined the first two descriptions of difficulties into one. It also adds an additional element to the third: an unusual interest in, and way of responding to, sensory stimuli in the environment. As Frederickson and Cline (2015, p. 283) note, this dyad is comprised of difficulties in:

- social communication and social interaction;
- restricted, repetitive patterns of behaviour, interests or activities including sensory difficulties.

The *Code of Practice* in England (DfE, 2015, §6.27) concurs with this description and suggests that 'young people with an Autistic Spectrum Disorder (ASD) may have needs across all areas, including particular sensory requirements'. They 'are likely to have particular difficulties with social interaction. They may also experience difficulties with language, communication and imagination which can impact on how they relate to others' (DfE, 2015, §6.29).

Assessment of 'autism'

Autism is a biological explanation of individual behaviour. It can be difficult, as Sheehy (2004) notes, to separate out the effects of autism from those of profound difficulties in learning, given that 80 per cent of children with autism score below 70 on norm-referenced intelligence tests (Peeters & Gilberg, 1999) and increasingly severe general learning difficulties are correlated with an increasing occurrence of autism (Jordan, 1999).

As Klin, Sparrow, Marans, Carter & Volkmar. (2000, p. 163) comment, 'There are no biological markers in the identification of autism, despite advances in neuro-science.' Hence a profile of symptoms and characteristics of autistic behaviour with agreed diagnostic criteria is used to identify autism in young people. The DSM criteria noted above are very influential and form the basis, for example, of the Autism Diagnostic Observation Schedule (ADOS) that is used in some local authorities in the United Kingdom as a diagnostic tool. However, DSM is an American publication and many assessments of autism spectrum disorders in the United Kingdom are based on the *International Classification of Diseases* (ICD), published by the World Health Organisation. In the ICD-10 (WHO, 1994, F84.0), autism is described as a disorder that is 'pervasive' and 'developmental', and that it is identified through 'abnormal and/or impaired development' that is evident before 3 years of age and by particular 'abnormal functioning' in social interaction, communication and 'restricted, repetitive behaviour'. Boys are affected three to four times more often than girls. Impairments 'in reciprocal social interaction' which manifest as 'an inadequate appreciation of socio-emotional cues' are always present. Impairments in communications include a 'lack of social usage of whatever language skills are present', as well as poorly developed 'make-believe and social imitative play'. During conversations, the ability to synchronise personal responses to the utterances of others is impaired as well as the ability to respond with feeling to other people's overtures. Autism is also said to be characterised by 'restricted, repetitive, and stereotyped patterns of behaviour, interests, and activities' that are demonstrated by 'a tendency to impose rigidity and routine on a wide range of aspects of day-to-day functioning'. The next version of the ICD is due to be published in 2018 (http://www.who.int/classifications/icd/revision/en/) and may well align this more closely with the DSM-V.

Reflective activity: Recognising autism spectrum disorders

The National Institute for Health and Care Excellence (NICE) (2011) has provided three 'Signs and symptoms' tables for use with preschool, primary and secondary-aged children in Appendix 3 of its publication, *Autism in under 19s: recognition, referral and diagnosis*. These are available at https://www.nice.org.uk/guidance/cg128/resources (accessed 24.06.16).

Access these tables yourself and compare the lists of signs and symptoms with the description of autism above.

What use do you think schools/colleges might make of these tables?

These tables 'are not intended to be used alone, but to help professionals recognise a pattern of impairments in reciprocal social and communication skills, together with unusual restricted and repetitive behaviours' (https://www.nice.org.uk/guidance/cg128/chapter/Appendix-C-Signs-and-symptoms-of-possible-autism, accessed 24.06.16). What might be some of the negative consequences of open access to tables such as these, do you think?

Do you feel there might be any danger of over diagnosis of ASD if tables such as these are used in schools? If so, why might this be the case?

The National Institute for Health and Care Excellence (NICE) (2011) has produced a very useful publication, *Autism: recognition referral and diagnosis of children and young people on the autism spectrum*, with scenarios to assist professionals to 'to improve and assess users' knowledge of the recognition, referral and diagnosis of autism in children and young people' (p. 4). It is available at https://www.nice.org.uk/guidance/cg128/resources/clinical-case-scenarios-183180493 (accessed 24.06.16). You might also choose to access this document and consider the advice given by NICE in relation to each of the young people whose experiences are described here.

Co-ordination between health agencies and other key services such as education, social care and the voluntary sector is important. NICE (2011) advises that a local autism multidisciplinary group (the autism team) should include, in its core membership, a paediatrician and/or child and adolescent psychiatrist, a speech and language therapist, and clinical and/or educational psychologist. Multi-agency staff should also work in partnership with the child or young person with autism and their family or carers. Once a concern about possible autistic tendencies has been raised, a member of the core autism team should advise on whether a referral should be made for a formal assessment.

Strategies to address autism

The Treatment and Education of Autistic and related Communication Handicapped Children programme (TEACCH) (Mesibov, Shea & Schopler, 2004) is designed to combine cultivating individual strengths and interests with structured teaching. The principles include improving skills through education and modifying the environment to accommodate individual autistic students, structured teaching rather than more informal approaches, and parents collaborating with professionals as co-therapists to continue the techniques at home.

Teaching communication skills

In a recent interview (Wearmouth, 2016a, pp. 45–6), Martha, the mother of an 8-year-old autistic child, N, described how she and her husband taught N to communicate with them at home, using PECS (see above) and other strategies. The hardest thing for the parents was how long every aspect of development in his ability to communicate took. They started with teaching him the purpose of communication. Up till then he had not seen the purpose of it because his mother had done everything for him. To teach him they used the technique of object exchange: at first his mother stuck a picture of a chocolate biscuit to a fridge magnet, put his hand on to the magnet, removed it from the fridge and put it into her own hand saying, 'Chocolate biscuit, please'. Then she gave him the biscuit, saying, 'Chocolate biscuit', to make the link between the picture and the sound symbols of the words. Finally she helped him to put the magnet back on the fridge as an end to that routine. Now there was strong motivation for N to want to communicate and he quickly learned to do it for himself. A 'stop' sign was put on the fridge to symbolise 'no more', also.

Signing in order to communicate became important at this point. Mother and child together learned Makaton signing from the CBBC programme 'Something special' which has an actor signing all the way through. They found Makaton simple and fun to use together. The mother encouraged the boy to connect words to signs by quite deliberately giving him the verbal equivalent every time she used one. 'Every time you sign, you also say at the same time, and he makes the connection'. Signing was also used at a special preschool group to teach him to transition between tasks – when to stop an activity, and so on.

At this point the speech therapist advised that he might become very anxious if activities were sprung on him without any warning. Next, therefore, came pictures to forewarn him what was about to happen, for example, pictures of a car and the local supermarket to show that they were about to go shopping. A picture of a timer to indicate 'time to go' proved to be of no use, probably because the concept of time was too complex.

Following this N's mother made line drawings on the pictures to make the link between pictures of the real thing and symbols to represent them. For example a line drawing of a red door represented the supermarket. The line drawings made the instigation of simple communication, through picture exchange (PECS, see above), possible for him. This was always around requests for food and drink.

Signing continued, accompanied by a running commentary from his mother on what was happening around N. To do this, she spoke in very short, punctuated sentences.

Subsequently, the use of PECS made scheduling possible. 'There is so much safety in schedules for an autistic child because one thing leads to the next.' After a while words can be written underneath the drawings to encourage literacy. N's mother described the family's use of scheduling as follows:

'We regularly use scheduling with picture cards at home. The cards have pictures of what we do during the day, places we visit, and tasks to be completed. At the beginning of the day, we choose pictures that represent what will happen that day. We stick the cards on a velcro strip, and as we complete activities through the day we unstick each card and 'post' it in a 'completed' box. The benefit is that my son can see the whole day's happenings and can predict what will happen next. I have found that using schedules has reduced my son's stress, and built his confidence and, over time, has increased his flexibility. If the schedule needs to change, it can be discussed and my son can see that the rest of the schedule remains unaltered, which can be reassuring to him.'

It is essential that an autistic child knows that s/he can communicate with others, so other members of the family and friends learned to sign too.

When he went to school at the age of nearly 5, N spoke three words: 'hippo', 'purple' and 'ten'. A very sensitive teaching assistant (TA) supported him through his first year by deliberately setting out to understand him as a person and how to communicate with him. There were times when he ran into problems, however. N's schedule for going to the toilet included washing his hands and turning off the tap, but one day the tap was stuck in the 'on' position. He would not leave the wash-room because he could not complete the activity as listed on his schedule.

By the end of Year One his vocabulary had increased considerably. The target on his individualised education programme (IEP) was to learn how to ask for help so he was given a card that said: 'Help me'.

Now N is about to move to a middle school, so the concern for his parents is how to liaise effectively with the special educational needs co-ordinator (SENCo) and other staff, and hope that they are all prepared to get to know, communicate with, and understand their son.

Addressing autistic tendencies in classrooms

In classrooms, to take account of the challenges facing autistic students, teachers can address needs of children in a number of ways:

- paying close attention to clarity and order, reducing extraneous and unnecessary material in order that children know where their attention needs to be directed and maintaining a predictable physical environment with very predictable and regular routines, ensuring that everything is kept in the same place;

- teaching children agreed signals to be quiet or to call for attention;

- providing specific low-arousal work areas free from visual distractions; headphones might be made available to reduce sound;

- providing a visual timetable with clear symbols to represent the various activities for the day, and a simple visual timer with, for example, an arrow that is moved across a simple timeline to show how much time has passed and how much is left.

- in order to develop greater understanding of personal emotions children might be taught in a very deliberate, overt and structured way;

- to name their feelings and relate these to their own experiences, predict how they are likely to feel at particular times and in particular circumstances, and recognise the signs of extreme emotions such as anger - a visual gauge showing graduated degrees of anger in different shades of colour can often be helpful here;

- to identify and name others' feelings and link these to possible causes, and identify appropriate responses to others' emotions. They might, for example, keep a feelings diary in which they record times when they feel happy, sad or frightened, and what they can do about this. Teachers might use art, drama and social stories to identify the different kinds of emotions and/or explore their physical aspects and/or talk through situations that need to be resolved.

Above all it is really important to get to know the pupil really well and to understand his/her individuality, strengths, weakness, likes, dislikes and so on.

Profound and multiple learning disabilities

For very many years there was a general assumption that children with multiple and profound difficulties were ineducable. However, since the 1970 Education Act, the right of all children to an appropriate education, irrespective of the degree of difficulty in learning, has been acknowledged. Some children with profound and multiple learning disabilities may have profound autism or Down's syndrome. Others may have Rett syndrome, Ttuberous Ssclerosis, Batten Disease or any other disorder. One common factor 4.3 for everyone is that they experience great difficulty communicating. Mencap (undated EM1_9781474287630.docx - CIT000259, p. 4) notes how many people with profound and multiple learning disabilities 'rely on facial expressions, vocal sounds, body language and behaviour to communicate'. Some people may only 'use a small range of formal communication, such as speech, symbols or signs'. Another factor is that learning is likely to be very slow. 'Short-term memory may well be very limited and children may need frequent repetition of the same concepts in the same situations' (ibid.). Some may not reach the stage where they can communicate intentionally. Many may find it hard to understand what others are trying to communicate to them.

Strategies to address profound difficulties in learning

> ### ? Reflective activities: Ways to address barriers to learning arising from profound difficulties in learning
>
> It is very important that those people who support people with profound and multiple learning disabilities 'spend time getting to know their means of communication and finding effective ways to interact with them' (Mencap, undated, p. 7). You might like to look back at some of the discussions above on ways to support the development of communication through, for example, AAC, including PECS, and the use of symbols such as Widgit Literacy Symbols available at http://www.widgit.com/parents/information/ (accessed 26.02.16).
>
> How might you use these systems to support communication skills among students whose profound difficulties in this area create barriers to their learning?

Down's syndrome

Down's syndrome is another condition often associated with some impairment of cognitive ability. A small number have severe to profound difficulties in learning, but children with Down's tend to have difficulties ranging from mild to moderate difficulties. The average IQ is around 50 (Dykens & Kasari, 1997). A 'syndrome' is a group of recognisable characteristics occurring together. Down's syndrome was first described by an English doctor, John Langdon Down, in 1866. It is a congenital condition – one present at birth. Down's is chromosomal. It occurs because each of the body's cells contains an extra copy of chromosome 21, and can be identified in a foetus with amniocentesis during pregnancy, or in a baby at birth. In the United Kingdom, around one baby in every thousand, around 775 per year (http://www.nhs.uk/conditions/downs-syndrome/pages/introduction.aspx – accessed 25.02.16), is born with Down's syndrome, although it is statistically much more common with older mothers. At maternal age 20, the probability is one in 1450 and at age 45 it is one in 35 (Morris, Wald, Mutton & Alberman, 2003). There is also data to suggest that paternal age, especially beyond 42, increases the risk of a child with Down's syndrome (Fisch et al., 2003).

The medical consequences of the extra genetic material are highly variable and may affect the function of any organ system or bodily process. Health concerns for individuals with Down's include a higher risk of congenital heart defects, recurrent ear infections, obstructive sleep apnea, and thyroid dysfunctions (Selikowitz, 2008). The incidence of congenital heart disease in children with Down's syndrome is up to 50 per cent (Freeman et al., 1998). Eye disorders are relatively common. For example, almost half have strabismus, in which the two eyes do not move in tandem (Yurdakul, Ugurlu & Maden, 2006). In the past, there was also a high incidence of hearing loss in children with Down's syndrome. These days, however, with more systematic diagnosis and treatment of ear disease, for example 'glue-ear' (see below), almost all children have normal hearing levels.

Language skills show a difference between understanding speech and expressing speech, and commonly individuals with Down's syndrome have a speech delay (Bird & Thomas, 2002). It is common for receptive language skills to exceed expressive skills. Overall cognitive development in children with Down's syndrome is quite variable which underlines the importance of evaluating children individually (Selikowitz, 2008). Fine motor skills are delayed and often lag behind gross motor skills and can interfere with cognitive development. Delays in the development of gross motor skills are variable. Some children will begin walking at around 2 years of age, while others will not walk until age 4. Physiotherapy and/or participation in other specially adapted programmes of physical education may promote enhanced development of gross motor skills.

Strategies to address difficulties associated with Down's syndrome

Down's syndrome cannot be cured, but the learning and other difficulties associated with it can be addressed if appropriate help is offered and other people accept and include. Above all it is important to stress that children with Down's syndrome are individuals and vary in their abilities and achievements as well as the barriers they experience to their learning.

Difficulties in social, emotional and mental health

Schools play a critical part in shaping a child's identity as a learner (Bruner, 1996), so interpretations of, and responses to, behaviour perceived as challenging or concerning at home and/or in schools often generate a great deal of heated debate.

Use of terms

The terms 'emotional and behavioural difficulties' (EBD), first formally used by Warnock (DES, 1978), or 'social, emotional and behavioural difficulties (SEBD), or, as now in England, 'social, emotional and mental health' difficulties are ill-defined. The use of these terms to explain why some students behave in a way that is seen as anti-social, related to emotional upset, withdrawn or otherwise disturbing is not always helpful to parents and/or teachers. Poulou and Norwich (2002, p. 112), for example, found from a review of international studies that the more teachers thought student behaviour stemmed from problems within the students themselves, such as the 'child wants to attract attention' or the 'child's innate personality', '. . . the more those teachers experienced feelings of 'stress', 'offence' and even 'helplessness', 'especially for conduct and mixed behaviour difficulties' (Poulou & Norwich, 2002, p. 125). Some behaviour that may be seen as inappropriate in a social context may actually stem from a neurological disorder, for example, actions associated with Tourette syndrome.

Anti-social behaviour

Young people's anti-social behaviour does not occur in a vacuum (Watkins & Wagner, 2000). Teachers see themselves as able to deal with a student's problematic behaviour if they consider that students' problems are generally caused by 'factors originating from teachers themselves, like their personality, manners towards the child with EBD, or teaching style' (ibid.) – in other words if they realise that they can take some control over the situation by changing some aspects of their own behaviour as it relates, for example, to pedagogy, or their relationship with students.

Strategies to address anti-social behaviour

 Reflective activity: Who should own disruptive behaviour in classrooms?

Bill Rogers is a very well known educator with a specialism in advising teachers and schools on ways of teaching students appropriate behaviour.

> To what extent do you agree with his view that we should not excuse students from 'taking ownership for their disruptive behaviour', or 'facing accountability for such behaviour by facing appropriate consequences' or 'learning that behaviour is not an accident of birth or location', and that 'one can learn to make better and more conscious choices about behaviour' (Rogers, 1994, p. 167)?
>
> How might teachers set about teaching students 'to make better and more conscious choices' about the way they behave?

Most commonly, understandings and strategies in classroom management are based on principles from a behaviourist psychology frame of reference (Skinner, 1938; Baer, Wolf & Risely, 1968). As we outlined in Chapter 1, behavioural methodologies hold that all (mis)behaviour is learned and, therefore, that learning and (mis)behaviour can be modified through intervening in a systematic, consistent, predictable way in the environment.

You will find further discussion on ways to address anti-social behaviour in Chapter 7.

Emotional concerns

Attachment and the nurturing of young children

One psychological theory of human development that has had considerable influence over educational provision for young children whose behaviour is of concern to teachers is that of attachment theory (Bowlby, 1952). Babies quickly attach themselves emotionally to their adult carers and progress through well-recognised stages of development towards maturity. Successful development depends on needs being adequately met at an earlier stage. Where this is not the case, then children will persist in inappropriate attachment behaviour, being over-anxious, avoidant or aggressive, or becoming incapable of warm attachment and positive human relationships (Harris-Hendriks & Figueroa, 1995; Bennathan, 2000).

Strategies to address insecure attachment

Attachment theory has influenced education in the early years through the development of 'nurture groups' in some infant schools, originally in the Inner London Education Authority in 1970–71 by Marjorie Boxall, an educational psychologist, and re-established more recently by some local authorities. Boxall (2002) argues that learning, personality and behaviour difficulties, which are more likely in the young children of families experiencing disadvantage and deprivation, can be the result of inadequate early care and support from parents who struggle with poverty, damaged relationships and harsh and stressful living conditions. The underlying intention of the nurture group is the recreation of the total experience of a normally developing child from babyhood onwards. Planning the routine of the nurture group day means providing a predictable, reliable structure through which children can go on to interact and learn in regular settings (Bennathan, 2000). The Boxall Profile is an observational tool that was developed as a way of assessing the level of skills children possessed to access learning and of identifying their developmental needs to support the work being done in nurture groups. It was originally standardised for children aged 3–8 years but has recently been developed for use in secondary schools.

Provision in a nurture group

Nurture groups attempt to create features of adequate parenting within school with the opportunity to develop trust, security, positive mood and identity through attachment to a reliable attentive and caring adult, as well as autonomy through the provision of controlled and graduated experiences in familiar surroundings.

Some features of such groups include:

- easy physical contact between adult and child;
- warmth, intimacy and a family atmosphere;
- good-humoured acceptance of children and their behaviour;
- familiar regular routines;
- a focus on tidying up and putting away;
- the provision of food in structured contexts;
- opportunities to play and the appropriate participation of the adults;
- adults talking about, and encouraging reflection by children on, trouble-provoking situations and their own feelings;
- opportunities for children to develop increasing autonomy. These opportunities incorporate visits outside the nurture group, participation in games, visits to regular classrooms and children's eventual full-time inclusion in a mainstream class. (Wearmouth, 2009, p. 167)

 4.5

Mental health

Sometimes children and young people experience emotional, behavioural and psychiatric problems, for example, extreme anxiety, eating problems, depression, obsessive-compulsive disorder and so on.

Addressing issues of mental health

Sometimes the difficulties experienced by young people are serious enough to warrant a referral to the local Child and Mental Health Service (CAMHS). CAMHS professionals deal with a wide range of mental health problems. In any one team they may well include:

- child and adolescent psychiatrists who are medically qualified doctors specialising in working with young people and their families;
- clinical psychologists qualified in assessing and assisting with young people's psychological functioning, and emotional well-being;
- child psychotherapists trained in therapies intended to support young people to deal with problems related to the emotions and mental health problems;
- family therapists one trained therapists who work with children and their families together to help them understand and manage the difficulties that are happening in their lives, by focusing on the 'systems' of interaction between family members and emphasising family relationships as an important factor in psychological health.
- social workers trained to help children and families affected by social disadvantages and needing extra support through social welfare, or needing to be kept safe.
- other professionals, for example, educational psychologists, art therapists, and speech and language therapists.

Bereavement in childhood

One of the events in childhood that is likely to affect children's behaviour very profoundly, and, indeed, may have resonances later on in life, is that of the death of the primary caregiver, most often the mother, or of close family members. According to Cruse (2016), 1 in 29 children aged 5–16 in the United Kingdom has been bereaved of a parent or sibling, and 1 in 16 has lost a close friend (http://www.cruse.org.uk/ – accessed 03.03.16). The deep distress that results from a child's bereavement may create a special educational need of a short- or long-term nature.

Some people may assume that a young person who loses a parent, caregiver, sibling or grandparent will not be affected too deeply as s/he is too young. However, emotional disturbances that are not immediately obvious may become apparent later and last for several years (Rutter, 1966). Cruse (2016) comments that it is common for 'some bereaved children and young people to delay their grief for months or sometimes years'. Subsequently, 'other life changing incidents such as moving home, acquiring a step parent or experiencing a further bereavement can serve to release the bereaved child or young person's delayed or unresolved grief'. There seems to be no way to divert grief, '... ultimately, regardless of how long the child or young person has managed to deny their grief, they will have to go through the grieving process eventually' (Cruse, 2016, http://www.cruse.org.uk/for-schools/symptoms, accessed 03.03.16).

As Cruse (2016) notes, above all, young people need to be given the opportunity to grieve. Ignoring or averting the child's grief is not supportive, but can prove extremely damaging as the child becomes an adult. Young people need to be allowed to talk about their feelings. Everyone has their own way of grieving. Not all young people will experience the same emotions, behave the same way and respond similarly to other people who have lost close friends or relations.

Addressing emotional or mental health difficulties through counselling

We have already noted above that young people identified as experiencing emotional or mental health difficulties might be referred to the CAMHS in their area. One approach available through this service might be counselling for the individual and, possibly, his/her family.

 Reflective activity: Awareness of what might be involved in counselling

Counselling can be seen as a complex learning process which takes place 'at a physical, bodily level and through language, and in the thoughts, feelings and memories of each participant' (McLeod, 1998, p. xvii) simultaneously.

What do you think this means in practice? Do you have any experience of counselling?

Who would have to be involved in taking the decision that a student should be offered counselling, do you think?

Talking therapies

One of the criticisms of the practice of counselling is that it tends to be protracted. In recent years there has been an attempt to address this criticism by offering brief series of therapy sessions, 'on average in less than 5 sessions', from a solution-focussed approach. This approach is justified as brief because it is focused on the future, and also because it works with the strengths of clients by making the best use of their resource. (http://www.barrywinbolt.com/solution-focused-brief-therapy/, accessed 19.02.16)

Cognitive behavioural therapy

One of the so-called talking therapies that might be used by a CAMHS therapist is cognitive behavioural therapy (CBT). This is described to young people as follows:

CBT helps you understand the link between your thoughts, emotions and behaviour. This is important because sometimes, when you talk about things that are difficult, you may feel worse to begin with. It teaches you skills:

- to overcome these problematic thoughts, emotions and behaviour
- to find ways of overcoming negative thinking and challenging unhelpful and inaccurate thoughts or beliefs.

CBT is not about thinking more positively!

CBT helps the way you feel to improve what you think and what you do.

By being able to approach situations in a more balanced way, you will hopefully be more effective in solving your problems and feel more in control of your life. (Royal College of Psychiatrists, 2016, p. 1)

Solution-focused brief therapy

'Solution-focused brief therapy' (SFBT) (de Shazer, 1985) that is employed in some places to focus on solutions rather than problems is an example of a cognitive-behavioural approach. The main task here is to help a student imagine how s/he would like things to be different, and what it would take for them to be so. The best known technique is the 'miracle question' (de Shazer, 1988). A paraphrase of this might be, 'If one night, while you were sleeping, a miracle happened and the problem that brought you here was solved but you didn't know that the miracle had happened because you were asleep, what would be different when you woke up in the morning that would tell you that the miracle had taken place?' As de Shazer et al. (2007, p. 40) comment: 'ultimately the miracle question is not so much about figuring out what would be a "dream come true" [...] as it is about discovering [...] and replicating the effects of it.'

Also important are the 'scaling questions':

- On a scale of 1 to 10 where 1 is the worst it's ever been and 10 is after the miracle has happened, where are you now?
- Where do you need to be?
- What will help you move up one point?
- How can you keep yourself at that point?

In the context of schools, students are invited to work out ways of reaching a positive outcome and to use their responses to learn ways of behaving more appropriately in school and/or achieve more highly in academic terms.

Sensory and physical difficulties and needs

A child who can see and hear will reach out and explore its surroundings naturally. A child with a sensory impairment will not necessarily do this and may need encouragement to explore and interact with others. The greatest challenge for a child with a sensory impairment is communication (Spencer & Marschark, 2010).

The 'best' communication approach for any child and family is the one which works for them, both fitting in with the family's culture and values and most importantly, allowing the child to develop good self-esteem, a positive self-image, successful relationships [...] in all aspects of her life. (NDCS, 2010, p. 50)

However much is known about a child's sensory or physical difficulties, though, as Miller and Ockleford (2005) aptly comment, that child is still an individual with his/her own personal strengths and needs, interests, experiences, background, and so on that, together with his/her own views, must all be taken into account when drawing up any intervention plan.

Hearing impairment

For a deaf child, early intervention in the child's life is clearly very important. Normal progress in language may be hard and necessitate intensive education and support throughout the child's life. Few children are totally deaf. There are different degrees of deafness, most often classified as mild, moderate, severe or profound (Spencer & Marschark, 2010). Deafness can be:

- conductive, when sound cannot pass efficiently through the outer and middle ear to the cochlea and auditory nerve. The most common type in children is caused by 'glue ear' (NDCS, 2010), a build-up of fluid in the middle ear which affects about one in five children at any time. For most children, the glue ear clears up by itself. A few need surgery to insert 'grommets' into the eardrums, tiny plastic tubes that allow air to circulate in the middle ear and help to prevent the build-up of fluid.
- sensori-neural, which is permanent and occurs when there is a fault in the inner ear or auditory (hearing) nerve.

Addressing barriers to learning associated with hearing impairments in mainstream schools

Delay in identifying deafness can mean delay in establishing effective communication with the child (Goldberg & Richberg, 2004; Moeller, Tomblin, Yoshinaga-Itano, Connor & Jerger., 2007). Children who do not hear clearly or whose hearing varies may be late to start talking, have difficulties with speech sounds, or fail to learn to listen well (Yoshinaga-Itano, 2003). They may also have poor memory and language-processing skills, poor basic vocabularies, difficulty with reading and spelling, sentence structure and comprehension and mathematics. Pupils with a conductive hearing loss have a higher tendency to behaviour problems, poor motivation and attention, shyness and withdrawal (Spencer & Marschark, 2010), especially those whose conductive deafness remained undiagnosed in early childhood.

Reflective activity: Engaging with barriers to learning associated with hearing impairments

Many young people with hearing impairments are in mainstream schools these days.

How might you begin to understand the barriers to learning that some of these students experience? What might you learn from what the students tell you?

How important is it to develop a mutually respectful relationship with students do you think?

As you read the approaches below, reflect on how you might establish a balance between respecting the individuality of the student and decisions about which technical supports might be available and supportive of learning and educational progress.

Non-specialist as well as specialist teachers should understand how to include them in classrooms most effectively. The three major 'types' of approach are Auditory-Oral (or 'Oral / Aural'), Sign-Bilingual or Total Communication.

> Generally the evidence for any one method working better than another for deaf children as a whole is unclear, and all the approaches can point to some evidence which shows successful outcomes for children. (NDCS, 2010, p. 45)

The aim of Auditory-Oral approaches is that deaf children should learn to use whatever residual hearing they may have to develop good listening and speaking skills which will enable them to communicate and mix with hearing people as part of the wider hearing community (Beattie, 2006). These approaches emphasise the use of amplification such as hearing aids, cochlear implants and radio aids to maximise the use of the child's 'residual' hearing (Spencer & Marschark, 2006). The most widely used of these approaches is the Natural Aural Approach. Here no sign language is used and children are not encouraged to rely on lip-reading (Lewis, 1996).

Sign Bilingualism in the United Kingdom uses British Sign Language (or Irish Sign Language in Ireland) and whatever is the spoken language of the home (Moores, 2008). This approach assumes that a visual language is essential for deaf children to have full access to language learning, education, information and the world around them, along with a strong positive deaf identity. British Sign Language (BSL) has its own grammar and linguistic rules which are different from English, so it is not used simultaneously with spoken language. It developed as a visual medium and uses body language, head position, facial expressions and gesture as well as the hands. It uses fingerspelling for words such as names which have no signs. Use of BSL can make a connection with Deaf culture and the Deaf community as well as the hearing world (Burman, Nunes & Evans, 2006).

Reflective activity: Using British Sign Language

Where a child uses BSL it is often useful if the rest of the family, classmates and teachers learn to sign also.

From your own experience, how, in practice, might this be arranged in schools and for the family?

Total Communication is based on the principle that deaf children can learn to communicate effectively by using whatever combination of means works best: sign, speech and hearing, fingerspelling, gesture, facial expression, lip-reading and cued speech. Signed/Signs Supported English (SSE) uses signs taken from BSL, together with fingerspelling (Moores, 2001) and is used in the word order of English to supplement what is spoken. Signed English, similarly, uses signs taken from BSL together with some specially developed 'markers' made with the hands, and fingerspelling, to give an exact representation of the word order and the grammar of English. It is mainly used to support the teaching of reading and writing. In fingerspelling, each letter of the alphabet is indicated by using the fingers and palm of the hand (Padden & Gunsals, 2003). Lip-reading is the process of reading words from the lip patterns of the person speaking (Spencer & Marschark, 2010). Lip-reading is never enough on its own, however. Many speech sounds are not visible on the lips, and lip patterns also vary from person to person. Further, lack of clarity around the face, for example, beards or moustaches that obscure the mouth, or eating whilst talking, can make lip-reading difficult. Cued Speech is a sound-based system that accompanies natural speech and uses eight hand shapes in four different positions (cues) to represent the sounds of English visually (Hage & Leybaert, 2006). Some spoken sounds cannot be fully lip-read: 'p', 'm' and 'b' all look the same on the lips; sounds like 'd', 'k' and 'g' cannot be seen on the lips. Hand shapes are 'cued' near to the mouth to make clear the sounds of English which look the same when lip-read. The association between the sounds and letters of spoken English is intended to help develop literacy skills as well as spoken language.

 Reflective activity: Using total communication in schools

As with the use of British Sign Language, it is often useful if the rest of the family, classmates and teachers learn to use total communication with students who experience hearing impairments of a severe nature.

How, in practice, might this be arranged in school and for the family?

Minimising barriers through assistive devices

As the NDCS (2008, p. 31) comments, deaf children often use assistive listening devices to assist them to hear what a speaker is saying, particularly in noisy listening conditions. Personal FM systems (often known as radio aids) are very useful, especially at school, college or at home. 'They can help reduce effects of background noise in, for example, a school classroom, and help a child to concentrate on one person's voice, often their teacher.' Radio aids have a transmitter with a microphone and a receiver. The person talking wears the transmitter and the sounds are transmitted by radio waves to the receiver. The deaf child wears the receiver which picks up the signal from the transmitter and converts it back to sound. The child's hearing aids or implants amplify the sound so that the child can hear what is said.

Classroom soundfield systems are designed for similar reasons as radio aids. Such systems include a microphone worn by the speaker that is linked to an amplifier by either an FM radio transmitter or an infra-red transmitter so that the speaker can walk around a room with no need for wires. Loudspeakers are fitted around the room. The soundfield system amplifies the speaker's voice to produce a clear, consistent level of sound above the background noise (NDCS, 2008). Most children with hearing aids or cochlear implants will still need to use a radio aid in a classroom with a soundfield system.

Sound waves reverberate and increase the amount of background noise in rooms with hard surfaces (Moeller et al., 2007). Soundfield systems and the acoustic treatment of teaching spaces can improve the listening environment for all students. It is important for class teachers to think carefully about the clarity of their spoken language (Wilkins & Ertmer, 2002). Teachers should use natural speech patterns and not exaggerate lip movements or shout. They should highlight key terms and key concepts and place themselves in a position appropriate for students to lip read or benefit from a hearing aid where the maximum range is often two metres. To acquire spoken and written English, students may also need the additional support of visual and written forms of language, as well as lip-reading or multi-sensory clues (Harris & Moreno, 2006).

Visual impairment

Visual impairment (VI) is a term indicating a continuum of sight loss (Mason, McCall, Arter, McLinden & Stone, 1997) affecting around 25,000 between the ages of 0 and 16 years in the United Kingdom (Tate, Smeeth, Evans & Fletcher, 2008), and 15,000 between the ages of 17 and 25 years. Visual difficulties may mean that children have had less opportunity to explore their environment before going to school and learn through observing and copying the actions of others (Douglas & McLinden, 2005). Academic progress and social skills may be influenced by this.

Addressing barriers related to visual impairment

Children may therefore need teaching of literacy development through specialist codes such as Braille or Moon or through print/modified print Braille and/or specialist

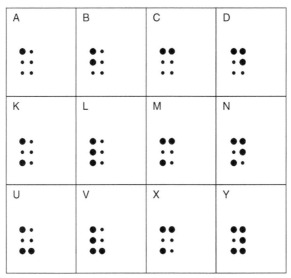

Figure 4.1 Braille alphabet

teaching of mobility, tactile and keyboard skills, as well as social and life skills generally. It is important to consider whether and when to withdraw the child from the mainstream classroom for specialist or additional teaching so that the pupil does not become socially isolated and the mainstream teacher maintains full responsibility for the pupil.

Braille is the alphabet and numbers, designed to be read by fingers rather than eyes through a series of raised dots on a page. A blind French schoolboy, Louis Braille, devised the code more than 200 years ago. This code is based on six dots arranged in two columns of three (see Figure 4.1). Different types of Braille codes use combinations of these dots, 63 in all, to represent letters of the alphabet, numbers, punctuation marks and common letter groups.

There are two grades of Braille: uncontracted (previously Grade 1) and contracted (previously Grade 2). Uncontracted includes a letter for letter and number for number translation from print. Contracted has special signs for common words and letter combinations. This usually increases the speed of reading. Particular subject areas, for example music, mathematics, science and foreign languages, have their own specialist codes.

 Reflective activity: Planning support for students with VI in classrooms

As Mason (2001) comments, in order to plan appropriate support for students with VI, teachers and support staff need to consider:

- whether the child has a preferred or dominant eye or a defect in field or colour vision. This is important for both seating and using appropriate teaching strategies;
- what kind of restrictions there might be on physical activities which may constrain the child's participation with peers;

- whether low vision aids have been prescribed and, if so, when they should be used and whether the student has been trained to use them;
- lighting levels as well as size and contrast of print to maximise the student's vision.

From your own experience, how do you think a school could ensure that all teachers are aware of what might be included on a student's learning plan?

Multi-sensory impairment

Multi-sensory impairment means difficulty with both vision and hearing resulting in limited and possibly confused experience of the world (Aitken, 2000). Taylor (2007, p. 205) notes the difficulties experienced by many of these children in communicating:

> These include: a reduced and confused experience of the world, becoming passive and isolated, and the tendency to be echolalic or repeating the last word said to them, all of which limit their ability to make choices. Aitken and Millar (2002) also highlight the effects of hearing impairment on individuals' communication, including isolation from information and from other people. A physical impairment in association with communication difficulties will also present additional challenges. The child with MSI has all these difficulties compounded.

Some children become skilled at using touch as a means of learning about the world and a means of communicating. Others may become skilled in using the sense of smell. Yet others may sense movement around them from differences in air pressure.

For those young people, many assistive devices are available to enable them to communicate: electronic language boards, voice synthesisers and voice recognition software.

Addressing barriers to learning through multi-sensory teaching

Multi-sensory teaching is simultaneous use of visual, auditory, and kinesthetic-tactile senses to enhance memory and learning. The use of such an approach for children whose senses are compromised or greatly reduced could be effective if careful planning takes account of their individual sensory needs. Helen Keller is, perhaps, the best known deaf-blind child in history. The breakthrough to communicating with her came when her teacher, Anne, pumped water over one of Helen's hands and spelled out the word 'water' in the other. Something about this made the connection between the word and its meaning. Helen made rapid progress after that. Anne taught her to read, firstly with raised letters and later with Braille, and then to write with both ordinary and Braille typewriters.

Tourette syndrome

 Reflective activity: What is known about Tourette syndrome?

Take a few moments to note down what you already know about Tourette syndrome:

- how it is identified;
- difficulties associated with it;
- approaches to addressing difficulties;
- how, in your experience, the general public tends to regard individuals with Tourette syndrome and why you feel this is.

Tourette syndrome is a neurological disorder characterised by motor and vocal tics: repetitive, stereotyped, involuntary movements and vocalisations. Across the world the prevalence among school children 'range from 1 to 10 per 1000, with a rate of 6 per 1000 replicated in several countries' (Piacentini et al., 2010, p. 1929). As NINDS (2005) outlines, motor tics are, commonly, sudden, brief, repetitive movements that may include eye blinking and other vision irregularities, facial grimacing, shoulder shrugging, and head or shoulder jerking, or, more dramatically, touching objects, hopping, jumping, bending, twisting, or motor movements that result in self-harm such as punching oneself in the face. Vocalisations often include repetitive throat-clearing, sniffing, or grunting sounds – or, at the extreme, 'coprolalia' (uttering swear words) or 'echolalia' (repeating the words or phrases of others). Tics tend to start in early childhood, peak before the mid-teen years and improve subsequently (NINDS, 2005).

People with Tourette syndrome often report that tics are preceded by an urge or sensation in the affected muscles, commonly called a 'premonitory urge' that builds up to the point where it is expressed. Excitement, anxiety or particular physical experiences can trigger or worsen tics. Medication can be prescribed for young people whose tics are severe enough to interfere with their functioning. However, as Piacentini et al. (2010, p. 1930) comment, this 'rarely eliminates tics and are often associated with unacceptable sedation, weight gain, cognitive dulling, and motor adverse effects', such as tremors.

Young people with Tourette syndrome often cope well in mainstream classrooms. However, frequent tics can interfere with academic performance or disrupt social relationships with peers. The author's own experience is that, in a well-managed classroom, other young people can be very understanding and supportive.   4.4

Supporting individuals with Tourettes

A number of approaches have been advocated for supporting individuals with Tourettes to manage their behaviour themselves. 'Habit reversal training', for example, acknowledges that tics have a neurological basis and also, in its design, takes into account the context in which the individual lives and works as well as the internal experience of premonitory urges. Piacenti et al. (2010, p. 1930) describe the main components of habit reversal as tic-awareness and 'competing-response training':

- Awareness training comprises self-monitoring of tics and the early signs that a tic is about to occur.
- Competing-response training involves deliberately engaging in a behaviour that is not physically compatible with the tic as soon as the premonitory urge is felt. Tics are not suppressed; the individual is taught to manage the urge and initiate an alternative socially acceptable behaviour that replaces the tic. The competing response can be initiated when the individual notices that a tic is about to occur, during the tic or after the tic has occurred. For vocal tics, the most commonly competing response that is taught is slow rhythmic breathing from the diaphragm. With practice, patients are able to complete the competing response without disengaging from routine activities.

 Reflective activity: Learning how to support young people with Tourette syndrome

All young people with Tourette syndrome, as with any other kind of special educational need, are individuals who benefit from a learning environment that is supportive and flexible enough to accommodate their individual learning needs. This may mean making special arrangements if the tics disrupt the pupil's ability to write, or problem-solving with the pupil on ways to reduce stress in the classroom or during examinations.

How might you set about learning how to support young people with Tourette syndrome most effectively in a school?

What might you learn from the young people themselves?

What might you learn from parents/families?

Who else, in your own context, would be in a good position to offer you sound advice?

Muscular dystrophy

Individual children with severe motor difficulties

> may have difficulties affecting some or all of their limbs, limited hand function, fine and gross motor difficulties and sometimes difficulties with speech and language. Most, though not all pupils will have a medical diagnosis. (Pickles, 2001, p. 290)

An estimated 8,000 to 10,000 people in the United Kingdom have a form of muscular dystrophy (Pohlschmidt, & Meadowcroft, 2010). The term is used to refer to a group of genetic muscle diseases associated with progressive weakness and wasting of muscles owing to the degeneration of muscle cells. Most of these involve a defect in a protein that plays a vital role in muscle cell function or repair. To take one example, Duchenne muscular dystrophy affects only boys, with very rare exceptions, about 100 boys born in the United Kingdom each year. A problem in the genes results in a defect in dystrophin, which is an important protein in muscle fibres. Most boys with this condition develop the first signs of difficulty in walking at the age of 1 to 3 years and are usually unable to run or jump like their peers. By about 8 to 11 years boys become unable to walk. By their late teens or early twenties the muscle-wasting is severe enough to shorten life expectancy (Pohlschmidt, & Meadowcroft, 2010). 4.6

Addressing barriers to learning related to severe motor difficulties

Regular supervision from a clinic is very important to manage the condition as effectively as possible. However, once again, the views and wishes of a young person as well as the family should be taken into account here.

(?) Reflective activity: Making reasonable adjustments for a student who experienced mobility difficulties

The current author has experience of a secondary school that made very appropriate provision on transition from primary school for a young lady who experienced mobility difficulties by supporting her to move right round the school buildings before the summer holidays and point out what would cause her problems. She used a wheelchair so the benches and sinks in the cookery room and science laboratory were at the wrong height for her, for example. It proved possible, with relatively minor adjustments, to ensure that she was included in classroom activities with her peers.

This is a very focused proactive approach to meeting needs based on the student's individual experiences and views. How useful and practical might this be to address barriers in an educational context with which you are familiar?

Summary

Students' views of themselves as capable of learning and achieving in schools make for powerful interactions for good or ill. However areas of need are described, for all students it is essential that ways of addressing difficulties are sought first in the learning environment and quality of differentiated teaching through the assess→plan→do→review cycle. Teachers and others need to maintain a commitment to working from strengths and interests and an understanding that everyone has strengths and/or interests on which approaches to learning can draw to make them more effective in many situations. Students in classrooms have rights to additional support based on assessments of past progress. For some students with communication and interaction needs, for students with sensory or physical impairment, for many dyslexic students and for students with social, emotional and mental health needs it is highly likely that what is needed is adaptations to teaching styles and the use of access strategies rather than different learning objectives. When planning for individuals, teachers first need to know whether the student or group can, with appropriate access strategies, work on the same learning objectives as the rest of the class. As discussed in Chapter 3, getting this right will depend on accurate assessment of what the student knows, understands and can do.

Chapter 5
Focus on literacy difficulties

The major question in this chapter is:

- How can teachers and others understand difficulties in literacy in ways that enable them to problem solve what they can do to support literacy acquisition for these young people at school and at home?

This includes the following questions:

- What might teachers need to know about different theories of literacy acquisition in order to understand and take a problem-solving approach to addressing the difficulties in literacy experienced by some students?
- What strategies can teachers and other adults and peers in classrooms use to support students to improve their literacy levels?
- How can teachers address the literacy needs of dyslexic students?
- What kind of family and community support might be appropriate for literacy learning?

Introduction

Having the ability to handle written text with confidence is a key part of coping with the day-to-day expectations of classroom life. It is highly likely that every teacher will meet students who experience difficulties in literacy in classrooms at some time or another and it is important to be well acquainted with ways to address such difficulties. However, we have noted at various points in the current book how additional intervention and support for individuals should not be expected to compensate for inadequate teaching. Good quality – 'Quality First' – teaching that predisposes to fewer difficulties arising in the first place applies in the area of literacy learning as much as in other areas of the curriculum. It is certainly the case that many of the approaches discussed here in relation to supporting the development of reading comprehension and accuracy, writing, spelling, and so on may well be appropriate for use with students who experience specific difficulties in literacy learning, such as dyslexia, as well as for classroom literacy learning for all students. Students who experience difficulties in learning, which in this instance is literacy acquisition, are likely to need not distinctively different teaching but more practice, more examples and more careful assessment than their peers (Norwich & Lewis, 2001, p. 326). One implication of this is that teachers should be thoroughly familiar with different understandings of the process of literacy acquisition as well as curriculum requirements in their own local and national area. They may then be in a good position to take an informed decision about how to assess difficulties and which approach to adopt to address barriers to learning.

We begin this chapter by reflecting on the attributes of an effective teacher of literacy for a diverse range of students in a classroom and go on to consider a range of understandings of the literacy learning process, and approaches that reflect these understandings. We then discuss issues of reading comprehension, accuracy and written expression, with suggestions of tried and tested ways to address these areas of literacy learning at different ages and stages. We conclude by examining the issue of difficulties of a dyslexic nature: theoretical explanations, policy implications and practical strategies for overcoming barriers to learning.

Attributes of successful teachers of literacy

One of the prime responsibilities of schools is to support students to see themselves as able to learn and achieve (Bruner, 1996). All students have different prior experiences of literacy learning. The individual teacher is highly influential in supporting the success – or otherwise – of teaching programmes. In reporting on research into around 8,000 students' perceptions of classroom learning in about 15,000 classes, Hobby and Smith (2002, pp. 8–9) discuss the importance of what it feels like, in intellectual, motivational and emotional terms, to be a pupil in any particular teacher's classroom. Feelings are very powerful in supporting, or preventing, learning. Feelings of success are often pleasant and/or exciting, but a history of failure is often upsetting and/or disturbing, especially when it is a frequent occurrence (Wearmouth, Glynn & Berryman, 2005). As already discussed in Chapter 1, young people will not make an effort if they see no value to themselves in doing so.

Particularly where the learner has experienced considerable difficulties in literacy development, it is important that support for literacy learning is offered in ways which are responsive and productive in classrooms. Research carried out in a New Zealand context (Wearmouth & Berryman, 2011) about the positioning of literacy learners and how they are 'fixed' into their status as high- or low-achieving writers resulted in similar conclusions about the attributes of an effective teacher of literacy. Students' writing identities were developing in a classroom where:

- the teacher had a very high degree of subject and pedagogical content knowledge;

- her whole approach to supporting writing acquisition of her students was determined rather than random;

- she had an immediacy of responsiveness in relation to every students' learning;

- she had a recognition of the overwhelming importance of positive relationships in the classroom, teacher to student and peer to peer;

- writing in the classroom focussed on the communicative aspects of the text and on completion of the whole text rather than discrete aspects of the mechanics of writing;

- spelling and grammar were not ignored but were highlighted and focussed on as the need arose for individual students;

- all students, high or low achievers, had been taught how to be a good 'writing buddy' in giving constructive feedback on peers' scripts;

- the authenticity of the writing tasks was reflective of the students' own experiences, interests and imagination.

A summary of this piece of research has been uploaded on the website that accompanies this book.

 5.1

Including the whole diverse range of students in classroom literacy activities

A sense of belonging and acceptance is a basic human need (Bruner, 1996). Children may also fail in their literacy learning if certain literacy practices are privileged over others, for example, when children's literacy achievements in family, home and community contexts are neither acknowledged nor affirmed in the literacy practices of the school. Children's learning goals and expectations often stem from the goals and norms of their own community. It is essential, therefore, that when young students enter school, classroom literacy practices should build on their own pre-existing experiences within their own families and communities.

? Reflective activity: Understanding and responding to conflict between home and school expectations

There is no possibility of making sense of what bears no relation to one's own ways of making sense of things.

Read the text below and consider how you might respond to barriers to learning created by unfamiliarity with local culture, customs and language on entering school that results in bewilderment and an inability to understand the expectations and norms of the literacy curriculum.

> The way in which a lack of understanding can feel threatening to oneself and can lead to feelings of anxiety or hostility is illustrated by an inmate of a UK prison who recalls in relation to his own school experiences, 'a cocktail of ... um ... conflicts there all the time' as he tried to cope with the expectations of a mainstream London school that conflicted with those of home:
>
> 'I was weak in certain subjects, like English mainly, because I tend to write the way I speak. I'm born here my parents are from the West Indies. I am in an English school I had to cope with the different ... criteria because at home it was like a cross between Caribbean where we tend to speak more Patois or broken English. School was like trying to do it faithfully.... You get to learn ... how important language is for you to fit ... and then, like ... I might get homework to do and I'll ask my dad and he will say no, it's done this way, which is, their schooling was from the old grammar, and it's always a conflict and I would always believe what my father had said because he was a father figure ... Yes, and then it was completely wrong, and eventually you get frustrated, and I am not going to do this, and you just sort of throw it out.' (Wearmouth, unpublished interview transcript)

Ways of responding to cultural and family differences

The implications of differences in literacy practices in students' families and cultures need particular consideration. Potential cultural resources that are of value to the students and supportive of their self-respect (Gay, 2010; Sleeter, 2011), for example, comic books, popular music, superhero figures from popular culture with powerful storylines, may or may not be seen by the school as legitimate supports for literacy learning. In this regard, respectful relationships between learners and between learners and adults that, again, may or may not be the case in classrooms, are really important to encourage students' feelings of safety in talking about themselves as well as asking and answering questions (Bishop, Berryman & Wearmouth, 2014).

Despite often rather negative views on the ability of families with little history of literacy to support their children's literacy development, studies have shown that parents from every ethnic and social group are often very keen to help their children with reading at home (Blackledge, 2000). The implications of this are, as Gregory (1996) notes, the need for teachers to be aware of the literacy practices in their pupils' lives outside school, to build on strengths that children bring to school, and to make interpretations of school literacy explicit to both children and their families. Having said that, however, it is clearly important to carefully consider how families are invited to participate in any home–school literacy programme, what they are being asked to do and the extent to which the programme is responsive to family circumstances. For example, home-based programmes have achieved higher mean take-up and retention rates than centre-based programmes.

Understanding models of literacy acquisition

Teachers' awareness and understanding of the process of literacy learning are fundamentally important in decisions about which approaches to employ in classroom activities to develop particular aspects of literacy learning for all students, that is, which approach will suit which student when focused at the individual level, and in which circumstances. Some countries, such as England, have national literacy curricula with close prescriptions of content, modes of teaching and forms of assessment. However, there is no simple recipe for a one-size-fits-all programme that is uniquely positioned to address literacy development (Bond & Dykstra, 1967; Adams, 1994). As Wearmouth (2009) and Glynn, Wearmouth and Berryman (2006) note, there are different understandings of what 'literacy' is all about, as well as of the process of reading and writing. These different views necessarily influence literacy teaching and interpretations of what constitutes best practice for all students as well as which programmes address literacy difficulties in the most effective way. There are many students whose literacy levels are consistently assessed as several years below what might be expected, given their chronological age, or length of time they have been at school. Individual students may experience difficulties in any one aspect of the process of reading, interpreting and writing text, or all of these. Interventions need to be tailored from an understanding of the particular difficulties experienced by the individual student within the context of 'Quality First' literacy teaching for all in classrooms.

In the section below we consider, first, various understandings of the reading process and programmes based on each model. We then move on to the process of writing together with approaches underpinned by the models that are discussed.

Views of the reading process

 Reflective activity: The reading process

Take a few moments to note down:

- your memories of how you learnt to read yourself, what helped you in this process, and any barriers you experienced;
- if you experienced barriers, what assisted you to overcome these;
- how, in your experience, young people learn to read most effectively;
- reasons why you think there is so much disagreement about the reading process.

Reading, fundamentally, is about the construction of meaning. However, there are a number of different views about the processes involved in the act of reading. Traditionally, two have dominated: the so-called bottom-up and top-down approaches.

'Bottom-up' approaches

From a 'bottom-up' view, reading comprises the process of decoding the abstract and complicated alphabetic code, and reconstructing the author's meaning. Fluent readers look first at the visual features of text such as component letters in the words, and identify symbols with sounds before they move on to consider the meaning of the print (Adams, 1994). This view sees reading as a series of small steps to be learned one by one. First, children must learn the letters of the alphabet and establish the principle of sound–symbol identification. Then they must learn to apply this in order to decode words. It implies teaching methods which emphasise the mastery of phonics and word recognition. With adequate practice, children will be able to understand written text.

> The process of learning about sound/symbol association, that is, the rules about letters and sounds in written language, is usually referred to as phonics.

The phonological system

Components of the phonological system include phonemic awareness and phonological knowledge:

- Phonemic awareness can be demonstrated by a literacy learner's ability to hear and manipulate sounds in speech. It therefore seems to provide a strong foundation for the development of decoding skills. There appears to be a link between the development of phonemic awareness and control over the alphabetical coding system which in turn provides the basis for fluent word recognition (Stanovich, 2000). Children identified as making poor progress in reading are frequently weaker in phonemic awareness than competent readers.

- Phonological knowledge usually includes larger segments of speech, for example, syllable and rhyme. There is strong experimental evidence that many students who experience difficulty in literacy learning exhibit deficiencies in phonological processing (Stanovich, 2000). It is crucial that children develop this knowledge early on in their schooling. Exposure to poems, rhymes, songs, shared books with repeated readings can encourage an interest in language and books and guarantee for most children that phonological training and word reading can effectively be linked together.

The implication of this view is to highlight the significance of phonics, writing and spelling of whole words, exercise with frequent blends and digraphs, practice with word families and attention to every letter of the word, in left-to-right order (Adams,

1994). It might seem logical to respond to the kind of visual and auditory difficulties listed above with a phonics-based approach. However, there is a strong argument for suggesting great sensitivity here. Depending on the age and interests of the young person, focusing on phonics, phonics and more phonics to the exclusion of other techniques may be experienced by students as extremely boring and demoralising (Wearmouth, 2004). For older students, for example, there were occasions when the current author, as a teacher, chose to turn to a 'whole book' approach (see below) for the sake of re-igniting students' interest in literacy learning, left aside phonics for a while and returned to it at a later date.

Understanding synthetic and analytic phonics

There are two main approaches to phonics teaching and it is important for teachers to understand the difference between them. As the National Institute of Child Health and Human Development (2000) notes, a crucial difference between synthetic and analytic phonics is that, in synthetic phonics, words are pronounced through sounding and blending. In analytic phonics letter sounds are analysed after the word has been identified:

- synthetic phonics where letter–sound correspondences are taught in isolation and students are required to blend individual letters together to form whole words. At the beginning of the reading process, a small number of letter sounds are taught, and children are shown how to blend these sounds to pronounce unfamiliar words. Other groups of letters are taught and then blended. Some writers insist that curriculum guidelines are required for specific exercises attending to letter/sounds and 'subsyllabic sound units'.

- analytic phonics which involves the analysis of consonants, vowels, blends, digraphs and diphthongs taught within the context of whole words. Teaching begins at the level of the whole word and involves pointing out patterns in the English spelling system. Typically, children are taught one letter sound per week and shown pictures and words beginning with that sound. Then they are introduced to letter sounds in the middle of words and so on. At some stage the teacher may show children how to blend consecutive letters in unfamiliar words, for example, 'buh-ah-tuh, bat'. Some writers contend that specific exercises are not necessary as children gather this information incidentally as they are exposed to text-rich environments and programmes.

'Top-down' approaches

The second approach views reading as the active *construction* of meaning, not simply the decoding of visual symbols into sounds. The reader is assumed to have expectations of what a text might be about, and then to test these expectations and confirm or reject them as s/he proceeds, the so-called psycholinguistic guessing game (Goodman, 1996).

Understanding a psycholinguistic approach to the reading process

'as we read, our minds are actively busy making sense of print, just as they are always actively trying to make sense of the world. Our minds have a repertoire of strategies for sense-making. In reading, we can call these psycholinguistic because there's continuous interaction between thought and language.'
(Goodman, 1996, pp. 110–11)

Everything readers do is part of their attempt to make sense and construct meaning out of print. According to Goodman, readers do not need to pay attention to every single part of every word to read a text. 'Readers become highly efficient in using just enough of the available information to accomplish their purpose of making sense.' (Goodman, 1996, p. 91)

Goodman is highly critical of phonic instruction for children with difficulties in the area of literacy development:

'much misunderstanding still exists about reading and written language in general. I believe that this confusion exists largely because people have started in the wrong place, with letters, letter-sound relationships and words. We must begin instead by looking at reading in the real world, at how readers and writers try to make sense with each other.' (Goodman, 1996, pp. 2–3)

This approach has been linked with the whole-book/whole-language approach based on the concept of learning to read through reading, even for students who experience literacy difficulties. There are many examples across the world of reading programmes of this kind which combine emphasis on meaning and interest in text with awareness of the part that others, including peers and parents, can play. In the United Kingdom, for example, Waterland, an infant teacher, operated from an assumption that reading may be learned by young children working alongside competent readers through the so-called the Apprenticeship Approach (Waterland, 1985).

Interactive approach

A third approach is the 'interactive' model which suggests that readers use information simultaneously from different sources. One set of information, for example identification of sounds with symbols, interacts with another, such as the anticipation of what the word is likely to be from the context of the text. During the development of reading skills, some readers may rely more heavily on visual and auditory cues, others on meaning and context. Readers' weaknesses can be compensated by her/his strengths. Stanovich (2000) calls this process the 'Interactive Compensatory' model because the various processes interact and also because the reader can compensate for weaknesses in one area by relying on strengths in the other aspects. Readers who are good at word recognition have less need to rely on context (Harrison, 1994). They can recognise the word because they have mastered the elements of the sound–symbol system. Readers who cannot easily recognise words at a glance need context to aid recognition.

Addressing difficulties in reading

Across the world there is a very wide range of teaching programmes and teaching approaches used to support the reading acquisition of those students who experience difficulties. Careful planning is required to address their learning needs within a broad, balanced view of literacy and a global understanding of them as individuals as well as within the context of the school and classroom curriculum within which the plan is to be realised. The interactive approach assumes 'a complex, multifaceted activity' which requires 'broad-based instruction':

> Children need to learn processing skills, using context and knowledge of syntax to focus on the general meaning of the whole, and also decoding skills focusing on individual letters and words. They need specific teaching of both 'top-down' and 'bottom-up' skills; a certain amount of phonic instruction; careful monitoring in order to give early help to those who make a slow start; interesting meaningful texts; teachers who are enthusiastic about literacy throughout the whole primary range; encouragement from home; and lots of practice. (Wragg, Wragg, Haynes & Chamberlain, 1998, pp. 32–3)

 Reflective activity: Choice of teaching approaches

For the sake of clarity it is useful to separate out ways to address teaching approaches related to bottom-up and top-down views of what constitutes reading whilst accepting the interactive nature of the process:

- bottom-up approaches, involving the teaching of phonics and phonological knowledge, and word recognition;
- top-down approaches, including the teaching of strategies for improving comprehension; vocabulary knowledge; and reading fluency.

As you read the sections below on programmes for teaching reading, consider which might suit classrooms and individual students within them with whom you are familiar.

Teaching phonics

To teach phonics well teachers have to be knowledgeable. The challenge is always to plan teaching approaches that will help to improve students' literacy skills and understandings. Hannell (2003, p. 23) suggests the following sequence of instruction:

1. three letter words in a consonant-vowel-consonant pattern sound *hot ham mud top*
2. four letter words, where two letters slide together to make a sound *flag step best tick*

3. four letter words where two consonants make a new sound *shop thin chat when*

4. four letter words where a vowel and a consonant make a new sound *corn fowl wam, quit*

5. four letter words with a final 'e' *mice date kite made*

6. three - and four letter words where two vowels make a new sound *rain out loud, meat*

7. silent letters *knee gnaw gnat know*

8. five letter words where three letters slide together *strap scrum strip judge squid*

9. five and six letter words where four letters make a new sound *fight dough nation*

10. longer words that combine two or more of the above patterns *jumper beach sprawl tribe*

11. prefixes, suffixes and compound words *predict disagree truthfully household*

Some popular programmes which can help to develop decoding skills and phonological processing include 'Toe by Toe' (Cowling & Cowling, 1993) and 'Sound Linkage' (Hatcher, 2000). This last focuses in particular on the sub-skills of reading with sections on syllable blending, phoneme blending, identification and discrimination of phonemes and activities on phonological linkage including multi-syllabic words and establishing links between sounds and the written form of words. 'Read Write Inc. Phonics' (Miskin, 2015) is a phonics-based programme 'for 4 to 7 year-olds learning to read and write and for 7 and 8 year-olds needing to catch up quickly' (http://www.ruthmiskin.com/en/read-write-inc-programmes/phonics/ – accessed 07.03.16).

A significant amount of research indicates that explicit teaching of the alphabetical code leads to improved outcomes in reading accuracy (Ehri, 2002). However, there is an issue about whether the gains are generalised to word recognition, writing vocabulary, text reading and reading comprehension. Many advocate instead an analytic approach to teaching phonics, that is, teaching phonics in the context of reading and writing whole words.

Multi-sensory approaches

One way to reinforce the links between sounds and symbols in order to develop skills in phonics is to take a multi-sensory approach to teaching. Multi-sensory programmes should focus on all modalities – auditory, visual, kinesthetic and tactile. This means that when teaching the sound of a letter or groups of letters, the teacher might encourage students to say the sound out loud whilst simultaneously writing the letter(s), perhaps on a textured surface to integrate the memory of the motor movement with the sound and look, that is the auditory and visual representation, of the letters.

Many reading programmes incorporate the multi-sensory principle, for example, the 'Hickey Multi-Sensory Language Course' (Crombie, 2000). Often teachers can develop supplementary materials to ensure that the activities are multi-sensory. This is particularly important when considering the learning needs of dyslexic students for whom the acquisition of phonics skills is often problematic.

Adopting a psycholinguistic approach

Two well-known, and 'tried and tested', whole-book programmes are 'Paired reading' (Topping, Duran & van Keer, 2015) and 'Pause, prompt, praise' (Glynn & McNaughton, 1985). Both have the advantage that they can be used in school with classroom assistants, more competent peers or volunteers from the local community as the tutors. Alternatively they can both be set up for use with families.

The example of 'Paired Reading' (Topping, 1996; Topping et al., 2015)

There are many examples of initiatives that involve reading tutors in or out of school listening to beginning or struggling readers and giving them some form of assistance. In the case of families using 'Paired Reading', Topping (1996) has set out a number of 'rules' that others acting as tutors might also follow:

The child should choose high interest reading material irrespective of its readability level (provided it is within that of the helper) from any source.

Families should commit themselves to an initial trial period in which they agree to do at least five minutes Paired Reading on five days each week for eight weeks or so.

Family members, friends and neighbours can be encouraged to help, but must all use the same technique. The beginning reader should be asked to feed back on the quality of the tutoring s/he receives.

The child should be encouraged to talk about a book s/he has chosen to encourage the motivation to read. Talk is also important to check on comprehension.

The child might wish to begin to read an easy text on his/her own. If s/he makes a mistake, there is a very simple way to correct this. After pausing for 4 to 5 seconds to allow self-correction, the tutor just models the correct way to read the word, the child repeats it correctly and the pair carry on.

Tutors should support children through difficult text by reading together – both members of the pair read all the words out loud together, the tutor modulating speed to match that of the child, while giving a good model of competent reading.

On an easier section of text, the child may wish to read a little without support. The child should signal for the tutor to stop reading together, by a knock or a touch. The tutor should go quiet, while continuing to monitor any errors, praise and pause for discussion. Sooner or later, while reading alone, the child will make an error which s/he cannot self-correct within 4 or 5 seconds. Then the tutor should apply the usual correction procedure and join back in reading together.

> The pair continue like this, switching from reading together to reading alone to give the child just as much help as is needed according to the difficulty of the text, how tired s/he is, and so on. Children should never 'grow out of' reading together but be ready to use it as they move on to harder texts.
>
> It is very important to praise children for their achievement and/or efforts where praise is due during paired reading sessions. (adapted from Topping, 1996, p. 46)

There is a technique, Glynn and McNaughton's (1985) *Pause, Prompt, and Praise*, that views proficiency in reading as resulting from the ability to use every relevant piece of information around and within a text to understand it. It is therefore based on the whole-book approach to the teaching of reading. Following Clay (1979, 1991), the authors of *Pause, Prompt and Praise* emphasise the importance of supplying reading material at a level appropriate to the learner so the learner meets some unfamiliar words but can read enough of the text to make sense of it. Tutors are taught to pause to allow for self-correction, prompt to offer word meaning or sound–symbol identification and praise to reinforce the use of independent skills. McNaughton, Glynn and Robinson (1987) found that pausing before correction leads to a greater degree of self-correction by the learner and an increase in reading accuracy. Careful consideration of the type of errors made enables prompting to focus on meaning, or on the graphical features of a word. The type of praise allows the tutor to focus on the desired reading behaviour.

Word recognition

There is a very strong argument for supporting learners to be able to recognise common words on sight. 'The 100 most frequently used words account for more than 55% of the words children read and write, and the 300 most frequently used words account for 72%' (Eldridge, 1995, p. 165). If word recognition is not automatic, then a lot of energy will have to be expended on this and comprehension will be hindered (Stanovich, 2000). Many commonly used words have irregular letter/sound associations, for example, 'they', 'what', 'are'. Learning letter sequences is challenging for children who have poor visual perception and retention.

Ways to develop word recognition

Most children learn to recognise commonly used words without any special 'drill' or systematic, sequential teaching through shared and guided and personal reading opportunities which may involve the rereading of familiar texts, daily writing practice, access to word charts of commonly used words, word games, use of dictionaries, and so on. However, others need specially focussed multi-sensory teaching.

Vocabulary knowledge

For most children vocabulary is acquired easily and rapidly, without any explicit instruction, a result of engaging in reading or what is sometimes called 'reading mileage' (Graves & Watts-Taffe, 2002, p. 142). Generally readers work out the meanings of around fifteen in every one hundred unknown words as they read along (Stahl, 1998; McNaughton, 2002). Clay (1979) demonstrated that by the end of the first year at school those children who made good progress had great exposure to numbers, and a wide range of words whereas those who were making low progress had less opportunity to learn new words in context. For some children, vocabulary knowledge that supports literacy development may therefore be limited. Sustained silent reading (SSR) can ensure readers get more opportunity to practise. However, the text must be neither too difficult so that it is frustrating, nor too easy so that the text does not provide opportunities to extend and consolidate word recognition and vocabulary knowledge. The reading task must also be enjoyable. SSR should not be the sole type of reading activity, however.

Ways to develop vocabulary

Strategies to support children's vocabulary acquisition

Although reading to children can provide an opportunity to discuss unknown words, just listening to stories may not always lead to vocabulary growth (McNaughton, 2002). Some children's attention may need to be engaged specially in discussion of new words. Teaching new vocabulary within the context of text may need to be carefully planned (Buikema & Graves, 1993). Pre-teaching of vocabulary (Nicholson & Tan, 1997) before reading can increase children's vocabulary knowledge using flash cards of words likely to cause difficulty, for example. Sorting and classifying words prior to reading a text can help students to focus their reading and support their understanding of new concepts (Whitehead, 1993). New vocabulary from the text can be used in advance for students to predict the content of the story or article. Questions can be set to clarify understanding of the vocabulary.

The definitions of words are vitally important but students must be involved in active discussion and use, not just look up, definitions and put them into a sentence (Wearmouth, 2009).

Teachers might support children's memory of new words by encouraging learners to think aloud about words in ways that are personally meaningful, for example: What category does it belong to? What is it like? What are some examples?

Teachers might also model ways to work out the meaning of new words from semantic and syntactic cues.

Important or interesting words that are relevant to the learner at the time might be a special focus in vocabulary selected from books that are read to, read with and read by children.

Responsive oral contexts for literacy

Teachers bear a huge responsibility for inspiring students in classrooms to become competent readers.

 Reflective activity: The importance of oral language for literacy learning

Take a few moments to note down what you feel is the contribution of oral language to literacy learning.

How far do you agree with the view that probably the most important prerequisite for competence in literacy is the development of oral language?

Children need oral language skills to acquire literacy. They will only want to read a text if they can understand what it is that they are reading. To do this they need prior knowledge and experience. Low performance on tests of reading comprehension can also reflect students' limited vocabulary, and/or limited experience in talking about characters and events within stories or concepts of various kinds, and relating these to their own knowledge and experience.

Talking is an essential intellectual and social skill that is shaped by how we think and forms part of how we communicate with others and make sense of the world. From birth, children appear to learn and use their first language in a natural and easy way from their immersion in oral language contexts (Ministry of Education, undated). Babies are able to communicate their emotions and have their needs satisfied long before they can talk. Vygotsky (1962) contends that all mental processes have social origins. The sense of words is rooted in experience with others. From what they hear and see, and how others respond to them, babies actively begin to construct language and to communicate their own ideas with those around them. People they know talk to them, talk about them and talk to each other. Sounds from music, rhymes and words are often a part of their very first intellectual and social experiences.

Young children first experience an activity with others, then internalise the experience through symbolising it in words:

> Any function in the child's development appears twice, on two planes. First it appears on the social plane, and then on the psychological plane. First it appears between people as an interpsychological category, and then within the child as an intrapsychological category. This is equally true with regard to voluntary attention, logical memory, the formation of concepts, and the development of volition. (Vygotsky, 1981, p. 163)

The young child's thought development begins through interpersonal negotiation with others, caregivers, teachers and peers at school and this is internalised into intrapersonal understanding. Vygotsky (1962) further suggests that at about the age of two the curves of development of thought and speech, till then separate, meet and join to initiate a new form of behaviour. (p. 43)

Learning to read and write, when interpreted as the ability to perceive and reproduce graphic symbols and make sound–symbol links, is often considered an individual, *intrapersonal* process. However, if learning to read and write is seen, in their broadest sense, as understanding and communicating meaning in the form of text, then the *interpersonal* dimension is crucial, that is, the understanding of the reading and writing tasks in company with others, caregivers, teachers and peers.

Strategies to develop oral skills

There is an important question about how learners can take the step 'from speaking to understanding writing on a page or screen, to realise that knowledge of life and language can help them make sense of words and texts' (Gregory, 1996, p. 95). Orally told stories, rhymes, songs, prayer and routines for meeting and greeting people, all have an important role in literacy acquisition and are promoted within many cultures long before children begin any form of formal education. Sarbin (1986) notes that it is through story that children learn to become functioning members of the society into which they are born:

> It is through hearing stories … that children learn or mislearn both what a child and what a parent is, what the cast of characters may be in the drama into which they have been born and what the ways of the world are. Deprive children of stories and you leave them unscripted, anxious stutterers in their actions as in their words. Hence there is no way to give us an understanding of any society … except through the stock of stories which constitute its initial dramatic resources. (Sarbin, 1986, p. 201)

Reading comprehension

Providing teachers and students with high-quality reading materials, representing a variety of genres, and written and illustrated by writers from students' home communities, can be crucial for engaging students experiencing literacy difficulties. Classroom and school programmes should provide students who are experiencing difficulties with access to a wide range of rich literacy texts and activities, including those from their own homes and communities as well as those originating in the classroom. Students need opportunities to talk about what they are reading, and to talk about what other people understand from reading the same text (Glynn et al., 2006). The difficulty or complexity of reading texts should be appropriate to the nature of the task. For example, texts taken home for 'demonstration' (Glynn et al., 2006) reading to one's family or for reading alone for leisure and pleasure may be at an 'easy' level for the reader. However, texts selected for one-to-one tutoring within the context of extra support and scaffolding by a trained and skilful tutor may be at a more demanding or challenging level. Students themselves need to have a real choice of texts to read to ensure that what they read is of high interest to them.

The teacher might decide to take a whole-book approach and tackle this from a psycholinguistic perspective, from an understanding that readers learn to read through reading (Goodman, 1996). Alternatively they might choose to follow those who consider that the best way to encourage understanding is to investigate strategies used by good comprehenders, and then teach these systematically.

Ways to develop comprehension skills

Good readers know what they have to do to get meaning from texts (Pressley, 2002). However, many readers who experience difficulties in literacy may need explicit teaching about comprehension strategies and guided practice in using them, as well as opportunities to engage with texts. We know that good comprehenders:

- search for connections between what they know and the new information they encounter in the texts they read;
- monitor the adequacy of their models of text meaning;
- take steps to repair faulty comprehension once they realise they have failed to understand something.
- learn early on to distinguish important from less important ideas in texts they read;
- are adept at synthesising information within and across texts and reading experiences;
- draw inferences during and after reading to achieve a full integrated understanding of what they read;
- sometimes consciously, and almost always unconsciously, ask questions of themselves, the author they encounter and the texts they read.

(Pearson, Roehler, Doel & Duffy, 1992, p. 154)

Difficulty in comprehension might occur at any of these points. Ways to help readers develop strategies to construct meaning from text include:

- preparing for reading
- thinking through ways to read and extract information
- ways to organise and translate the information that has been read.

Preparing for reading

It is essential to make young people aware that they have knowledge that they can draw upon to make the act of reading meaningful. This is especially important where learners experience difficulties. Learners might be encouraged to ask:

- What do I know?
- What do I want to know?
- What have I learnt?

Teachers might identify and discuss the vocabulary of the text that may be difficult, and/or overview the topic of the text.

Ways to construct and organise meaning

It is the current author's experience that, where students have severe difficulties understanding text, it is useful to shorten the amount read before questions are asked. This may mean a page by page reading, or even a paragraph by paragraph reading. However, as students pay more attention to the messages conveyed by the text the amount of text read before questions are asked can be lengthened.

'Three Level Guides'

The so-called Three Level Guides are statements about a text written by teachers to help students become more aware of different levels of deriving meaning from texts. These statements are intended to help students to think about the text, what statements are important and can be verified directly from the text, what statements require them to make inferences from their prior knowledge, and how they can apply information from texts.

The three levels are:

- literal (reading the lines)
- inferential (reading between the lines)
- applied (reading beyond the lines).

The purpose is for students to use their understanding of a passage to decide whether:

- a statement represents what is actually stated in the text;
- the statement could be true, or not, dependent on making an inference;
- the statement is something that the author might agree with.

The students should first try to decide by themselves and then discuss and justify their choice with a partner or a small group. The reading activity is intended to be completed collaboratively, so that students learn from each other as they discuss the statements.

Creating a Three Level Guide

'In creating a *Three Level Guide* it is important to first determine your content objectives. This gives the guide a clear focus and informs the development of your statements. In this way, the statements will lead the reader to focus on the relevant parts of the text. Your content objectives will determine your applied level statements.

These third level statements should be written first as they influence the development of the statements at the other levels. The third level statements encourage the reader to think beyond the text to its wider implications. These statements reflect the main ideas and concepts you would like the students to explore through the text.

Once you have written the applied level statements, write your literal statements. These statements guide the reader to the information in the text related to the issues explored in the applied level statements. The literal statements support the students by focusing their attention on the relevant information in the text. This teaches the students to be selective in their reading by encouraging them to disregard irrelevant information.

Finally, develop your interpretive level statements which guide the reader to draw inferences from the information in the text. These statements focus on the author's intent behind the words and information selected. Interpretive level statements can also encourage the reader to explore what is omitted in the text.' (http://www.myread.org/guide_three.htm, accessed 17.02.16)

Collaborative reading and writing activities can provide children with the opportunity to support peers' learning through observing, guiding or offering assistance, while the less skilled learner is motivated to respond to and initiate language interactions as well as respond to peer questions and challenges.

'Reciprocal teaching'

Palincsar and Brown (1984) and Palinscar (1998) report a seminal research study into the successful use of 'reciprocal teaching' to enhance reading comprehension with pupils who experience difficulties in literacy development. Teachers and pupils took turns to lead discussion about the meaning of a section of text that they were jointly trying to understand and memorise. This technique focused on four strategies to assist understanding of the text and joint construction of its meaning: generating questions from the text, summarising its content, clarifying areas of difficulty and predicting the content of subsequent sections of text based on the content and structure of the current portion. Learners were taught the terminology of reciprocal teaching through direct instruction in each of the four strategies prior to the start of the procedure. This technique emphasised the role of the teacher in modelling expert performance and the role of the learner as active participant in his/her learning in addition to the function of social interactions in learning. Assessment of learners' progress was ongoing and judged through their developing contributions to discussion of the texts.

'The basic procedure was that an adult teacher, working individually with a seventh-grade poor reader, assigned a segment of the passage to be read and either indicated that it was her turn to be the teacher or assigned the student to teach that segment. The adult teacher and the student then read the assigned segment silently. After reading the text, the teacher (student or adult) for that segment asked a question that a teacher or test might ask on the segment, summarised the content, discussed and clarified any difficulties, and finally made a prediction about future content. All of these activities were embedded in as natural a dialogue as possible, with the teacher and student giving feedback to each other . . .

'Gradually, the students became much more capable of assuming their role as dialogue leader and by the end of ten sessions were providing paraphrases of some sophistication.' (Palincsar & Brown, 1984, pp. 124–5)

The success of that initial research project has been replicated many times with pairs of tutors and tutees and within small groups at school level and in higher education (Doolittle, Hicks, Triplett, Nichols & Young, 2006; Spörer, Brunstein, & Kieschke, 2009).

A similar repeated reading strategy (Samuels, 2002) using a mutual peer tutoring approach involved a student and teacher reading together, the student alternating between being the teacher and the learner.

Reading fluency

Some researchers have noted how repeated reading, 'reading mileage' (Davey & Parkhill, 2012) can assist and develop reading speed and fluency.

Supporting reading fluency

A number of researchers have built upon Chomsky's (1978) tape-assisted reading approach that involved students practising until they can read a passage at the same rate as the tape recording or the story. Fluency can be enhanced through opportunities to read along with a recording of the text and lead to positive responses to text which can enhance children's reading confidence and attitude to reading (LeFevre, Moore & Wilkinson, 2003). Repeated exposure to text, aurally and visually, can reinforce word recognition, thus freeing up cognitive 'energy' for comprehension.

Teaching reading through reading

'Jason' was a very dyslexic, but highly articulate, non-reader, aged 12, in a secondary comprehensive school. Previous teachers in his primary school had adopted a phonics approach to teaching him to read, but to no avail. By the time he reached secondary school he was quite a disaffected, and depressed, young man. He was quite reticent about himself to start with, but when he finally talked about how he felt about literacy learning he said that all his friends had read *Hitchhiker's Guide to the Galaxy*, and *The Hobbit* and he wanted to be able to join in their discussions. As the school's special educational needs co-ordinator (SENCo), the current author decided that, given his age and status as a non-reader, there was nothing to lose by setting phonics instruction on one side for the time being and trying to teach him to read by engaging with his interests instead. She made an agreement with him that she would systematically record 30 minutes' worth of *Hitchhiker's Guide to the Galaxy*, followed by *The Hobbit* five days a week, with the agreement that he would collect the recording from her every day, take it home and listen to the recording twice whilst following it with his eyes. After seven months the young man's father phoned the school to tell the author that his son had sat and read *The Daily Mirror* newspaper over Easter at the breakfast table for the first time ever. Several years later, and with a lot of support for his spelling and writing in general, he was accepted at university.

If choice of reading material is important, so too is listening to children read.

The importance of attentive listening to children's reading

In order that meaningful interactions can take place between reader and listener, classroom conditions must predispose to attentive listening. The adult or peer should be responsive to the learner's understanding of, and interest in, the text and any difficulties that are experienced in reading and understanding. When the current author first began to teach in the area of special educational needs she noticed how listening to young people read seemed at best a perfunctory activity and became quite concerned about this. She strongly agreed with the views of Wragg et al. (1998, pp. 264–5) who highlighted research findings which are important in listening to children's reading in the classroom:

> we concluded, in the light of observations of what seemed to be successful practice, that there were six ingredients that were needed if teachers were to derive maximum benefit from hearing children read and conversing about the chapter. These were:
>
> - Orderliness – disruptive behaviour by other pupils can be a powerful distractor.
> - Focus – a strong focus on reading as the major activity of the moment, so that maths or other problems do not take the teacher away from the principal domain.
> - Independence – children reading alone need to be able to make their own decisions, so they are not too dependent on the teacher; equally, those reading with the teacher need independence, so they can guess intelligently at unfamiliar words.
> - Priority – the child being heard needs to have top priority, except in emergencies.
> - Importance – reading must be made important, so that interruptions are frowned upon.
> - Worthwhileness – the chapter needs to be engaging and worth talking about.
>
> (Wragg et al., 1998, p. 152)

Understandings of the writing process

Reading is clearly closely linked to writing. Readers and writers use their knowledge in complementary ways: readers to construct meaning from existing texts and writers to construct meaning in the new texts that they create. As a reader, the learner interacts with words (and letters or letter clusters in words), grammatical structures, and other language patterns in texts in order to construct meaning. As a writer, the learner starts with ideas and represents these in grammatical structures and other language patterns in texts in order to construct meaning (Ministry of Education, 2006, p. 123).

In the same way as reading, approaches to writing might sometimes be classified as either:

- a traditional focus on the product, that is, surface features and the mechanics of text, grammar and spelling (Smith & Elley, 1997), or
- a focus on the process: that is, for example, processes such as brainstorming, drafting, revising, editing, and publishing content and meaning (Graves, 1983).

Focusing on the product of writing

The question of whether it is important to learn to spell accurately is one which is fraught with controversy. The English language has an alphabetic writing system in which the symbols bear only some relationship to the sounds of the language:

> It is not a direct relationship ... the symbols (the letters) may best be described as providing a clue to the sounds. (Barton, 1995, p. 97)

Some words have clear sound–symbol correspondence – but even then, there is often confusion for speakers whose speech does not conform to Standard English or Received Pronunciation.

English also uses meaning in its spelling system. The similarity of spellings of word parts often indicates meaning: 'sign', 'signature', 'assign' and 'signal' all relate to the Latin word 'signum'. In addition, as Barton (1995) points out, English contains some logographs where one character is a unit of meaning, for example, '&' and 'etc'. Many spellings are idiosyncratic and the particular combinations of letters serve as logographs, for example, 'right', 'rite' and 'write'. In this case, homophones indistinguishable in speech are differentiated in writing by their spellings, and each has to be learned separately:

> we are never sure of the spelling of a new word we hear until we have seen it written down; we are often unsure of how to pronounce a word we come across in reading until we hear it spoken. (Barton, 1995, p. 100)

Addressing spelling acquisition

Given the complexity of English orthography and the difficulty experienced by some students in learning to spell accurately, it is hardly surprising that there is a diversity of approaches both to teaching spelling and to the need for doing so.

Spelling can be approached from a holistic, whole word approach, or from an approach that identifies individual sounds and letters and combines these into words. Choice of words to be spelt can be made on the basis of what the learner needs and wishes to spell for the purpose of his/her reading. This approach may require students to construct personal spelling lists from the errors they make in their written work. In contrast, choice of words to be learned can be made from word lists. Some spelling approaches group words to be learned in terms of similar letter–sound patterns within words. These may be hierarchical, phonically regular combinations of letters and sounds that the learner is already expected to know. This approach may group words to be learned in terms of similar letter–sound patterns within words. Students may spend a great deal of time learning large lists of words, and getting them correct, but may still show little or no generalisation of these patterns into similar words that they may encounter in their writing.

Schools' spelling and marking policies can stimulate a fair amount of controversy. Bentley (2002) argues that, for the most part, class or group spelling tests are a waste of time since learners will be at different stages in spelling acquisition. However, spelling tests may be a required part of a school's approach to supporting students' literacy development. Teachers may feel that set spelling tests are very important to assess the development in spelling of a whole class or group. On the other hand, they may feel that the degree to which spelling tests are a waste of time may depend on how spellings are chosen for students to learn and how far they are tailored to the needs of the individual child.

Bentley argues that, additionally, schools should have very clear marking policies. On the one hand it can be argued that, for some students, repeatedly receiving back scripts covered with marks indicating errors is very demoralising. On the other, there has to be a rational, structured approach to ensuring that students make progress in recognising mistakes and learning how to correct them. Some teachers may feel it is appropriate to encourage students to proofread their own, or peers', work before handing it in and/or, perhaps, to correct only words or sentence structure with which they feel students should already be familiar. Whichever strategy schools choose should be supported by reasoned argument. Whatever decisions are made, they have both advantages and disadvantages which need to be recognised.

Reason and Boote (1994) outline four developmental stages of spelling acquisition. At Stage One, students can recognise rhyme, blend spoken sounds into words and make some attempt to represent phonic structures at the beginning of words in letter form. At Stage Two they can write single letter sounds, simple, regular single syllable words and the more common single syllable irregular words. At Stage Three they can write words with consonant blends (for example 'tr-', '-nd') and digraphs (for example 'sh'), vowel digraphs (for example 'ea', 'ow') and the 'magic' 'e', and at Stage Four they can spell most common words correctly (Reason & Boote, 1994, p. 133). In order to identify the stage of development a student has reached in his/her spelling it is very important to take the time to scrutinise samples of writing very carefully. Bentley's (2002) comments that students' spelling errors often span the developmental stages indicate that there is much overlap between one stage and the next. A student who is tired and/or is in a hurry may well make more mistakes than s/he would do otherwise. There is probably no single rule about how long a student might remain at one stage of spelling development. Perhaps the most important issue is to ensure that, overall, a student is making progress towards greater competence in spelling and if s/he is 'stuck' at one stage to work out ways of supporting him/her to move on to the next.

In order to avoid difficulties in spelling later on, children need to be familiar with vowels and syllables at an early stage and to be taught techniques for learning the spelling of words they want or need to use in writing. Students should never simply copy words but should always be encouraged to memorise them and then write them down.

 Reflective activity: Strategies for learning correct spelling

Read the text below and consider whether you might employ either of the multi-sensory strategies below to support the spelling acquisition of young people and, if so, which one(s).

Multi-sensory approach 1

For students who find particular difficulty with spelling, Reason and Boote (1994) describe a multi-sensory approach which, whilst lengthy at first, can, in their view, be slimmed down as students gain confidence and competence in spelling:
'Look at the word, read it, and pronounce it in syllables or other small bits (re-mem-ber; sh-out)
Try to listen to yourself doing this
Still looking at it, spell it out in letter-names
Continue to look, and trace out the letters on the table with your finger as you spell it out again
Look at the word for any 'tricky bits'; for example, gh in right. (Different students find different parts of a word 'tricky'.)
Try to get a picture of the word in your mind: take a photograph of it in your head!
Copy the word, peeping at the end of each syllable or letter-string
Highlight the tricky bits in colour (or by some other means)
Visualise the word again
Now cover it up and try to write it, spelling it out in letter-names
Does it look right?
Check with the original
Are there some tricky bits you didn't spot (i.e. the parts that went wrong)?
Repeat as much of the procedure as necessary to learn the words thoroughly.'
(Reason & Boote, 1994, p. 138)

Multi-sensory approach 2

The author has used a slightly different version of a multi-sensory approach (Bradley, 1981) very successfully with students of a range of ages:
The method consists of a series of steps in the following order:
The student proposes the word he (sic) wants to learn.
The word is written correctly for him (or made with plastic script letters).
The student names the word.
He then writes the word himself, saying out loud the alphabetic name of each letter of the word as it is written.

He names the word again. He checks to see that the word has been written cor-rectly; this is important, as less able readers are often inaccurate when they copy (Bradley, 1981). Repeat steps 2 to 5 twice more, covering or disregarding the stimu-lus word as soon as the student feels he can manage without it.

The student practises the word in this way for six consecutive days. The procedure is the same whether or not the student can read or write, and whether or not he is familiar with all the sound/symbol relationships, but it must not deteriorate into rote spelling, which is an entirely different thing.

The student learns to generalise from this word to similar words using the plastic script letters. (Bradley, 1981, quoted in Bentley, 2002, p. 342)

Many parents or families may not know how most appropriately to help their child to learn new spellings. Guidelines that include a description of Reason and Boote's or Bradley's methods may help to reduce their anxiety levels and may well be very welcome.

'Cued Spelling' (Topping, 2001)

Another method of supporting spelling acquisition is what Topping (2001) terms 'Cued Spelling'. Students are encouraged to select target words for themselves and manage their own spelling programme. When students are familiar with the technique speed in spelling is emphasised in order to overcome the difficulty with generalisation over time and contexts. 'Cued Spelling' uses words the student wishes to spell and relies on praise, modelling, and swift support procedures to avoid the fear of failure. The tech-nique comprises ten steps (Topping, 2001): (Step 1) The learner chooses words of high interest to him/herself, irrespective of difficulty level. (Step 2) Tutor and learner check the spelling of the word and put a master version in a 'Cued Spelling Diary'. (Step 3) The pair read the word out loud together, then the learner reads the word aloud alone. (Step 4) The learner chooses cues (reminders) to enable him or her to remem-ber the written structure of the word. These may be sounds, letter names, syllables or other fragments of words, or wholly personal mnemonic (memory) devices. (Step 5, The pair repeats the cues aloud simultaneously. (Step 6) The learner then repeats the cues aloud while the tutor models writing the word down while it is 'dictated'. (Step 7) Roles then reverse, the tutor saying the cues aloud while the learner writes the word down. (Step 8) The learner repeats the cues and writes the word simultaneously. (Step 9) The learner writes the word as fast as possible and decides for him/herself whether to recite the cues out loud. Finally (Step 10), the learner reads the word out loud. Each session ends with a 'speed review' where the parent dictates all the target words for that session as quickly as possible. The learner then checks the accuracy of the words against the master copy. Target words which are incorrect are learned again using the 10 Steps, and different memory cues may be chosen. At the end of each week, the parent dictates all the target words for the whole week as quickly as possible. Parent and child together decide what they wish to do about mistakes and whether to include them in the next week's target words.

Spelling approaches such as cued spelling, with their clear breakdown into specific steps would lend themselves to being implemented in either peer-tutoring or cooperative learning contexts in schools. Each pair can be encouraged to keep a spelling diary, each page including space to write the master version of up to 10 words on all days of the week, with boxes to record daily Speed Review and weekly Mastery Review scores and spaces for daily comments from the tutor and weekly comments from the teacher.

Focusing on the process of writing

Focusing on the process may mean taking a holistic approach as, for example, in 'Responsive Written Feedback' (Ford, 2015). Or sometimes it can help teachers to imagine the human mind as processing information rather like a computer and to see the writing process as driven by a series of goals which are organised in a hierarchy (Hayes & Flower, 1986).

Supporting writing development through responsive written feedback

Ford (2015) describes how, in an attempt to respond to the wishes of families and a local community to support their children's acquisition of writing, she suggested 'Responsive written feedback' as an appropriate intervention. In the session with the families and their community it was explained 'that they did not need to concern themselves with correcting and evaluating the writing, but rather focus on providing a response to the messages contained within the student's writing' (p. 192). The importance of focusing on students' motivation to write is very clear in the underpinning assumptions where it was anticipated that:

> By modelling correct spelling, punctuation and structure in their own response they would be supporting the students with their written language development, and most importantly they would also be demonstrating to the students that their writing communicated messages that were understood and valued by another person. (Ford, 2015, p. 192)

In the students' own 'Responsive written feedback session', they were '[…] required to write something of their choice. They have five minutes to plan their writing, 10 *[sic]* minutes to write, and five minutes to proofread and edit their writing'. The teacher and family members could negotiate the number of students to whom they were prepared to respond and whether they wished to respond to their own children. 'The writing exchanges happened each week for a period of one school term (10 weeks)' (Ford, 2015, p. 192).

In this particular study writing samples were analysed across the student sample. They indicated an increase in the length of students' writing over the 10-minute period from a mean of 70 words at the beginning of the term to 94 words at the end. The accuracy improved from a mean of 6.7 correct words per minute to 9.4 at the end. This was accompanied by an increase in students' use of vocabulary that was both more interesting and more challenging. Just as importantly, the opportunity to strengthen the relationship between the school and the local community and families led to an intention on the school's part to maintain this and broaden the initiative.

Supporting the planning process

Those engaged in the writing task achieve their goals through processes of planning, translating and revising what has been written:

- planning involves generating information to be included in the script, selecting and organising what is relevant, and deciding on criteria for judging successful completion of the script;
- translation means converting the plan into the script;
- revising includes editing for both grammatical errors as well as structural coherence.

Seeing the process of writing like this can be very useful because it enables teachers to focus on the individual processes of writing production. An area that has been researched thoroughly in relation to students with difficulties in literacy development is the use of strategies intended to highlight planning processes. An example of this is the use of writing frames to generate and organise ideas (Englert & Raphael, 1988; Graves, Montague & Wong, 1990). 'Writing frames' are a way of providing learner writers with a support or 'scaffold' that offers, for example, some headings, subheadings and connectives for linking paragraphs when writing an explanatory information text, the layout, greeting, opening sentence and closure when practising a letter; sentence openings for making contrasting points when presenting an argument. The theory behind this is that, by expressing these thoughts in a visible way we can subsequently rethink, revise and redraft, and we are allowed, indeed forced, to reflect upon our own thinking (Wray, 2002).

'Paired Writing'

Topping (1995, 2001) has piloted a 'Paired Writing' technique which he suggests should be used for three sessions of 20 minutes per week for six weeks:

'Paired Writing is a framework for a pair working together to generate ... a piece of writing – for any purpose they wish ... Paired Writing usually operates with a more able writer (the Helper) and a less able one (the Writer), but can work with a pair of equal ability so long as they edit carefully and use a dictionary to check spellings.'

The structure of the system consists of six steps, 10 questions (for ideas), five stages (for drafting) and four levels (for editing). Further details will be found in Topping (1995).

- Step 1 is Ideas Generation. The Helper stimulates ideas by using given Questions and inventing other relevant ones, making one-word notes on the Writer's responses.

- Step 2 is Drafting. The notes then form the basis for Drafting, which ignores spelling and punctuation. Lined paper and double spaced writing is recommended. The Writer dictates the text and scribing occurs in whichever of the five Stages of Support has been chosen by the pair. If there is a hitch, the Helper gives more support.

- In Step 3 the pair look at the text together while the Helper reads the Draft out loud with expression. The Writer then reads the text out loud, with the Helper correcting any reading errors.

- Step 4 is Editing. First the Writer considers where s/he thinks improvements are necessary, marking this with a coloured pen, pencil or highlighter. The most important improvement is where the meaning is unclear. The second most important is to do with the organization of ideas or the order in which meanings are presented. The next consideration is whether spellings are correct and the last whether punctuation is helpful and correct. The Helper praises the Writer and then marks points the Writer has 'missed'. The pair then discuss – and agree on improvements.

- In Step 5 the Writer (usually) copies out a 'neat' or 'best' version. Sometimes the Helper may write or type or word-process it, however. Making the final copy is the least important step.

- Step 6 is Evaluation. The pair should self-assess their own best copy, but peer assessment by another pair is very useful. The criteria in the Edit levels provide a checklist for this.

Developing metacognitive strategies

The deliberate conscious control of one's actions and thought is called metacognition. 'Metacognitive' strategies are designed to enable students to think about their own cognitive processes so that those who experience difficulty in particular areas of learning can develop alternative routes to accessing these areas. Children can be taught strategies at an early age to help develop metacognitive skills. For example, teachers might model how to approach the writing process that children can then copy. A typical example of teacher modelling of writing might comprise four stages: prewriting; composing/drafting; revising; and editing (Tribble, 1996, p. 39).

'Mind mapping'

'Mind mapping' (Buzan, 2000) is an example of a way to begin planning a structure for producing extended text. Learners first think about and then produce a visual representation, a mind map, of all those topics to be covered in the text before beginning to develop the structure. Once students have produced their mind map they can arrange the elements in it in a coherent order and then produce the structure for their text. Mind mapping assumes that those who experience difficulties in writing are likely to benefit by being able to separate out content from the technical aspects of structuring and then producing the text by focusing on one before the other. Of course there is likely to be considerable overlap between these processes.

Using narrative to plan writing

'We dream, remember, anticipate, hope, despair, love, hate, believe, doubt, plan, construct, gossip and learn in narrative' (Westby, 1991). It is important for students to learn to express these feelings in written as well as oral form. Narratives can be seen as an early step towards later expository text since they contain a number of essential elements such as: comparisons, problem-solving, exhortation and persuasion, and so on (Montgomery & Kahn, 2003). Some students who experience difficulties in literacy may need support to reproduce story grammar. Montgomery and Kahn (2003) note an interactive oral teaching strategy 'scaffolded story writing' that has been used as an interactive group activity to support struggling writers:

> In the scaffolded narrative method, questioning is used to help students build their comprehension, organisation, sequence of ideas, and metacognition. This questioning encourages students to become 'meaning makers'. (Montgomery & Kahn, 2003, p. 145)

The learning support teacher introduces the idea of an author, what s/he does and why students might want to be one. The students are taught five elements of an effective narrative: interesting character(s), context, a credible problem, possible solutions to the problem and a good ending (Apel & Masterton, 1998). The support teacher sets up a series of questions to support the students in thinking about the stories they want to write and the students discuss possible approaches with each other.

Using the 'scaffolded story-writing' technique

The approach comprises five steps:

'**Step 1: Draw a sequence story**. The [teacher] divides an 8" x 11" blank sheet of paper into six sections and tells the students to draw their stories on the paper in correct sequence, using as many sheets as are necessary … The students may use stick figures and simple drawings … Some students need help in sequencing their stories properly

Step 2: Describe the main characters. Students should list descriptive details for the main characters, including age, height, weight, body build, hair color and style, eye color, clothes, family, favourite foods, things they like to do …

Step 3: Begin writing the narrative. The students begin their narratives with an interesting opening sentence or two to catch the reader's interest. The [teacher] might read opening paragraphs from stories he or she has enjoyed to the students. Students should follow their picture sequence when writing their narratives. They should also incorporate the information they compiled before they started writing the story, including the character descriptions'.

The [teacher] uses a questioning technique throughout this intervention. She or he must facilitate the student's ability to come up with creative, independent ideas . . .

The dialogue between the student and the [teacher] continues until the student is certain about what he or she wants to write . . . The [teacher] needs to ask questions until a coherent story emerges, which sometimes occurs in stages. The [teacher] may get the first part down and then move on to the next part. Some stories change in the process as better ideas occur and the student revises his or her initial thoughts. It is best to get a first draft completed and then rewrite.

Step 4: Write the story. From the beginning, the [teacher] reinforces the idea that the story belongs to the student, and changes are never made without consulting the student. . . . .

Step 5: Rewrite and correct. Some students require corrections and help throughout the writing process. They need words to be spelled for them, or they want to try out a sentence or two orally before they write . . . Grammar is often incorrect, and syntax is sometimes awkward. Editing the final draft is the point at which these areas must be addressed.

'Many students approach the editing process with trepidation . . . suggestions for change must be given diplomatically. When the [teacher] suggests a possibility and the student does not like it, the change should not be made' (Montgomery & Kahn, 2003, pp. 146–7).

Montgomery and Kahn suggest that punctuation and spelling should be taught within the context of such stories:

> The editing process is an ideal point at which to teach language structure to students who want to learn, because it pertains to their stories. They want to make their stories the best that they can be. It is nice to have a final product of which they can be proud. (Montgomery & Kahn, 2003, p. 148)

The case of dyslexia

Some young people experience difficulties with written texts that appear to be unrelated to their overall ability. One area of difficulty is dyslexia.

Reflective activity: Awareness of dyslexic difficulties and their implications

Note down what you think dyslexia might be.

Do you have any friends or acquaintances who call themselves dyslexic? If so, what kind of difficulties do they experience? What, if anything, have they done to help themselves?

Dyslexia is most commonly explained as difficulties in learning where the information-processing system of dyslexic individuals is seen as different from that of non-dyslexics in ways which have an impact on a number of areas of performance. Some definitions relate only to difficulty in acquiring literacy as reflected by its derivation from Classical Greek: δυσ (dys), meaning 'bad' or 'difficult', and λεξίς (lexis), meaning 'word', or 'speech'. The British Psychological Society (BPS) working party adopted this narrower view of dyslexia related solely to literacy:

> Dyslexia is evident when accurate and fluent reading and or spelling develops very incompletely or with great difficulty. This focuses on literacy learning at the 'word level' and implies that the problem is severe and persistent despite appropriate learning opportunities. It provides the basis for a staged process of assessment through teaching. (British Psychological Society, 1999, p. 8)

Other definitions are wider and include reference to difficulties in co-ordination, personal organisation, balance, patterning, directionality (right/left confusion), sequencing, rhythm, orientation, memory, and so on. The wider definition espoused by the British Dyslexia Association (BDA) includes difficulty in the development of literacy and language related skills, particularly in phonological processing, and also in working memory, the speed of processing information and the automatic development of skills that may not reflect the level of other cognitive abilities.

> Dyslexia is a specific learning difficulty that mainly affects the development of literacy and language related skills. It is likely to be present at birth and to be life-long in its effects. It is characterised by difficulties with phonological processing, rapid naming, working memory, processing speed, and the automatic development of skills that may not match up to an individual's other cognitive abilities. (http://www.bdadyslexia.org. uk/dyslexic/definitions – accessed 14.03.16).

Conventional teaching methods may not suffice in addressing such difficulties but information technology and individual counselling may lessen the effects.

The Rose Review on identifying and teaching dyslexic children is in accord with this wider view (Rose, 2009, p. 30) and identifies dyslexia as a learning difficulty associated with 'difficulties in phonological awareness, verbal memory and verbal processing speed' that 'affects the skills involved in accurate and fluent word reading and spelling', but also acknowledges a wider range of information-processing difficulties in various 'aspects of language, motor co-ordination, mental calculation, concentration and personal organisation'. However, these aspects alone are not seen as markers of dyslexia. A 'good indication' is the extent to which 'the individual responds or has responded to well-founded intervention'. In other words, as the BPS (1999) implies also, if a child experiences difficulties but has not received good teaching, then it cannot be assumed that s/he is dyslexic.

In terms of literacy acquisition, the difficulties experienced by dyslexic students are usually related to difficulties in processing either visual or/and auditory information and making the connections between the visual symbols and the sounds they represent, commonly called 'decoding'. In relation to visual factors, learners may experience difficulty in recognition of the visual cues of letters and words, familiarity with left–right orientation, recognition of word patterns and recognition of letter and word shapes (Wearmouth, 2009). Or they may encounter problems with auditory factors: recognition of letter sounds, recognition of sounds and letter groups or patterns, sequencing of sounds, corresponding sounds to visual stimuli, discriminating sounds from other sounds and/or discriminating sounds within words.

Theories explaining dyslexia

A number of theories attempt to explain difficulties experienced by dyslexic learners.

Visual-based theories

Some theorists propose that dyslexia may be the consequence of an abnormality in the neural pathways of the visual system (Everatt, 2002). Others suggest a lower level of activity in the areas of the visual cortex thought to be responsible for identifying the direction of movement (Eden et al., 1996). There is also a view that visual difficulties may be caused by over-sensitivity to certain wavelengths (or colours) of light, sometimes referred to as scotopic sensitivity syndrome (Irlen, 1991). Coloured filters, overlays or lenses which are said to alleviate reading problems for some learners (Wilkins et al., 1994) have increasingly been incorporated into teachers' practice, with variable results.

Phonological deficit hypothesis

Since the 1980s the dominant theory used to explain dyslexia has been the phonological deficit hypothesis (Bradley & Bryant, 1983; Snowling, 2000; Stanovich, 2000). Difficulties experienced at the level of phonological representation and the relationships between symbols and the sounds they represent constrain reading development (Hatcher & Snowling, 2002). Activities such as non-word reading are problematic because of the difficulties associated with sound–symbol relationships. Dyslexic children with poorer phonological representations have fewer compensatory word attack strategies to draw on and this further undermines their reading performance.

Effects on performance

At pre-school level dyslexic children may experience a delay in spoken language, including difficulty in learning nursery rhymes and verbal sequencing, for example, days of the week and letters of the alphabet (Riddick, Wolfe & Lumsdon, 2002, pp. 12–13). There may also be poor gross motor co-ordination, for example, in learning to ride a bicycle or swim; poor fine motor skills, for example, in copying shapes and letters; and poor short term memory, for example, remembering a sequence of instructions and/ or names. At primary age a child is likely to experience difficulties in reading, writing, spelling and number work. The child may be unable to identify rhythm and alliteration, or read single words accurately. S/he may reverse some words, for example, 'pot' and 'top', miss out whole lines and read some sections of text twice without realising it, and have better understanding of text than word accuracy. Reading age for fluency and accuracy is likely to be below chronological age. Difficulties in encoding the phonological features of words (that is, the sound system of a language) is core to dyslexic children's difficulties, so children who begin school with poor letter knowledge and poor rhythmic ability may be at risk of developing difficulties in reading (Snowling, 2000, pp. 213–14). A child may spell the same word differently in the same text, spell incorrectly words learnt for spelling tests, make several attempts to spell words with frequent crossings out, spell phonetically but incorrectly, use what look like bizarre spellings, for example, 'bidar' for 'because', leave out syllables, for example, 'onge' for 'orange, or part of a letter blend especially when there is a blend of three letters, for example, 'sred' for 'shred', reverse letters, especially 'b' and 'd', 'p' and 'q'. S/he may experience difficulty copying from the board, produce work that is chaotic or very untidy, begin writing anywhere on the page, confuse upper and lower case letters, produce very little output and what there is may be unintelligible even to the child.

Policy related to literacy difficulties

Families and carers of children and young people who experience difficulties in literacy acquisition may feel alarmed at the focus on the testing of their children's achievement in literacy against national norms. Currently, in England, a high-stakes assessment regime that is used to make significant educational decisions about students, teachers and schools (Heubert, 2000) regulates the teaching of literacy in schools. Effectively, now, literacy policy in schools is driven by the requirements of the particular Key Stage in English with the whole system held in place by schools' accountability for publicising their pupils' progress and assessment outcomes, and also for their rating by Ofsted during school inspections (Ofsted, 2015). There is also a requirement that children should take a systematic synthetic phonics test at Key Stage One.

Whilst parents and carers of children with literacy difficulties may, as noted above, feel alarmed at the effect on their offspring of such a high stakes testing environment, there is also a formal recognition that severe dyslexic difficulties are likely to create a barrier to learning. Severe dyslexia might also constitute a disability and be covered by the Equality Act (2010) under which schools and local authorities have a duty to be proactive in providing 'reasonable adjustments'. Advice about 'reasonable adjustments' given to schools by the Equality and Human Rights Commission (2016) reads:

> You cannot justify a failure to make a reasonable adjustment; where the duty arises, the issue will be whether or not to make the adjustment is 'reasonable' and this is an objective question for the tribunals to ultimately determine.
>
> The duty is an anticipatory and continuing one that you owe to disabled pupils generally, regardless of whether you know that a particular pupil is disabled or whether you currently have any disabled pupils. You [...] should plan ahead for the reasonable adjustments you may need to make, regardless of whether you currently have any disabled pupils. (http://www.equalityhumanrights.com/advice-and-guidance/education-providers-schools-guidance/key-concepts/reasonable-adjustments/ – accessed 18.02.16)

As the Equality and Human Rights Commission (ibid.) comment, this duty runs alongside schools' responsibilities under education legislation. Some students may require reasonable adjustments in addition to the SEN provision or additional support they are receiving. For some this may imply special consideration during external examinations, for example, additional time or access to an amanuensis or a word processor.

Addressing dyslexic difficulties

Teaching approaches for dyslexic students can be grouped into those that are designed to enable the child to overcome the difficulties that are experienced as far as possible – almost to train the personal information-processing system to become more organised in a deliberately systematic and focused way (personal reflections) – and those that enable the young person to cope (Wearmouth, 2009). Many of the techniques described above are suitable to address dyslexic-type literacy difficulties.

Training to overcome difficulties

Hatcher and Snowling (2002) outline examples of phonological awareness training: playing rhyming games, making up nonsense rhymes, repeating rhyming strings, and playing other games which require the manipulation of sounds such as identifying words as units within sentences, syllable awareness and blending tasks. Interventions that rely exclusively on training in phonological awareness are less effective than those that combine phonological training with print and meaning in the context of sentences in text, however.

At almost any age, paired reading arrangements as outlined above can enable dyslexic individuals to gain more experience in reading ('reading mileage', Clay, 1993, 1998) and in visual tracking of the text in order to increase word identification, knowledge of letter/sound combinations and use of contextual information and inference. Students might be encouraged to choose reading material of high interest to themselves, irrespective of its readability level, and the child and the reading partner might read out loud together, with the reading partner modulating his/her speed to match that of the dyslexic pupil. Or children might be encouraged to use recordings of books that they really want to read, tracking through the text with their eyes while listening to the CD.

Allowing students to dictate his/her thoughts onto a digital recorder and then transcribing them for him/her, or allowing him/her to dictate thoughts to the teacher/an older child/the parent may be the first step in writing. Subsequently listening to the recording of his/her own thoughts and then writing the text from this is one way to separate out the conceptual thinking around content and the mechanical aspects of writing with which the young person experiences difficulty.

Provision of writing frames can support extended writing and encourage logical sequencing (Wray, 2002).

Multi-sensory approaches that introduce visual, tactile, auditory and kinaesthetic modes to teaching and learning enable students who need extra reinforcement in their learning to see, touch, hear and move, sometimes simultaneously, in their learning activities. The principles of multi-sensory teaching which apply to language work also apply to the mathematics field, for example, introducing new mathematical concepts and processes using concrete materials, diagrams, pictures and verbal explanation. Progress should be carefully monitored at each stage, checking that a particular concept has been thoroughly mastered and understood before moving on to the next step.

'Metacognitive' strategies can also help dyslexic and other students to think about their own thinking processes to build on their own strengths. 'Mind-mapping' (Buzan, 2000), for example, as we noted above, encourages learners first to produce a visual representation of all those areas to be covered in the text to develop a structure for producing extended text.

Coping strategies

Research stresses the motivational value of computer-assisted learning, for example, word-processing which can increase the time that students are willing to practise writing (Florian & Hegarty, 2004). Spell-checkers can remove much of a pupil's inhibition about writing that comes from poor spelling. Drafting and correcting becomes less laborious and the printed copy can be corrected away from the machine by the student or the teacher and improved versions created without difficulty. Everything can be saved and reused easily, allowing work to be done in small amounts. Presentation is improved; when the final version is printed it is legible and well presented. Optical
 5.2   comfort is also important. A choice of screen colours can be helpful to students.

'Reasonable adjustments': examination concessions

Where a young person has a formal assessment of severe dyslexia it may be the case that this is interpreted as a disability under the terms of the 2010 Equality Act. If this is the case then, as discussed in Chapter 1, s/he is entitled to 'reasonable adjustments'

Table 5.1 An example of a dyslexic student's learning and teaching needs

Identification of difficulties

A 13-year-old student was identified as experiencing a number of difficulties in learning of a dyslexic nature:

- significant difference between verbal comprehension abilities and reading accuracy;
- significant weakness in the area of short-term memory processing;
- weakness with the sequencing and organisation of information;
- difficulties with tasks requiring the integration of fine motor skills, visual tracking, spatial analysis, visual discrimination and speed of information processing;
- extreme lack of confidence in personal, intellectual and academic abilities.

Area of need	Intervention
Increase word identification, knowledge of letter/sound combinations and use of contextual information and inference.	Paired reading arrangement at school and home, with high interest reading material from school, the library and from home, irrespective of its readability level. Training in the RR technique given to school reading buddy and parents.
Improve the speed of her reading, left–right working, orientation, hand–eye coordination, sequencing, sound–symbol recognition, and speed and accuracy of scanning.	Following text with the eyes while listening to a CD of choice at home.
Improvement in speed and accuracy of tracking skill.	Timed left to right tracking through pages of unwanted magazines or books, crossing out letters of the alphabet in the right order. Copy of alphabet supplied to support this.
Improvement in spelling.	Multi-sensory approach 2 as described above. Five new spellings taken from own work introduced daily as appropriate.
Improvement I content, length and grammatical accuracy of free writing.	1. Dictation of stories on to digital recorder, or to classroom assistant, and transcription of them by teaching assistant. Later, encouragement for student to transcribe. 2. Provision of writing frames. At its simplest level this comprised three steps – a beginning, a middle and an ending – moving towards a six-part structure which included:

(Continued)

Table 5.1 (cont.)

	• introducing the people • describing the setting/place • something beginning to happen • the exciting part • things sorting themselves out • the ending. This structure was gradually differentiated into using the following questions: • What is the title? • Who are the main characters? • Describe the main characters. What did the main characters try to do? • Who were the other characters in the story? • What was the story about? • What was the main part of the story? • How did the story end?
Improvement of appearance of written work and motivation to write.	Use of word-processor with spell check facility with encouragement to the student to change text, change, move it around and corrected as often as necessary until the work was acceptable.
Improvement to short-term memory.	Teaching of simple mnemonics to aid memory. Multi-sensory approach to maximise effect of repetition of learning accomplished through oral, visual, auditory and kinaesthetic modes.
Improvement in spatial analysis and visual discrimination.	All visually presented materials kept simple in format and uncluttered by excessive stimuli. Visual cues provided to assist student in planning and organising assigned tasks. Specific and concrete cues used when giving directions.
Examination concessions required.	Examination concessions granted (extra time, answers in note form, oral test to support written examination, use of word-processor in course work, examinations etc.) and 25% additional time. Examination papers duplicated to see both sides of a page at the same time, enlarged or printed on coloured paper, along with the use of highlighting pens to help with the analysis of questions.

to enable access to the school or college curriculum, including internal and external examinations. The school might give internal examination concessions (extra time, answers in note form, oral test to support written examination, use of word processor in course work, examinations etc.) and 25 per cent additional time. Examination papers might be duplicated so that the pupil can see both sides of a page at the same time, enlarged or printed on coloured paper, along with the use of highlighting pens to help with the analysis of questions. Guidelines for access arrangement during external examinations have been issued by some qualifications bodies to ensure compliance with the 2010 Equality Act, for example, the Joint Council for Qualifications (JCQ) (2014) in relation to secondary students.

5.3

Table 5.1 above offers an example of the learning and teaching needs of a 13-year-old dyslexic student.

Summary

In schools, becoming literate is often thought of as acquiring basic technical skills in order to be able to read, write and spell competently. Difficulties in literacy that are experienced by students have been seen as the result of deficiency in developing these skills and interventions have been designed to remedy this deficiency. More recently, however, many educators have recognised that it is not just the individual abilities of the learner that matter when students learn to read, write and spell. Particular social features of the learning contexts are important too.

As Cambourne (2003) comments, what is learned cannot be separated from the context in which it is learned. The experiences and contexts in which literacy learning is embedded are critical in determining the learner's understanding, and ability to use literacy skills such as reading, writing and spelling. If students learn to read in contexts where competent reading is assumed to be the errorless reproduction of texts, they will understand the purpose of reading differently from those taught in ways which stress that reading is the construction of meaning from texts.

At the same time, each student with literacy difficulties is an individual. Each situation is unique. Each requires its own solution. There is no one easy option. As practitioners, teachers need to bear in mind the wider cultural and social factors, the school and curriculum context, and also factors related more specifically to the individual child.

Chapter 6
Focus on numeracy difficulties

> The major questions in this chapter are:
>
> - What are some of the characteristics of inclusive pedagogy that support effective mathematics learning for all students?
> - How can teachers and families understand difficulties in numeracy learning?
> - What kind of interventions can address difficulties in the acquisition of skills, knowledge and understandings of mathematics?

Introduction

Many students in schools experience difficulties in learning mathematics. The challenge for those with an interest in mathematics education is to understand what teachers might do to break this pattern.

We take the view in this chapter, as elsewhere in this book, that the cause of difficulties in mathematical learning is not simply a deficit in the learner's thinking. The learning environment and the teaching approaches are also crucial factors in influencing whether a student is likely to experience difficulties greater than those of his/her peers. In many ways the variety of approaches to teaching mathematics illustrate some of the differences in the views of learning discussed in Chapter 1 and the consequences for teachers' pedagogy that are derived from these, for example:

- behaviourism, with an assumption of children as vessels to be filled with mathematical knowledge and skills by the expert teacher;
- social constructivism, with its view of children as active agents in their own construction of knowledge and who need scaffolding by the expert other, and time and dialogic space for discussion and interthinking (Littleton & Mercer, 2013) on the interpersonal plane. The purpose of this is to bridge the variety of understandings and personal frames of reference and histories that each student

brings to the mathematics lesson (Clay & Silverman, 2009) so that all students can clarify and elaborate their new understandings on the intrapersonal plane (Vygotsky, 1978).

There are ways of structuring the environment and planning activities in mathematics that are likely to facilitate all students' mathematical learning. Having said this, however, even with the best organised classrooms there are likely to be some students who continue to experience difficulties and may need extra support.

We begin this chapter with a brief overview of the attributes of effective mathematics teachers and the importance of the learning environment for successful mathematics learning. We go on to consider the skills needed to be a good mathematician in school and reflect this against some of the cognitive difficulties experienced by students. We then look in more detail at areas of mathematics learning with which some students may struggle and some of the ways to begin to deal with these. We draw the chapter to a close with a discussion of specific numeracy difficulties of a dyscalculic nature that may be seen to parallel those of a dyslexic kind in the area of literacy learning.

Attributes of effective teachers of mathematics

 Reflective activity: Memories of mathematics acquisition

Think about your own learning of mathematics and reflect back on:

- how successful you were;
- to what you attribute your own achievement, or lack of achievement, in mathematics;
- what might have helped you to gain an even higher standard of achievement;
- what is it about this area of the curriculum that seems to cause some students so much anxiety and/or so many problems.

Effective mathematics teaching requires a number of attributes on the part of the teacher. To begin with, of course, there is the issue of teachers' subject knowledge. Then there is the question of teaching approaches in relation to knowledge, awareness and understanding of the learning process and the approach to teaching mathematics that is dependent on this. Further, there is the matter of teacher expectations.

Teacher knowledge and understanding

As Wearmouth (2009) comments, what teachers do in mathematics classrooms is largely dependent on:

- what they know and believe about mathematics and its teaching;
- what they understand about the teaching and learning of mathematics;
- what they know about their students.

Teachers' subject knowledge

Unless teachers themselves are able to understand the relevant mathematical concepts, they may not be able, or confident enough, to identify points at which they can elaborate on students' current understandings and help them to move towards more complex and sophisticated appreciation of mathematical concepts.

Teachers must have sound content knowledge if they are to recognise the conceptual understandings and misunderstandings that students are using in their methods and if they are to realise where those (mis)understandings might be leading (Hill, Rowan & Ball, 2005; Kilpatrick, Swafford & Findell, 2001; Shulman & Shulman, 2004; Warfield, 2001; Ball & Bass, 2000). Teachers who are unclear in their own minds about mathematical ideas may struggle to teach those ideas and often use examples and metaphors that prevent, rather than help, students' mathematical understanding (Bliss, Askew & Macrae, 1996). Limited teacher knowledge of mathematics can lead to misunderstandings of students' solutions and to giving feedback that is inappropriate or unhelpful (Ruthven, 2002). In a study of whole-class teaching episodes at three schools, Myhill and Warren (2005) found that many strategies used by teachers worked more as devices to enable students to complete tasks than as learning support mechanisms that would help move them towards independence. In the Year 2 and Year 6 lessons observed, teachers often used 'heavy prompts', pointing students to the 'right' answers. Using this strategy, the teachers in the Myhill and Warren study tended to miss critical opportunities for gaining insight into students' prior knowledge or level of understanding.

Teachers' knowledge of appropriate teaching approaches

Effective teaching is not necessarily related to higher formal qualifications, however (Askew, Brown, Rhodes, Johnson & Wiliam, 1997). In the Effective Teachers of Numeracy Project in the United Kingdom it was the teachers who were able to make connections between different aspects of mathematical knowledge who recorded high academic gains for their students. 'Highly effective teachers of numeracy themselves had knowledge and awareness of conceptual connections between the areas which they taught in the primary mathematics curriculum' (Askew et al., 1997, p. 3).

Teachers who are effective in teaching mathematics to the whole range of student learners take developing of students' mathematical thinking very seriously and are committed to it (Anthony & Walshaw, 2007, p. 1). It seems that teachers' beliefs, expectations and understandings of all students as active agents in their own learning are as important in the area of mathematics as in any other area of the school curriculum. Each young person who experiences difficulties in mathematics learning is different, and it is really important to engage with each one individually to tease out the root(s) of the problem. These might be, for instance:

- a history of failure to learn and succeed in mathematics resulting in 'learned helplessness' (Seligman, 1975): an attitude of 'I'm useless at maths' learned early;
- a poor memory for mathematics, for example, for number facts and formulae needed for rapid mental arithmetic. Or perhaps fundamental concepts were never understood in the first place, for example, place value, so it is hardly surprising if a student does not remember what s/he does not understand;
- inability to see patterns and relationships in numbers;
- difficulty in remembering and manipulating mathematical symbols;
- poor spatial awareness;
- poor organisational/directional/sequencing ability;
- low teacher expectations leading to low achievement (Skinner & Belmont, 1993; Wearmouth, 2016b) and so on.

To teach mathematics effectively it is important for the teacher, as the more expert other in the learning process, to listen to what students have to say and re-frame student talk in mathematically appropriate language. There is now a large body of evidence that demonstrates the beneficial effects of students being encouraged to articulate their mathematical thinking (Fraivillig, Murphy & Fuson, 1999; Lampert, 1990; O'Connor, 1998). By expressing their ideas, students provide their teachers with information about what they know and what they can learn next with support in the zone of proximal development (ZPD). This provides teachers with the chance to scaffold new learning by highlighting connections between mathematical language and conceptual understanding. As we have discussed in relation to socio-cultural views of learning, constructive feedback has a powerful influence on student achievement (Hattie, 2002). There is evidence (Wiliam, 1999) that constructive feedback makes a comparison between where a student is currently at and a standard as interpreted by the teacher.

Hiebert and colleagues (1997) have found that teacher talk effective in supporting mathematical understanding and competence involves:

- drawing out the specific mathematical ideas that students are using to work out the answers to problems;
- sharing other methods and ways of working through mathematical problems;
- supporting students' understanding of the accepted conventions in mathematics.

However, for students to be prepared to volunteer their answers in mathematics lessons they need to feel safe and know that they will not be humiliated by either the teacher or their peers if they are wrong. Many students who experience difficulty in mathematics lack the confidence to speak out in the classroom, however. The current author well remembers the occasion when teaching mathematics to a bottom set of 14-year-old students in a secondary school she was asked by one boy: "'ere, Miss, why do you bother with us when you can teach them clever kids?'

Effective teachers neither embarrass students nor ignore wrong answers. They use mistakes to enhance the teaching. They might, for example, comment on the strategies students are using and/or talk about the mathematical concepts that students are learning. They encourage students to monitor their own progress and set their own goals. In a study of effective practice in a Year 10 classroom, Angier and Povey (1999) noted how students' academic and social outcomes were improved by the inclusive ethos that the teacher had established in the mathematics classroom.

In summary, teachers who are effective in supporting the mathematical learning of those students who experience difficulties show an interest in what students have to say, listen to their ideas, avoid sarcasm and do not allow students to put each other down. Stipek et al. (1998) note that these teachers appear genuinely to like and respect their students and make an effort to make mathematics problems interesting and give the impression that they value all students' contributions. In this way they create an environment where students are prepared to take risks because they know that it is safe to do so.

Opportunities for 'interthinking' with peers

 Reflective activity: The importance of space for thinking

Effective mathematics teaching for the full range of learners in classrooms means creating a space for both individuals and groups. It is undoubtedly also the case that sometimes students need opportunities and time to work quietly away from the demands of a group to enable reflection and elaboration of mathematics understanding on the intrapersonal plane.

A number of research projects have concluded that small-group work can provide the context for social and cognitive engagement and dialogic space for 'interthinking' (Littleton & Mercer, 2013) to share ideas and elaborate understandings on the interpersonal plane. Look back at the discussion of social constructivist approaches to understanding learning in Chapter 1 and note down ways in which peers might support the learning of new mathematical concepts.

Peers can serve as an important resource for developing mathematical thinking and for finding out about the nature of task demands and how those demands could be met. Collaborative activity within a small supportive environment allows students not only to exchange ideas but also test those ideas critically. Helme and Clarke (2001) found in their secondary school classroom study that peer interactions, rather than teacher–student interactions, provided opportunity for students to engage in high-level cognitive activity. These researchers stressed the important role the teacher played in establishing social rules governing participation in the classroom. These rules can serve to make the engagement in mathematical learning tasks by lower attaining students possible or impossible. Alton-Lee (2003) reports that the teachers who set aside time to guide students in effective group processes invariably enhance students' outcomes. Students need to have sufficient competence and experience to allow them to ask appropriate questions of themselves and each other in order to elaborate mathematical thinking and understanding.

There have been successful projects, for example, the Improving Attainment in Mathematics Project (IAMP) (Watson & de Geest, 2005), that show how focusing on developing students' understanding and introducing them to the kinds of practices that distinguish mathematics learners from others can lead to improved student achievement and level of interest in the subject. The kinds of practices that Watson and de Geest are referring to here are

> choosing appropriate techniques, generating their own enquiry, contributing examples, predicting problems, describing connections with prior knowledge, giving reasons, finding underlying similarities or differences, generalising structure from diagrams or examples, identifying what can be changed, making something more difficult, making comparisons, posing their own questions, giving reasons, working on extended tasks over time, creating and sharing their own methods, using prior knowledge, dealing with unfamiliar problems, changing their minds, and initiating their own mathematics. (Anthony & Walshaw, 2007, pp. 18–19)

What teachers had in common was a very purposeful approach in setting meaningful activities in lessons, and a deliberate effort to support students to think of themselves as able to become competent mathematicians. During the two years of the IAMP, students showed a greater willingness to engage with mathematics, concentrate on mathematical tasks that might be quite complex for longer periods, take risks and discuss alternative ways of working on mathematical problems.

Influence of teacher expectations

Opportunities to learn depend to some extent on what is 'normal' in classrooms, what is allowed and disallowed, teacher and peer expectations, and the way that the learning environment is organised. Since the seminal study of Rosenthal and Jacobson (1968), which concluded that children's academic school performance can be positively or negatively influenced by the expectations of teachers, sometimes called the 'observer-expectancy' effect, there has been a great deal of work on the importance of positive teacher expectations in promoting student achievement. Very importantly students' learning and behaviour are influenced by the kind of relationship s/he has with a teacher which develops over time and is itself affected by the teacher's construction of a student's value and worth.

Reflective activity: The damaging effects of low teacher expectations and devaluing of students

Read the text below and, as you do so, reflect on:

● the effect that the teachers' approaches to teaching mathematics to the various groups were likely to have on the students concerned;

● what might be done to enable these teachers to adopt a different attitude to the students who experienced difficulty.

Teachers do not always value students' mathematical contributions equally. Unfairness in the way teachers treat different groups of students can affect students badly (Nash & Harker, 2002). Teachers who give less attention to some students than to others tend to offer less encouragement to students who they have labelled as 'not mathematical'. One student in the Nash and Harker (2002) study said: 'Like when you ask the teachers you think, you feel like you don't know, you're dumb. So it stops you from asking the teachers, yeah, so you just try to hide back, don't worry about it. Everyday you don't understand, you just don't want to tell the teacher' (p. 180).

Bartholomew (2003) found that mathematics teachers at a London school valued top-stream students more highly than others. The messages conveyed to students about the way they were valued were clear. In contrast with friendly interactions with a top-stream class at the same year level, a teacher behaved in an authoritarian manner with his low-stream class:'insisting that students queue outside the room in absolute silence and eventually counting them in and seating them alphabetically. They had to remain in their seats in silence, were given no opportunities to ask questions, with the result that many students were extremely confused as to what they were meant to be doing' (Bartholomew, 2003, p. 131).

Do you consider that enabling teachers to hear the views of students might be one way to change hearts and minds? If so, how might this be arranged, do you think?

Research suggests that teachers who create effective classroom communities care about student engagement and work hard to find out what helps and what hinders students' learning (Cobb & Hodge, 2002). At the same time they make sure that students do not become overly dependent on them and encourage them to ask questions about why the class is expected to do certain things in mathematics lessons, and what the point is of doing that (Noddings, 1995). There is an implication that learning should be reciprocal. While students have something to learn from teachers, teachers may also have something to learn from their students (Perso, 2003).

Every task or activity in mathematics supports some kinds of thinking and hinders others. Many studies (Boaler, Wiliam & Brown, 2000; Sullivan, Mousley & Zevenbergen, 2003) reflect the author's own experiences of ways in which low attainers are often presented with a very limited 'diet' of activities in mathematics lessons, where the four rules of number customarily dominate and there is little focus on students constructing their own understandings. In a study of the views and experiences of nearly 1,000 students, Boaler et al. (2000) found that those in lower streamed classes had fewer instructional opportunities to learn. Teaching strategies were very narrow, resulting in profound and largely negative learning experiences. Teachers often seemed to ignore students' backgrounds and needs and, similar to those in Bartholomew's (2003) study, talked to them in ways that highlighted the difference between these students and those achieving highly in mathematics.

Significance of the mathematics learning environment

Walshaw (2004) identifies a number of components of the learning environment which help to bring about mathematical learning and the way in which mathematical knowledge is constructed by students:

- how activities are organised and mediated to develop mathematical understanding so that students feel a sense of forward movement in their mathematical knowledge;
- classroom 'discourses' in mathematics, that is, the kind of language that is used and the way that mathematics is talked about and arguments are made and understood. It is really important that all students learn this mathematical language and that specialist terms are both taught to the students at whichever level is appropriate and deliberately used to scaffold the students' mathematical thinking. Mathematical language is not simply the vocabulary and technical usage of mathematics. It also includes the ways that expert and novice mathematicians use language to explain concepts. 'Teachers who make a difference are focused on shaping the development of novice mathematicians who speak the precise and generalisable language of mathematics' (Anthony & Walshaw, 2007, p. 204). Zevenbergen, Mousley & Sullivan (2004) argue for a very definite, clear approach to teaching mathematics, one where the teacher:
  - helps students to 'see through' the language that is wrapped around the mathematical problem to the problem itself;
  - offers very clear, intelligible explanations of the mathematics that is required to work out that problem;
  - is sensitive to class and cultural differences among the group of students, and between the students and the teacher, and works hard not to alienate students by insensitive trampling on these differences;
  - understands that responses to the particular activity might be different from what was anticipated, but nevertheless acceptable mathematically.
- the tools and resources that are made available for students to use. Some students will need concrete materials to aid their mathematical thinking, as

discussed elsewhere in this chapter, for far longer than others. Choice of task, tools and activity significantly influences the development of mathematical thinking. Mathematical tasks should be focused on the solution of genuine mathematical problems. The most productive tasks and activities are those that allow students to access important mathematical concepts and relationships, to investigate mathematical structure and to use techniques and notations appropriately.

An important synthesis of 600 studies of effective mathematical pedagogy (Anthony & Walshaw, 2007) confirms the importance of these components and adds a non-threatening classroom atmosphere to this list.

Skills in effective mathematics acquisition

 Reflective activity: Prerequisites for successful mathematics learning

In your experience what do learners have to be able to do to be successful mathematicians?
   Why do you think some young people appear to experience particular difficulties in this area of the curriculum?

In reflecting on problems associated with learning mathematics it is useful to consider what learners need to be able to do to be successful. Chinn (2012, p. 9) cites the Russian psychologist Krutetskii (1976) in setting out these skills as an ability to:

- 'formalise maths material', in other words to think in the abstract rather than in 'concrete numerical relationships';
- make generalisations and 'abstract oneself from the irrelevant';
- operate with numerals as well as other symbols;
- conduct 'sequential, segmented, logical reasoning';
- cut short the process of reasoning;
- reverse mental process;
- be flexible in thought;
- use spatial concepts.

It should be clear why some students experience problems from the discussion of difficulties in information-processing, memory, sequential reasoning, use of symbols, moving from concrete to abstract thinking, and so on, related to cognition and learning in Chapter 4. However, solving learning problems in mathematics is not a straightforward matter of importing more one-size-fits-all cures. The task of the teacher is 'demanding, uncertain, and not reducible to predictable routines' (Anthony & Walshaw, 2007, p. x) for a number of reasons. For example, the choices that teachers make about organisation, management, and the area of the mathematics curriculum on which to focus at any one time, as well as the cognitive demands of mathematics teaching are all part of the complexity of practice in the classroom. As Chinn (2012, p. 9) notes, '[…] maths can be a written subject or a mental exercise. It can be formulaic or it can be intuitive. It can be learnt and communicated in either way [...]. Maths can be concrete, but fairly quickly moves to the abstract and symbolic. It has many rules and a surprising number of inconsistencies. In terms of judgement and appraisal, maths is quite unique as a school subject'.

Barriers frequently experienced in the acquisition of mathematics

 Reflective activity: Common barriers to mathematics acquisition and strategies to address these

In the section below we discuss barriers to learning that are commonly experienced in particular areas of mathematics: language, concepts of number-ness and quantity, written recording of number work, relational signs, place value and 'zero', number bonds, multiplication, negative numbers, money and time. The discussion of each topic includes suggestions for addressing possible barriers. As you read this discussion, reflect on:

- your experience of working with students who face difficulties similar to those that are described here;
- whether, and how, you might make use of the suggested approaches to addressing these difficulties.

The language of mathematics

Many students who experience difficulties in understanding and using number symbols also experience difficulties in the use of language. The language of mathematics may prove difficult, with new words, signs and symbols to be learned and considerable ambiguity of meaning in the way words are used outside the context of mathematics.

Reflective activity: Ambiguity and complexity on the use of mathematical language

As Weavers (2003, p. 35) notes, there are many mathematical terms that are synonymous.

In your experience, how often do teachers use these terms to mean the same thing?

- +, add, sum of, plus, and, altogether, addition, more than, positive
- −, subtract, take away, minus, difference between, less, smaller than, negative
- x (often confused with +), times, multiply, product of, lots of
- ÷, divide, share, how many in, how much each, quotient
- =, equals, becomes, is the same as, makes
- >, greater than, often confused with <, less than.

How do you think you can teach students the meaning of these synonyms?

Sometimes the same word can denote a completely different calculation. For example: 'What is 6 more than 30?' requires a different operation from: 'How many more than 6 is 30?'

How can you explain the different calculations required here to a student, do you think?

Some words have a variety of meanings: 'volume' can refer to quantity or sound, the 'face' of a person is very different from a clock 'face' or the 'face' of a three-dimensional shape.

What can teachers do to ensure students understand the differences here, do you think?

Addressing difficulties in mathematical language

The number of new words that are introduced really needs to be restricted to a very few that the student can remember the next day and the next week and practised very regularly, rather than introducing too many so that the student cannot remember any clearly. If we introduce two things that are very similar at the same time, it is highly likely that our students will forever confuse them. Mathematical problems may need to be read very slowly with an emphasis on each individual word so that the student has an opportunity to think about what the problem means before s/he can consider how to work it out. It can also be very helpful to assist students to estimate an answer first by saying whether it should be bigger or smaller than the first number in order to narrow down the possible calculations.

Many students adopt mathematical symbols and algorithms without having grasped the concepts that underpin them (Chinn, 2012). Activities involving reading and writing numbers may tell us something about children's ability to read and write numbers. They do not necessarily tell us anything about children's conceptual understanding of 'number-ness' (Wearmouth, 2009). Learners' ability to understand symbolic representation depends on understanding what the symbolic representation refers to. We might well think about Piaget's seminal work (1969) on the four stages of learning to justify the handling and counting of everyday items to support developing understanding of number-ness.

Concepts of number-ness and quantity

There seems to be a preference in the United Kingdom and the United States for teaching number in the early years through the use of number sequences (Grauberg, 2002). Children usually learn to count in a sequence of one-digit numbers. 'An ability to recite these numbers is a perfect example of the child giving the parent or the teacher an illusion of learning, of knowing' (Chinn, 2012, p. 81). In some other countries in Europe and the Far East, for example Japan, it is different, however, and the preference is for emphasising cardinal aspects, that is recognition of small quantities without counting. Recognising a small number, for example four, as a quantity involves one operation of matching a sound symbol or visual symbol to an amount. This seems, logically, easier than recognising four from a number sequence. This latter involves remembering that four comes after three and before five, and simultaneously counting up to the total amount. Hughes (1986, p. 45) exemplifies this point from an interview with a boy named Ram:

MH: What is three and one more? How many is three and one more?
Ram: Three and what? One what? Letter? I mean number?
[. . .]
MH: How many is three and one more?
Ram: One more what?
MH: Just one more, you know?
Ram: (Disgruntled) I don't know.

Addressing difficulties in acquiring concepts of number-ness and quantity

It will take a lot of activities in a variety of different contexts before a child such as Ram:

will be able to grasp the powerful abstract qualities of a number – which means the concept of 'twoness', 'threeness', 'nness'. Through his experience with many different materials we want him (sic) to see what is common to all (the fact that there are, for instance, 'two' of each) and we want him to learn to ignore what is irrelevant (e.g. size, colour, feel). (Grauberg, 2002, p. 12)

It might be appropriate to concentrate on establishing the idea of quantity first – a lot, a little, more, less, and so on – and then small numbers as a specific quantity for the child who experiences difficulties in language. As Grauberg (2002) comments, this approach has the potential to establish the concept of 'numberness', before starting on number lines.

Written recording of number work

Children who experience difficulty in language and symbolic representation are also likely to find it problematic to acquire and use written symbols for numbers. As Grauberg (2002) comments, 'Where is the 'f' in 5?'

Addressing difficulties in written recording of number work

It is possible to use other number systems, for example tally charts, first, where one bundle represents five and is clearly made up of five. Or, for some children it might be important to use concrete aids to establish number learning, for example Cuisenaire rods and/or an abacus, for much longer than for other children.

Relational signs: 'plus', 'minus', 'equal(s)'

Adding and subtracting both imply actions. Without an understanding of what the action is there is little point in trying to encourage the use of the symbol. '=' is often interpreted to children as 'makes', but, as we are all aware, a child's notion of 'makes' is clearly not what the symbol '=' means, mathematically. Having said this, primary schools in particular have a lot of equipment that can be used to play games in adding, subtracting and balancing.

Addressing difficulties in remembering relational signs: 'plus', 'minus', 'equal(s)'

A major question is how to move from the act of adding, taking away or balancing to competent use of the abstract symbols. One way to do this might be to encourage children to devise their own symbols for the actions first. It may be that students will suggest the use of arrows pointing in one direction or another, and that these can gradually be substituted with the conventional symbol.

Place value

The role of place value in mathematics learning cannot be overestimated. It is the author's experience that difficulties with the concept of place value and 'zero' are experienced not just by children with language difficulties but by other students also, to the end of their secondary education. Whilst teaching in a secondary school, she realised that place value was not properly understood by many of the teenagers who were expected to cope with the concept of hundreds, thousands and millions in other curriculum areas while she was still trying to support them to develop a basic understanding of place value. She thought it was hardly surprising that students found concepts such as population density expressed in thousands per square mile so frustratingly complex and difficult in their geography lessons that their behaviour became disruptive. They could not handle the concepts of thousands and millions competently and confidently, either in an ordinal or cardinal sense, and became very disruptive when expected to apply these concepts.

Addressing difficulties in acquiring the concept of place value

One way to start to address problems with place value might be to continue to use concrete equipment such as base ten blocks, Dienes materials – unit cubes, 'longs' of 10 cm cubes, and 'flats' of 100 cm cubes – or similar Numicon (Oxford University Press) materials for much longer than the teacher might have anticipated, providing that this can be done without embarrassing the child(ren). Alternatively, as Grauberg (2002) notes, the numbers may be written on transparencies and then superimposed. For example, 54 might be written down at first as 50 with the 4 superimposed over the 0. 504 would be written down as 500 with the 4 superimposed over the last 0.

Concept of 'zero'

Zero may be another problematic concept, mathematically. The use of zero as a place holder in a multi-digit line can be difficult to comprehend – without understanding the whole concept of place value.

Addressing difficulties in the use of zero

The current author was once asked by 14-year-old students in a bottom mathematics set: 'How can 44 times nought possibly equal nought? How can something equal nothing when you've started with 44 and made it bigger by multiplying? (Wearmouth, 2009, p. 138). She replied by taking a handful of nothing and putting it down on the desk 44 times to prove the point.

Number bonds

The learning of number bonds is really important in the initial stages of mathematics acquisition. This may be quite problematic for students who experience difficulties in short-term memory, however.

Addressing difficulties in learning number bonds

Number bonds for ten can be presented in a number of ways. Students who have little idea of the meaning of numerals or number terms might be supported to develop their understanding through using dice and/or dominoes. Using the arrays of dots from 1 to 10 can provide a clear way to comprehend and acquire number bonds. Card games can be used to practise these number bonds. Number bonds should be remembered as number facts, for example $7 + 3 = 10$, and also as an 'addend', a number that should be added to another to make ten, for example $7 + \square = 10$. The extension from $7 + 3 = 10$, to $70 + 30 = 100$ and to $300 + 700 = 1000$ is straightforward.

The number bonds for 9 and 11 can be taught with regard to their relationship to 10.

Number bonds for 10 and 100 are useful in subtraction, given that this can be done by counting on through tens, hundreds and thousands.

Teaching pupils, and making sure they remember, number doubles for digits less than 10 can be a useful strategy for rapid recall for some students. An extension of this is doubles plus or minus one, for example $6 + 5 = (6 + 6) - 1$ or $9 + 8 = (9 + 9) - 1$.

Multiplication

Both the concept of multiplication and the learning of multiplication tables can be problematic for some students.

Addressing difficulties in multiplication

As Chinn (2012) points out, it is a relatively straightforward progression from addition to multiplication when it is seen as repeated addition of the same numbers: 5 x 3 can be seen as $5 + 5 + 5$, so 3 lots of 5. Times table facts are important and should be learned if at all possible. One way to do this that the current author has found very successful is to teach students in short sequences that overlap. One sequence should be practised until the student is very confident with it. For example:

1 x 4 = 4
2 x 4 = 8
3 x 4 = 12
4 x 4 = 16
5 x 4 = 20

The next overlapping sequence will be then be:

5 x 4 = 20
6 x 4 = 24
7 x 4 = 28

8 x 4 = 32

9 x 4 = 36

The final sequence will be:

9 x 4 = 36

10 x 4 = 40

11 x 4 = 44

12 x 4 = 48

Sequences can be shortened if necessary, but should always overlap. The purpose of this is that when the student recites the whole table the overlaps will carry him/her through into the next sequence.

If necessary students can be encouraged to draw their own table squares and use these, *provided they remember that the top left-hand square is left blank*. Number facts for the 0 times, 1 times, 5 times and 10 times can be filled in first because they are the easiest. 2 times can follow next. *Students might need to be reminded that 0 x anything is 0.*

	0	1	2	3	4	5	6	7	8	9	10
0	0	0	0	0	0	0	0	0	0	0	0
1	0	1	2	3	4	5	6	7	8	9	10
2	0	2				10					20
3	0	3				15					30
4	0	4				20					40
5	0	5	10	15	20	25	30	35	40	45	50
6	0	6				30					60
7	0	7				35					70
8	0	8				40					80
9	0	9				45					90
10	0	10	20	30	40	50	60	70	80	90	100

Figure 6.1 Example of table square to be completed by students

Or the harder tables can be taught as derived from easier tables, for example

- 4 x is double 2 x;
- 8 x is double 4 x;
- 3 x is (2 x) + (1 x);
- 6 x is (5 x) + (1 x);
- 7 x is (2 x) + (5 x);
- 9 x is (10 x) – (1 x).

Negative numbers

Counting backwards can be quite challenging for some learners (Chinn, 2012), so understanding and dealing with the concept of negative numbers can be even more so.

Addressing difficulties with negative numbers

The use of real life situations can be a very important aid to learning here. For example, talking to students about going up and down in a lift can help: 'If you get into a lift two floors below ground level, at floor -2, how many floors will you have to go up to get to ground level at floor 0?' Or 'If you get into a lift two floors below ground level (floor -2) and want to go to the floor two levels above ground level (floor 2) how many floors will you go up?' This problem can be represented on a vertical line:

$$
\begin{array}{c}
4 \\
3 \\
2 \\
1 \\
0 \\
-1 \\
-2
\end{array}
$$

Temperatures can be represented in the same way above and below zero. When the students fully understand this concept the number line can be presented in the conventional way as a horizontal line:

$$
-2 \quad -1 \quad 0 \quad 1 \quad 2 \quad 3 \quad 4
$$

Money

Money is another concept that all students need to acquire, but can be extremely problematic in its acquisition. Firstly, there is the issue of all the difficulties with number that might be experienced by the child. Secondly, there is the question of understanding money as a system of tokens.

Addressing difficulties associated with money

One way to approach problematic issues associated with money might be, again, through the use of Diennes equipment or Numicon (see reflective activity on p. 177 below). Rods and cubes can be made up into bundles representing the value of the money in the decimal system first, and used as long as necessary until the transition to, firstly, toy money and then to the real thing.

Time

Supporting a student to acquire a concept of time is not the same as teaching him/her to tell the time. As Piaget (1969) noted, time is a complex concept. It can refer to points in time, duration and sequence of events, frequency of events and intervals between them. The point of reference in relation to many indicators of time is not consistent. For example, 'late' could refer to a point in the morning, if a student should have arrived earlier, or to a point at night. Even our sense of the passage of time seems to distort depending on the activity and our engagement with it, or lack thereof.

Addressing difficulties with the concept of time

It is not a straightforward matter to see how to use Bruner's framework of the three modes of representation – enactive, iconic and symbolic – to differentiate activities and approaches for students who experience difficulties in the area of time because no concept of time is concrete, as Grauberg (2002) points out. However, using a timer or some sort, perhaps one invented by the students themselves, might help in the initial stages. Students might be asked to see how much of an activity they can complete before a sand timer – or their own timer runs out. A way to encourage a sense of the duration of time is to focus on the intervals between events – for example, the silence between the sounds emitted after striking a percussion instrument. Concentrating on the sounds themselves might encourage a sense of time when understood as the frequency of events. To encourage the concept of sequence, a teacher might first organise an activity for children to act out a regular sequence of events in their own lives. Then s/he might represent sequence as a series of pictures (Bruner's iconic mode of representation) and ask children to arrange the cards in a logical order and talk about it.

In terms of telling the time, use of a digital clock or watch is a simpler option than a traditional clock face. However, to do this is to lose the context of the passage of time. The hands of the traditional clock face move in the twelve-hour cycle, but the numbers on a digital timepiece simply change. These days the concept of a visual timetable for use in schools with young children and older children who experience cognitive difficulties is quite common (Selikowitz, 2008).

Specific numeracy difficulties

Many students identified as dyslexic often have good conceptual understanding in general terms. However, in the area of mathematics, up to around 60% of these students experience difficulty in understanding mathematical concepts and learning computational skills (Joffe, 1983; Henderson, 1998; Miles & Miles, 2004). Mathematics covers a range of topics: size, time, shape and space, but all these aspects require competence in basic arithmetical skills. The term 'dyscalculia' is often used to describe difficulty in grasping computational skills and, despite ability in other areas, difficulty in reasoning and understanding of basic mathematical concepts. Many of the difficulties experienced by dyslexic students in information processing also affect their progress in mathematics learning:

- left–right orientation difficulties;
- sequencing problems;
- memory weakness;
- poor spatial awareness and skills of perception;
- slow speed in information processing;
- poor understanding of mathematical concepts.

Addressing orientation difficulties

For some students, differentiating between words indicating direction may be problematic: up and down, in and out, and so on. We learn to read English from left to right. However, in mathematics lessons, they are often expected to work in columns down the page, and from right to left. Writing letters and figures the correct way round may be inconsistent. To address this, teachers might encourage students to use multisensory strategies, for example, by tracing over large letters or numerals or drawing them in sand, with clearly marked beginnings and ends, simultaneously saying the name of the letter or number aloud.

Addressing sequencing problems

Sequencing days of the week and months of the year, and setting out work in a logical progression, may all prove tricky. Sequences may be chanted or practised rhythmically, or tapped on a hard surface very regularly to address this problem.

Addressing memory weakness

Learning and remembering tables, the alphabet, and so on may well be problematic for some students. To develop more immediate concentration and memory, they might be asked to look at a variety of objects or geometric shapes on a tray, or sheets with pictures or numbers written on them, for a minute or two, then asked to recall what they saw. They might also discuss with each other what strategies they used for memorising the objects, shapes or numbers. These strategies[1] might then be practised deliberately.

---

[1]Memory strategies are often called mnemonics.

Students may experience difficulties in making simple calculations without the support of fingers or marks on paper. Mathematics relies heavily on previous learning, so those students with a poor memory can have major problems. Constantly emphasising understanding can assist students whose memory for rote learning is poor because it gives them a way to start from 'first base' rather than relying on memory. Sometimes students can benefit from working in collaborative groups with peers to discuss the question first to ensure that they have all understood it.

Lever (2003) offers a way of supporting pupils to work out their tables that she calls 'finger tables'. To use this method, the pupils have to know their tables from 2 times to 5 times. Then the teacher might instruct the pupils to:

> Put their hands, palms up, in front of them. Begin to number the fingers and thumbs – for example with a small white label of felt tipped pen – starting with the thumb on the left hand side. The left hand thumb is '10', the forefinger is '9', middle finger '8', ring finger ''7' and little finger '6'. On the right hand the thumb is also '10', forefinger '9' and so on.
>
> To multiply two numbers, first put the relevant finger tips together, for example 7 x 7. The two fingers touching and the two on the far side of these should be totalled (2 + 2 = 4) and used as the 10s (i.e. 40). The nearside fingers on the left hand (i.e. 3 of them) should be multiplied with the nearside fingers (i.e. 3 of them) on the right hand – 3 x 3 = 9. Then the two numbers 40 + 9 should be added together – 40 + 9 = 49.
>
> To multiply 7 x 8, put the relevant finger tips together. There are two fingers touching and three on the far side = 5 fingers (50). Multiply the three nearside fingers on the left hand with the two nearside fingers on the right hand: 3 x 2 = 6. Then 50 + 6 = 56. (Wearmouth, 2009, p. 142)

Weavers (2003) also suggests that children should use a 'table square' (see above) rather than a calculator for multiplication of two numbers up to 10. Table squares contain obvious patterns of numbers which students might find interesting and memorable.

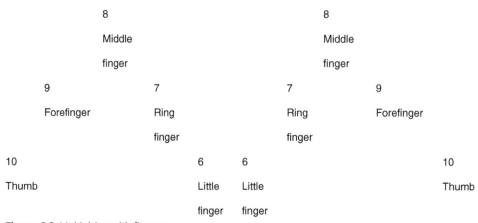

Figure 6.2 Multiplying with fingers

Addressing poor spatial awareness and organisational skills

Not all dyslexic students have poor visual perception skills, but a considerable number do. Some students find it difficult to interpret maps, outlines, block graphs, the representation of three-dimensional shapes on two dimensional paper, and so on, as well as the copying of data from the board or from a text. The current author has experience of teaching a number of secondary-aged pupils who might begin their work anywhere on the page: in the middle, to the right or left, without apparently noticing. Her dyslexic students might draw bar charts of any height or width seemingly at random or might be unable to understand what is meant by a term such as 'right angle' because they could not easily recognise the shape at sight or recognise it when drawn in perspective. Quite often it helps to enable access to concrete objects first, for example building bricks and blocks of all sizes. The author remembers teaching a severely dyslexic, but otherwise very intelligent, young man to recognise the shape of a right angle. First, she asked him to look straight down at the sharp-edged corner of his desk and run his hands round the right angle many times until he was used to the shape, feel and sight simultaneously. Then she transferred attention on to representing the right-angled corner on to paper.

Some students experience difficulty – sometimes extreme – in organisational skills which may manifest itself in perceiving and, therefore, using structures to organise personal thinking and working. In terms of mathematics, those who experience difficulties of this sort may well experience difficulty in

- understanding and using the decimal system;
- organising:
- quantities;
- word problems in mathematics;
- spatial arrangements.

Eleven-year-old Matt, for example, was one of the author's students who would begin his work at any point on the page. He could not easily 'see' pattern and organisational structure, so it is hardly surprising that he had not grasped the idea of the regular arrangement of base 10 and the decimal system.

Grauberg (2002, p. 66) suggests that, where students experience this kind of difficulty, it is important to provide them with

> a working model that can illustrate the underlying structure of the decimal system clearly and memorably. They need a tool at their fingertips, a picture in their minds, ready for use.

One way to do this is to support the student to conceptualise a 'field of 100', consisting of a square with ten rows of ten dots marked on it, each row of ten with a gap in the middle.

Students can then see straightaway that ten is made of 5+5. Then, by covering two of the dots in one row, that it can consist of 8+2, and so on. Similarly, numbers can be counted in tens and students can see the relationship between 10, 20, 30 and so on to 100:

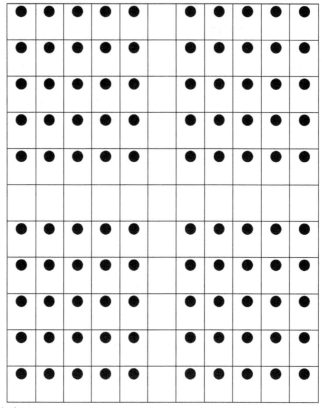

Figure 6.3 Field of 100

Seven, for instance is seen as five-and-two and is instantly recognised as such; 70 is recognised as five-rows-of-ten-and-two-rows-more. Numbers are thus seen as two-dimensional geometrical shapes, as 'quantity pictures' rather than as points on a number line. (Grauberg, 2002, p. 66)

This arrangement of dots is useful for supporting students' understanding of the position of numbers under 100 within this arrangement of dots.

Using Cuisenaire rods is another way to build up a concept of base 10, using groupings of 1, 5, 10 and 50.

 Reflective activity: Recognising spatial difficulties

How might you recognise the degree to which a student experiences spatial difficulties?

● Do you have experience of working with students who experience difficulties similar to those described below?

● If so, what did you do about it?

Spatial difficulties might manifest themselves, to start with, by inability to match shapes or line up piles of wooden blocks easily. Eleven--year old Matt, mentioned above, could never set out work straight on a page, could not discriminate between the left- and right-hand pages of his exercise books, and had terrible problems in drawing and interpreting any kind of graphs. He was also very clumsy. The author saw him once trying to stack tables in a school dining hall and he somehow managed to trap his head in between them in the awkward way in which he was working.

A number of studies (Bishop, 1983; Choat, 1974; Wheatley & Wheatley, 1979) together with anecdotal evidence from personal experience lead the author to believe that supporting children to work with concrete materials together with a multi-sensory approach of finger tracing and/or handling different sorts of geometric shapes whilst simultaneously verbalising appropriate terms relating to the activity can have some very positive results in developing spatial awareness. Later, children can be supported to recognise the significant features of graphs and charts, again by finger tracing over the features that have significance to the meaning and interpretation whilst verbalising these.

 Reflective activity: Considering theoretical underpinnings of mathematics programmes

There is a popular mathematics programme, Numicon, built on a multi-sensory approach to teaching maths that is designed for

- developing conversation, mathematical reasoning and problem-solving;
- exemplifying the principles of maths mastery with concrete apparatus and imagery to ensure deep understanding is embedded.

Details of this can be accessed at: https://global.oup.com/education/content/primary/series/numicon/?region=international, accessed 22.02.16.
  How do you think these principles reflect the concepts of

- interthinking to support learning, from a socio-cultural understanding of learning (see page 159 above);
- Piagetian understandings of stages of learning, and/or Bruner's modes of representation (see pages 15–16 *and* 18–19 above)?

Addressing slow speed in information processing

 Reflective activity: Time to complete work

Pressure on dyslexic/dyscalculic students to complete work in a given period of time may cause undue stress, anxiety, and further mistakes in the effort to finish on time. Many of these students take a long time to process information thoroughly. Inability to recall information instantly and difficulty in learning number bonds and tables by rote is likely to disadvantage them. One secondary student told the author, for example, that he was 'always exhausted' at the effort it took to do the same work that others coped with easily and that he needed a lot of sleep as a consequence.

As a teacher, how would you ensure that such students are encouraged to work at their own pace so that they can complete what they start, take pride in their achievements and not become discouraged?

Addressing poor understanding of mathematical concepts

A dyslexic/dyscalculic student may spend a long time on repetition and drill with the result that s/he has little understanding of mathematical concepts or the conventions used in mathematical problem-solving. Mathematical word problems are complex because students need to understand the context in which the problem is set, the logic of the word problem and also the mathematical procedures that are required to reach a solution.

For many students, the very fact that the teacher is aware of the specific difficulties that students may face may well be a relief. A useful starting point is to ensure that pupils understand the problem in the first place. It might be helpful to encourage them to talk to each other about what they think it means – to inter-think – partly to check understanding of the logic of the problem and partly also to ensure that they have read the text properly. Alternatively, or in addition, students might close their eyes and visualise the problem. Then they might either use concrete objects such as counters or blocks, or draw a picture, to represent the problem before attempting to work out the solution.

Multi-sensory teaching by using all the senses simultaneously wherever possible, will, again, help many students. For example talking students through processes while they are carrying them out, repeating the sequences they should follow aloud and encouraging them to do this also can be very helpful.

Assessing specific difficulties in mathematics

Assessment should seek to build on strengths – to identify what the pupil can do and understands – and also identify the procedures, concepts and skills where s/he experiences barriers to mathematical learning. In an assessment, knowledge of a mathematical term is no guarantor of understanding. Including practical apparatus may be important, for example in assessing spatial concepts such as opposite and between, or the concept of a fraction.

Expressing a mathematical problem in written form may create barriers for some students in demonstrating what they know and can do mathematically. Many students present their own idiosyncratic layout of mathematical operations, for example column displacement in setting out computations. Coping strategies might include using tally charts or fingers.

As El-Naggar (2001, p. 11) advises, where assessment uses written symbols to obtain a result that reflects the student's ability it may need to be carried out not just by checking written examples but also by

- listening to the pupils read symbols aloud;
- presenting a task in written symbols for the pupil to carry out (using apparatus);
- asking the pupil to write down in symbols a problem presented orally;
- observing the way a pupil approaches a problem;
- asking the pupil how s/he reached an answer;
- analysing error patterns.

Understanding, and use, of space and shape may also be problematic for some pupils. A lot of the assessment of pupils' strengths and weaknesses might be carried out with objects rather than diagrams.

El-Naggar (1996, pp. 20–1) offers some specific examples of children's mathematical errors. Ten-year-old Sally:

> was working horizontal additions and producing some very strange answers without discernable patterns.
>
> e.g. 5+4=8
>
> When asked to explain how she arrived at her answer Sally verbalised, 'Five add four ... you take the five and then you take six (pencil traced the down stroke of the numeral four), seven (pencil traced the horizontal stroke of the four), eight (pencil traced the horizontal stroke of the four), so the answer is eight.'
>
> Sally was confusing the numeral four with tally marks. What was really alarming was the length of time that the errors ... had gone undetected.

Analysing mathematical demands of learning activities

In a previous chapter we suggested that addressing the difficulties in learning experienced by students may be a question of problem-solving where the teacher makes a deliberate effort to get to know the student, thinks about the difficulties s/he experiences, reflects on the demands of the particular area and then matches the learner's strengths and areas of difficulty against the demands of the curriculum area.

 Reflective activity: Analysing the demands of a mathematics task prior to planning a lesson

In terms of mathematics, in order to be proactive, it may well be worthwhile to carry out a task analysis of a new topic, in other words to analyse the particular demands of the task before teaching the lesson (Chinn, 2012).

Look carefully at Table 6.1, think about a mathematics activity that you might wish to carry out in a classroom, and list what you think the demands of that activity might be for those students who experience difficulties in mathematics learning.

How might you take account of those demands when planning how you can differentiate the activity in a classroom context?

Table 6.1 Analysis of potential areas of difficulty and possible teacher strategies

Area of difficulty	Possible teacher strategies include:
Confusion with directionality. This manifests itself in starting computations in different places, confusion with place value, writing numbers the wrong way round, insecurity with right and left, difficulty with the concept of rotation, working with decimal points, and so on.	• Making calculators available; • Making squared paper available with left and right marked on it; • Writing headings 'HTU' for each computation; • Practising estimating by teaching students to round up and down so that they can check if their answers are approximately correct.
Problems with vision and perception, in particular the recording of symbols, for example, numerals and function signs.	• Teaching the symbols for numbers in small groups where numerals with similar shapes, for example, 6 and 9, are not introduced at the same time; • Writing the symbols +, −, × and ÷ on different coloured cards; • Encouraging students to trace over the symbols +, −, × and ÷ whilst simultaneously saying their names; • Verbalising the signs < and > and showing how they can relate to movement on a number line.
Problems with reading texts. Omissions, errors or reversals of words may mean that a mathematical problem is unintelligible.	• Encouraging a reciprocal teaching approach where students work in groups, expect the text to make sense and discuss mathematical problems and possible solutions together; • Using correct terminology while talking about mathematics; • Supplying reading lists of mathematical terms essential to the concept being taught and helping students to learn them by the same method that the school uses to teach reading; • Helping students to highlight the core parts of written questions.
Problems with remembering terms such as 'circumference', 'radius', 'diameter', 'hexagon' and so on.	Encouraging students to develop their own systems of mnemonics for these terms.
Problems with organisation that might relate to sequencing and spatial issues. These problems might present themselves in keeping books and files organised in a systematic way, untidy page presentation, loss of pens, pencils and other equipment.	• Giving very clear instructions about page layout, and model that is expected; • Giving clear exemplars to individuals, or to all students in the class; • Insisting that lines are drawn with a ruler by all students and that drawings are done in pencil; • Encouraging students to use squared paper and to write one digit per square; • Allowing sufficient time for the work to be completed neatly; • Ensuring that tasks are completed.
Acute anxiety about mathematics which might show itself as working very slowly, or even work avoidance.	• Considering how to include the students who experience the greatest difficulties in mathematics in whole class activities such as questions and answers, or practice of tables, without humiliating them publicly; • Listening to students' worries and concerns and taking account of them; • Creating opportunities for working in well-organised collaborative peer groups.

Support from parents and families

It may very well be worth considering how to form working partnerships with parents and families to support young people to overcome barriers to their mathematics learning. The concept of home–school mathematics boxes with games and/or other mathematics materials has become increasingly popular. A number of published materials, for example Numicon, are available for such initiatives and some schools will already have access to these. In other schools it may be that the teacher has to create them him/ herself. Some schools will already have very good, effective partnerships with parents and parents and families may be accustomed to coming into the school to discuss with teachers what they can do to help their offspring, while others will not. Whatever the case, it is really important that families are thoroughly familiar and confident with the materials and how to use them before working with them at home with their children, and also that they have access to the school to talk through any issues that may arise. Achieving a positive working relationship with families often requires a great deal of sensitivity on the part of schools, especially if parents or carers are not confident in mathematics learning themselves.

 Reflective activity: Enabling families to support their children's mathematics learning at home

Think about a school context with which you are familiar. Note down all the factors that you would have to take into consideration if you intended to set up a home– school initiative for those young people who experience difficulties in mathematics learning. Among the factors you might consider are, for example:

- your aims in establishing such an initiative in the first place;
- which school/college staff should, or might, be involved;
- how to establish the nature and degree of difficulty in mathematics experienced by the student(s) and what kind of programme would best meet their needs;
- available resources;
- ways to make contact with parents and families, some of whom may not feel confident in discussing their children's mathematical difficulties with teachers, or may feel that this is an intrusion on their privacy;
- who, at home, whether parents/carers or other family members including siblings, might be prepared to spend time helping the child to overcome the difficulties they experience;
- what kind of support these family members would need to enable them to assist the child effectively and over which period of time.

From your own experience and knowledge of the context you have in mind, you may well feel that there are also other very important issues to take into account.

Summary

There is evidence that the mathematics curriculum for students known to experience difficulties can be very narrow and restrictive. However, as the Cockroft Report (1982, para 243) advocated many years ago, certain elements that are required in mathematical teaching to all other pupils should also be apparent in teaching those who experience particular difficulties:

- explanation by the teacher;
- discussion between the pupils and the teacher, and between pupils themselves;
- practical work appropriate to the concept being taught;
- reinforcement and practice of basic skills and routines;
- application of mathematics to everyday situations;
- problem solving;
- investigations.

🖉 6.1

El-Naggar (2001, p. 9) suggests that teaching in mathematics follows the sequence below:

Step 1: a clear explanation of what we expect our pupils to do, inviting questions and discussion.

Step 2: Provision of materials and time for them to understand that explanation in their own way, while working together and discussing (through games, puzzles, problems and role playing).

Step 3: Recording and reinforcing through the use of work cards, text books and recording individual/group results.

Difficulties in learning of the sort described in this and previous chapters that are not recognised or acknowledged by the teacher can be important contributors to poor classroom behaviour by some students. The following chapter picks up on this issue as well as others in outlining approaches to understanding and addressing student behaviour that may be experienced as challenging in schools and classrooms.

Chapter 7
Focus on behaviour in schools and colleges

The major questions in this chapter are:

- What kind of classroom organisation and approaches to teaching can predispose to positive behaviour so that fewer problems arise in the first place?
- How can behaviour experienced as anti-social or challenging be understood in the context of schools and colleges?
- When does such behaviour create barriers such that special or additional provision is required to meet them?
- How can such behaviour be addressed?

Introduction

The discourses used in schools around problematic behaviour really matter because they can have a strong effect on the way teachers deal with students and their parents or carers. This chapter adopts a position that all young people, including those whose behaviour in classrooms can be experienced as challenging, have a fundamental need to belong. It is crucial for teachers – and everyone else, for that matter – to understand that belonging is a fundamental human need (Maslow, 1943; Bruner, 1996).

🖱 7.1

As we discussed in Chapter 1, the human mind actively makes its own sense of every situation. It is very easy to blame a young person for poor behaviour, especially when it disrupts lessons and other students' learning. However, schools themselves play a critical part in shaping a young child's identity as a learner (Bruner, 1996; Wearmouth, Glynn & Berryman, 2005). As Cummins (2009) notes, the more learn the more we want to learn. Students are more likely to make an effort and engage in learning when their sense of self is affirmed through interactions with teachers (Glynn, Wearmouth & Berryman, 2006).

Careful account should be taken of students' own sense-making and ways in which young people's behaviour relates to the way that they make sense of their worlds, even if this may be experienced by teachers and families as uncomfortable at times. Young people spend a third of their day at school (Rogers, (2003). During that time teachers are in a position to provide structured frameworks within which these young people can be taught alternatives to unacceptable behaviour that offer a sense of belonging and increase self-control.

It is clear that teachers and families can put themselves into a much stronger position to deal with problematic behaviour by recognising that the way children behave occurs in interaction between the learning environment and the individual and therefore may be addressed by factors within classrooms and within schools as well as factors associated with those children (Wearmouth, Glynn & Berryman, 2005). We begin this chapter with a discussion of the links between school failure, disaffection and challenging or otherwise socially inappropriate behaviour. In this discussion we consider the importance of ensuring that the learning environment predisposes to positive learning and behaviour and thus reduces the probability of disaffection in the first place and reflect on frameworks to underpin this at school and classroom level. We offer an overview of the theories that we draw on to discuss understandings of behaviour experienced by peers and teachers as anti-social, and go on to discuss ways to address the issues, in particular as these relate to attention deficit/hyperactivity disorder (AD/HD), physical aggression and bullying.

Links between school failure and challenging behaviour

Across the United Kingdom teachers are expected to take responsibility for promoting good behaviour in classrooms and elsewhere, have high expectations and maintain good relationships with pupils. Individual student behaviour should be understood within the context of the school as a whole, as well as the classroom or other location where the behaviour occurs.

 Reflective activity: Links between school failure and challenging behaviour: interview with 'Katherine'

Take a few moments to read the extract below from an interview transcript in which a young adult, 'Katherine', describes her feelings about the difficulties in learning that she experienced all through her schooldays, her consequent disaffection from all things related to schooling and the socially unacceptable behaviour that accompanied this. At the time of the interview she had just decided that, as an adult, she wanted to learn all those things that she had failed to learn at school and that were, in her view, currently holding her back. As you read this, reflect on the point(s) at which Katherine's difficulties might have been addressed and how.

What, then, do you want to do all this [learning to read, basic number work, etc.] for?

To prove to myself that I'm as good as anybody else, to get better grades, to be able to stand there and write things down, to write letters – and also, for people in the same situation as myself, to say to them: 'Why don't you go and do something?' […] Everybody should have a chance.

Can you think of one thing that happened that made you suddenly stop and say to yourself: 'Right, I'm going to do something about this'?

Yes. I was standing in Halford's and I wrote out a cheque three times. I was totally embarrassed. It was in front of a queue of people and the shop assistant. In the end I just gave her my credit card and walked out. I felt everyone was looking at me and thinking: '[…] "Oh, she's thick." […]'

How old were you then?

I was twenty.

How old were you when you realised that you had a problem with reading?

Spelling to me now is very, very important. When you first leave school, if you can't spell you con your way through it somehow. But when you get to my age, you get to thinking that there's not always going to be someone around to help you writing letters to friends, applying for jobs, writing cheques, quite a varied range of stuff.

I remember one time – I must have been about 6. I got no spellings right at all, and I just sat there and cried. Everybody else knew about it as well because she read the spellings out. Then I got people taking the mickey because they thought it was really funny. [They said] Oh, she's thick, she's stupid. She doesn't know what she's doing. Really cruel things like children say to one another.

Did it affect your reading as well?

Oh, yes. I wouldn't read anything. I used to do anything to get out of reading aloud. When we used to choose books from the library, I used to pretend that I'd read them. I'd read the back cover, and then make the rest up. If I was made to read aloud, I'd read really quietly and then the teacher would get really annoyed. She'd say she couldn't hear, and tell me to stop reading. I didn't want people laughing at me, so whatever I could do to protect myself I would do. I'd make her get fed up, and then she wouldn't ask me to read. That was the way of it. I've missed out so much by not reading books. Some of the children's books – I've really missed out by not being able to read them. I suppose to read a book you need to use your imagination, but my mind has not been trained to imagine things, so I can't do it. That's just my little theory.

[…] By the age of 13, at upper school I totally and utterly gave up – on school, on teachers. I just thought they were there to give you a hard time. Everyone seemed to be against me, whatever I was doing, and in the end I just mucked around. To get a bit of attention. I never did any homework. I got into trouble, but I just gave up – and they gave up. They just put me in the group of other kids who just mucked around. Obviously, you've always got people in the class who want to muck around. You're blaming the teacher, so if you can wind them up enough […] I used to write all over the tables because they hated it. I'd take the mickey of them by calling them names out loud in class. We knew one teacher's Christian name, so we called it out loud. Whatever you could do to disrupt the class, you'd do it. The French teacher used to go out of the class, so we'd get hairspray and set light to it as it sprayed out.

One French lesson, my friend got this little bottle of gin and we just sat there drinking it under the table. I don't think it's right that some teachers just used to come in, set the work, and then go off for 45 minutes. If you've left a bunch of 15 year olds, they're not going to do the work, are they? I think if I had had the proper help with reading and spelling I would not have dropped back as much as I did.

Looking back at school, what sort of things could teachers have done with you that would have helped?

They did the best thing by taking me out. I would not have done the work with other children watching me. It would have been worse. What should have happened is that the teachers should have found out what the problems were properly, sat down and listened to me, talked to my parents, and got everybody involved – for me and other children like me. I knew what I was doing, but trying to write it down on paper was totally different.

I would read all the sentences wrong. It never made sense.

So you just sat there in this world of semi-nonsense?

Yes.

What are you doing now?

A nanny.

Is this what you really want to do?

No. I want to do some work with children with learning difficulties. I want to visit homes and see what parents want and need for the child. I need more college training. I need to be able to write reports. I need more independence. (Adapted from Wearmouth, 2015)

Katherine's is an individual account and we cannot generalise from it. However, her comments serve to reinforce some of the assumptions that one might hypothesise about the potential long-term consequences and effects on life chances of not addressing children's difficulties in literacy, or any other kind of learning, at an early stage. As an adult she felt humiliated at the public display of her poor literacy skills. She also felt cheated of opportunities that she might have had if she was competent in reading and writing. Her recollections of school experiences also reflect many of the comments recorded in Riddick's (1996) study of the personal experiences of 22 children, aged from 8 to 14 years and identified as 'dyslexic', and their families. Here, for example, children reflected on similar feelings of disaffection and of dread of 'visible public indicators' (Riddick, 1996, p. 124) of their difficulties in literacy, such as reading aloud and always being the last to finish work.

Establishing school and college environments predisposing to positive learning and behaviour

The link between the quality of teaching and student behaviour was clearly acknowledged in a report on behaviour in schools: the *Steer Report* (DfES, 2005) *Section*

2: Principles and practice. What works in schools that identified practical examples of good practice that promote good behaviour and that can be adopted by all schools. The report notes the importance of consistently applied policy and practice, and an understanding that good behaviour will not necessarily just happen. It needs to be taught by staff who model what they want through their own behaviour and who have access to training and support in behaviour and classroom management.

You will find a summary of the main points of the Steer Report uploaded on the website that is linked to this book.   7.2

Establishing positive classroom environments

A previous report into behaviour in schools, the Elton Report (DES, 1989) remains pertinent to today's schools and colleges despite the fact that it was written nearly three decades ago. It stresses (chapter 3) two important principles in terms of classroom activities:

> The classroom is the most important place in the education system. What happens there every school day decides how well the purposes of the system are being achieved. (para 1)
>
> In order to learn well, children need a calm and purposeful classroom atmosphere ... Teachers must be able to keep order. If they cannot, all the children in their charge will suffer. (para 2)

Elton, like a number of other authors since that time, found that the most frequent and wearing form of misbehaviour in class is 'talking out of turn and other forms of persistent, low-level disruption' (DES, 1989, chapter 3, para 3). Elton also commented that it is not always older or stricter teachers who are able to control classes most effectively. It is teachers who can command respect and, often but not always, those whom pupils like. These teachers know how to get the best out of children. (The current author remembers how, as a young teacher organising a trip for pupils to London Zoo, the coach driver nearly refused to drive the group when he realised that the two organisers were both young women. 'Where's the man?' he said, meaning the *older* man. The author's young female colleague and she were not amused, especially as the point was made in front of their pupils.)

Elton (DES, 1989) concluded that, to be effective, teachers have to:

- have good subject knowledge;
- be able to plan and deliver lessons which are coherent and engage pupils' attention;
- be able to relate to young people and encourage good behaviour and learning;
- deal calmly and firmly with inappropriate behaviour.

Teacher behaviour that relates most directly to pupil behaviour is group management skills where those teachers:

- establish positive relationships with their classes based on mutual respect;
- are able to create a classroom ethos in which pupils lose popularity and credibility with classmates by causing trouble;
- recognise potential disruptive incidents, choose an appropriate means to deal with them early on and prevent escalation;
- know what is going on around them;
- know how pupils react to each other and to teachers;
- are in full control of their own behaviour and model the good behaviour they expect of pupils.

Examples of teachers whose behaviour predisposes to poor pupil behaviour are described as

teachers who lack confidence in their own ability to deal with disruption and who see their classes as potentially hostile. They create a negative classroom atmosphere by frequent criticism and rare praise. They make use of loud public reprimands and threats. They are sometimes sarcastic. They tend to react aggressively to minor incidents. Their methods increase the danger of a major confrontation not only with individual pupils but with the whole class. (DES, 1989, chapter 3, para 8)

Applying the principles of positive classroom learning environments

 Reflective activity: Organising lessons predisposing to positive learning and behaviour

There is a lot of agreement in the literature that lessons that are organised and taught well support good standards of behaviour in classrooms.

Have a look at the list below and consider the extent to which you recognise Elton's list of teacher behaviours as useful in thinking about how to organise lessons that predispose to positive learning and behaviour.

Elton (DES, 1989, chapter 3) considers that classroom teachers should:

- know pupils' names, personalities, interests and who their friends are;
- organise the classroom environment and the lesson to keep pupils engaged and reduce opportunities for disruptive behaviour. [A student of mine once reduced the incidence of disruption in her primary classroom simply through having equipment, including stationery for the pupils, properly organised and available prior to the start of the lessons];

- pay attention to pupil groupings;
- match work to pupils' attainment levels;
- be enthusiastic;
- use humour to create a positive atmosphere in class;
- continually 'scan' the behaviour in the classroom;
- be aware of their own behaviour, including stance and tone of voice;
- model the standards of respect that they expect from pupils;
- emphasise praise for good behaviour as well as work;
- make the rules for classroom behaviour explicit from the first time they meet pupils in class, and explain why they are needed;
- be consistently firm but not aggressive or sarcastic, target the right pupil not the whole class, criticise the behaviour and not the person, be sparing but consistent with punishments, reprimand pupils in private not in public, and follow through whenever a consequence has been specified;
- avoid punishments that humiliate pupils;
- analyse their own performance in classroom management and learn from it.

Elton (DES, 1989) recommends the introduction of peer support groups to develop the trust and confidence needed for mutual observation and consultancy,

Reflective activity: Learning from colleagues in a safe environment

How might you self-audit your own classroom organisation and behaviour?

Are you in a position to ask a trusted colleague to observe and audit a lesson for you? If so, how might you create a safe context for your colleague to do this and discuss the observations afterwards?

It is important to note Elton's advice that such classroom observation should not be inspectorial but involve commenting on each other's teaching. 'This is probably the most effective method of classroom skills training available' (DES, 1989: Chapter 3, para 42).

7.4

Classroom provision that supports social and emotional aspects of learning

Some educators consider that, in classrooms, all children can benefit from support to understand and manage their feelings, work cooperatively in groups, motivate themselves and develop resilience in the face of setbacks. Difficulties in these areas are likely to have a negative influence on learning and achievement. In the mid-1990s the Department for Children, Schools and Families (DCSF) in England commissioned curriculum material to be used as part of schools' personal, social and health education programmes. This material is known as *Social and Emotional Aspects of Learning (SEAL): Improving behaviour, improving learning.* Primary SEAL has been available since 2005, and secondary since 2007. The programme is based on a number of social and emotional aspects of learning: self awareness, managing feelings, motivation, empathy and social skills. For primary schools the programmes include: *New Beginnings, Getting on and falling out, Say no to bullying, Going for goals!, Good to be me, Relationships and changes.* Secondary SEAL in Year 7 provides materials, and makes them relevant to the secondary context, to build upon Primary SEAL. It also includes approaches to promote professional development for whole school development.

 Reflective activity: Reducing the likelihood of student conflict and school exclusions

The authors of the SEAL materials claim: 'Evidence shows that well-designed SEAL programmes contribute to school improvement through better academic results, more effective learning, better behaviour and higher school attendance. SEAL supports inclusion and contributes to reducing the need for exclusions providing staff and pupils with ways of managing and resolving conflict' (http://www.pshe-association.org.uk/uploads/media/27/7415.pdf, accessed 19.02.16).

Access the website noted above to view the range of available materials for yourself.

How straightforward do you think it would be to evaluate the extent to which the implementation of a programme such as SEAL has met its aims in a school?

To do this, of course, you would need to have a baseline of behaviour, academic achievement, attendance levels and exclusion rates against which to assess progress over time.

Theories underpinning approaches to understanding and addressing anti-social behaviour

Understanding and addressing behavioural issues related to groups of, and individual, students is, as in other areas of educational need, complex. As we discussed in Chapter 1, there are a number of different theories of learning that are commonly used to underpin classroom management techniques as well as programmes designed to address individual needs arising from anti-social behaviour. One in particular that we refer to here is behaviourism.

Use of behaviourist approaches to establish a consistent learning environment

Most commonly, understandings and strategies in teaching socially appropriate behaviour in classrooms are based on principles from a behaviourist psychology frame of reference (Skinner, 1938; Baer, Wolf & Risely, 1968). As we saw in Chapter 1, behavioural methodologies hold that all (mis)behaviour is learned and, therefore, that learning and (mis)behaviour can be modified through intervening in a systematic, consistent, predictable way in the environment.

Classroom and school rules are examples of antecedent conditions (or setting events) that are intended to signify behaviour that is acceptable or appropriate. Such rules can also provide punishing consequences for behaviour that is unacceptable.

Ways to teach appropriate behaviour to individual students in the classroom

 ### Reflective activity: Use of behaviourist principles to underpin planning in the assess→plan→do→review cycle (DfE, 2015)

When a young person's behaviour in the classroom is experienced as anti-social and in order to take action during an early stage in the assess→plan→do→review cycle (DfE, 2015), a teacher may well decide to draw up a behaviour plan for an individual of a group that is based on behaviourist principles.

As you read the section below, think about and then note down whether and how you might incorporate suggestions of Rogers (2013) and/or Sproson (2004) into the plan.

As Rogers (2013) comments, a child's background is no excuse for poor behaviour. From a behaviourist perspective socially acceptable behaviour is learned and can, therefore, be taught as part of day-to-day classroom activities. Strategies to maximise students' learning of new behaviours include 'shaping' which breaks complex tasks down into a series of steps, and ensures that each step is reinforced in a particular sequence. Other procedures include modelling, where students are rewarded for matching the behaviour being displayed for them.

Key to motivating pupils to choose appropriate behaviour are 'positive reinforcers': teacher praise, rewards of various sorts and positive communications with parents. If children disrupt the lesson they should take ownership of this and be given a reminder what the rules are: 'Jayson … you're calling out … Remember our class rules for asking questions, thanks' (Rogers, 2013, p. 238). In classrooms, younger children can be given a non-verbal cue to appropriate behaviour and shown clearly what is expected.

Adults' behaviour is very important in modelling and reinforcing specific ways of behaving in particular situations. In doing so it is really important not to allow oneself to be drawn into a power struggle that some young people find rewarding and that is likely to reinforce the way they are behaving. Students may imitate negative as well as positive behaviour however, so, for example, the use of abusive or sarcastic language should be avoided at all costs. This might entail modelling ways of resolving conflict which respect the rights of students to learn and feel safe, and

- meet the needs of both parties, that is, provide win-win outcomes wherever possible
- bring an end to the conflict, or at least reduce it
- do not leave either party "wounded" . (Sproson, 2004, p. 319)

There are a number of techniques based on behaviourist principles that can enable teachers to avoid power struggles with individual students in classrooms and prevent the escalation of anti-social behaviour:

- Some young people may take pleasure in not doing what they are asked immediately, especially if there is an audience of peers. In this situation Rogers (2013, p. 240) among others advocates that, in the classroom, teachers build in a brief 'take-up' period for pupils to respond. Make the request, walk away so as to imply compliance, and acknowledge compliance when it happens.
- The 'broken record' approach (ibid.) also encourages teachers to repeat a request a number of times, calmly, without being drawn into the kind of argument.
- Pupils bringing inappropriate objects into classrooms, or engaging in inappropriate activities might be given what Rogers (2013, p. 242) calls 'directed choices'. As a newly appointed teacher, my own sister was once in a situation where teenage girls brought long sticks into her mathematics lesson in a class where every student had been suspended the previous term – to test her out, as they later admitted. She simply responded by directing their choices: 'Shall I put them in this cupboard or that one? I'll keep them safe for you till the end of the day.' They never asked for them back.
- Where, on evaluating progress, it is clear that a young person's behaviour has not improved following the first iteration of a behaviour plan, it might be appropriate to review the plan and take further measures in the next iteration, again using behaviourist principles in so-called Multi-Element Planning (Pitchford, 2004).

Taking further action through Multi-Element Planning (MEP) (Pitchford, 2004)

Multi-Element Planning (MEP) is one practical approach currently used in parts of the United Kingdom as well as in other areas of the world. It involves a very systematic approach to identifying the apparent stimuli for the behaviour, adopting preventive strategies and/or drawing up a further behaviour plan. This approach takes account of the following:

- potential causes of difficulties experienced by the child;
- factors that appear to maintain the behaviour seen as challenging or otherwise of concern;

- strategies related to improving the learning environment, the teaching skills that will be useful to the child;

- strategies that will prevent the recurrence of the problematic behaviour or provide a way of safeguarding the child, peers and staff when the behaviour does recur.

One of the issues to be considered in MEP is that of ethics. Where teachers deliberately set out to change students' behaviour then there is always a question of how that teacher's power is exercised, what behaviour is seen as preferable and why, and in whose interest it is that the behaviour should be changed in this way. Pitchford (2004) poses the following questions before any assessment or intervention is devised:

> What gives us the right to manipulate or change someone's behaviour?
>
> How certain are we that the problem behaviour is not a perfectly reasonable response to unreasonable circumstances?
>
> If we do intervene, how ethically sound are our techniques and what is their record of effectiveness [...]? (Pitchford, 2004, p. 311)

In his work Pitchford references the MEP described by LaVigna and Donnellan (1986) which has four main components:

- Strategies that 'examine whether there are mismatches between the child and his/her environment that require a change in the environment not a change in the child' (Pitchford, 2004, p. 312). Change strategies should be considered in relation to interpersonal, physical, and instructional contexts in which the behaviour occurs.

- Positive Programming which involves 'teaching children skills that will have a positive impact on their lives working on the assumption that learning is empowering, gives dignity to the individual, helps them get their needs met and helps them cope with an imperfect world' (Pitchford, 2004, p. 313). Three areas of skill development are addressed: general, functionally equivalent and coping:

  - general: 'academic or life skills that the child has not mastered that are having a negative impact on his/her quality of life' (Pitchford, 2004, p. 313);

  - functionally equivalent: that is, socially acceptable skills or behaviour that will serve the same purpose for the student as that which is seen as unacceptable. 'No matter how strange, behaviour always has a purpose or a function (LaVigna and Donnellan, 1986). If we understand that purpose or function we are more likely to be able to channel it in a constructive way' (Pitchford, 2004, p. 314). Pitchford offers examples of 'problem behaviours and their functions together with the functionally-equivalent skills that could be included in a multi-element plan to help the child achieve the same end'. If, for example, the function of 'shouting out' behaviour is understood as initiating social contact, then the child might be taught to raise his/her hand and wait quietly, or raise his/her hand and say: 'Excuse me Miss/Sir. I've finished my work.' If the function of making a silly noise is to raise classroom excitement levels and make other children laugh, then the child might be taught how to tell jokes and/or the right and wrong places to tell jokes;

○ coping skills designed to help students 'manage and tolerate the frustrations and difficulties in their lives'.

● Preventive Strategies, comprising the antecedent control strategy and the use of reward strategies (LaVigna and Donnellan, op. cit.):

○ antecedent control strategies include removing those events that act as a direct trigger to problem behaviours (Glynn, 1982);

○ reward strategies only work well when they are used in the context of the types of positive programming and ecological strategies described earlier. Rewards can be artificial. The teacher will not always be there to reward the child and since our aim is to teach the child to be independent, rewards may only be a short term expedient . . . From a behavioural perspective, basically there are three ways of rewarding children (LaVigna and Donnellan, op. cit.):

1. Rewarding children for being 'good'

2. Rewarding children for not being 'naughty'

3. Rewarding children for being 'naughty' less often than they were before. However, as Pitchford comments, this technique may be inappropriate for behaviour seen as dangerous.

● Reactive Strategies which 'are included in the plan in order to safeguard the child, his or her peers and staff when things go wrong . . . In particular we should know what safe non-punitive techniques will be used if the problem behaviour occurs and what support will be given to the child. Just as important is consideration of the practical and emotional help or support that should be given to the member of staff' (Pitchford, 2004, p. 321).

 Reflective activity: Including the four components of MEP in a behaviour plan

Now reread the four main components of MEP listed above and reflect on:

● ways in which MEP clearly reflects the principles of behaviourist approaches to understanding learning;

● how much training it would need for you to be able to use MEP effectively;

● how much time you think it would take to use MEP to work out a plan that would address an individual student's anti-social behaviour;

● how you would take the ethical issues noted above into account when carrying out MEP.

Understanding attention deficit/hyperactivity disorder (AD/HD)

One kind of anti-social behaviour that may be at the extreme end of the continuum is so-called attention deficit/hyperactivity disorder (AD/HD). Sometimes this is addressed through programmes based on behaviourist principles, but often it also includes the use of medication.

 Reflective activity: What is known about attention deficit/hyperactivity disorder?

Take a few moments to note down what you already know about AD/HD:

- how it is identified;
- difficulties associated with it;
- approaches to addressing difficulties.

AD/HD is one of the conditions that is sometimes attributed to a biological cause. It is described by Norwich, Cooper and Maras (2002, p. 182) as '... a medical diagnosis of the American Psychiatric Association' that is 'characterised by chronic and pervasive (to home and school) problems of inattention, impulsiveness, and/or excessive motor activity which have seriously debilitating effects on individuals' social, emotional and educational development, and are sometimes disruptive to the home and/ or school environment'. According to the British Psychological Society (BPS, 1996), between two and five per cent of British school students are believed to experience this condition. There are interesting differences in the reported incidence of AD/HD internationally which are explained by some researchers as related to prevailing variations in cultural practices.

In Britain and Europe, the tradition has been 'to use the diagnostic systems of the International Classification of Diseases (ICD) published by the World Health Organisation' (1994, p. 13) where there is a strict requirement for 'pervasiveness and persistence'. This means that behaviour seen largely in one context only does not constitute grounds for a diagnosis. The criteria for diagnosis in the ICD-10 manual (World Health Organisation, 1994) are that the child should have demonstrated abnormality of attention and activity at home and at school or nursery, for the age and developmental level of the child. The 'directly observed abnormalities of attention or activity' must be 'excessive for the child's age and developmental level'. The child should 'not meet criteria for pervasive development disorder, mania, depressive or anxiety', the difficulties should have begun 'before the age of 6 years' should last 'at least 6 months'. The child should have a measured 'IQ above 50'.

While checklists of behaviour in diagnostic manuals might be an expedient way to classify adults' perceptions of students' behaviour, defining AD/HD as a mental disorder may be problematic. The BPS (1996, p. 23) comments that 'The pattern of AD/HD-type behaviour might be maladaptive to environmental requirements, but it is not necessarily the result of psychological dysfunction.'

Ways to address AD/HD

 Reflective activity: Ethical issues associated with the use of psycho-stimulants to regulate behaviour

As you read the discussion below of the various ways commonly used to address AD/HD, think about and note down the ethical issues that are involved.

In some cases, a medical diagnosis of the cause of serious challenging or inappropriate behaviour in schools may result in a prescription for particular kinds of medication. The use of psycho-stimulants is based on a theory of biochemical imbalance: 'The medication stimulates areas of the brain regulating arousal and alertness and can result in immediate short-term improvements in concentration and impulse control. The precise mechanism is poorly understood and the specific locus of action within the central nervous system remains speculative' (BPS, 1996, pp. 50–1).

Some researchers suspect that stimulants work through the release of neuro-transmitters, powerful chemical messengers. Neurons in the brain do not actu-ally connect to each other. There is a gap between them. Neurons communicate through neurotransmitters that are passed between them. Many researchers have suspected that AD/HD may result from problems related to communica-tion between neurons. Of the most commonly used stimulants, methylphenidate (Ritalin) is most widely prescribed. It is usually administered in the form of tablets to be taken regularly.

Defining AD/HD as a mental disorder is problematic, however. As the BPS (1996, p. 23) notes: 'We have evidence that children given the diagnosis ADHD don't attend, don't wait and don't sit still. But just because they don't do all these things does not mean that they cannot do them.'

In any case, although the prescription of a chemical psycho-stimulant is fairly common, as noted by the BPS (1996), prescribing a drug provides an insuffi-cient response. 'Medication must not become the first, and definitely not the only, line of treatment' (BPS, 1996, p. 2). Students' core values associated with self-identity, self-esteem and a sense of purpose as a functioning member of a social and cultural group must also be considered in addressing overall well-being. Arguing from a behaviourist position, Rogers (1994a) suggests that effect-ive approaches should focus on the effects of consequences through positive reinforcement, response cost and training in the reduction of behaviour viewed as problematic. Individualised behaviour management strategies should make clear to pupils what behaviours are unacceptable and also provide opportunities for modelling, rehearsing and reinforcing behaviours that are acceptable (Rogers, 1994a, pp. 167–9).

In a summary of 150 intervention studies of students with AD/HD (BPS, 1996, pp. 47–8), seven approaches were identified which reflect Rogers' (1994a) view. These approaches focus on the effects of consequences through positive reinforcement, response cost and training in the reduction of behaviour viewed as problematic. Positive reinforcement or token reinforcement was shown to result in reduced activity, increased 'time on task' and improved academic performance. 'Several studies showed that behaviour management and medication were most effective when combined'(BPS, 1996, pp. 47–8) Mildly aversive procedures (reprimands or redirection) should be effective with primary-age children, especially when combined with positive reinforcement. A combination of positive and negative reinforcement procedures and 'response cost', that is mild punishment designed to make the undesirable behaviour more difficult and more of an effort to perform, was also identified as successful in some studies.

Responsibility for administering chemical psycho-stimulants

One major concern about the use of such psycho-stimulants relates to the effects and side effects of these drugs. There is also an ethical issue concerning the lack of adequate monitoring of the day-to-day classroom learning and behavioural outcomes of medication prescribed for many students:

> [E]ducational practitioners are concerned about the so-called 'zombie' effect (Sharron, 1995) which may be the result of inappropriate doses and poor monitoring. There is also evidence of 'behavioural rebound' in the afternoons when the medication wears off. These concerns illustrate the practical issues of managing medication at home and at school [as well as the ethical risks in relying on medication alone, without providing appropriate learning tasks and activities that attract positive reinforcement, to bring about behaviour change at school]. (BPS, 1996, pp. 51–2)

 Reflective activity: Responsibility for administering medication

It is really important that you are aware of statutory guidance in relation to where the responsibility lies in schools and colleges for administering medication to students.
  The publication below applies only to schools and colleges in England. Check this point in your own geographical area if this lies outside England.

In England, schools' governing bodies have the responsibility for ensuring effective implementation of policy, including provision of a named person with overall responsibility for policy implementation. Statutory guidance (*Supporting pupils at school with medical conditions. Statutory guidance for governing bodies of maintained schools and proprietors of academies in England*, DfE, 2014e, §19) makes it clear that any member of school staff may be asked to support pupils with medical conditions and they should take into account the needs of pupils with medical conditions that they teach. This includes administering medicines, but they cannot be required to do this:

> School staff should receive sufficient and suitable training and achieve the necessary level of competency before they take on responsibility to support children with medical conditions. (DfE, 2014e, p. 12)

Guidance is also available for schools in Scotland, Northern Ireland and Wales at www.medicalconditionsatschool.org.uk/documents/Legal-Situation-In-Schools.pdf – accessed 27.06.16 .

Physical confrontation and aggression

On occasions, students may be aggressive, out of control and a danger to themselves and others, whether or not their behaviour has been identified as of concern, and whether or not a behaviour plan has been drawn up for them. Whatever label might be given to difficult behaviour, dealing with severe behaviour incidents is far more challenging and stressful for a teacher or others than dealing with mildly disruptive incidents. However, an appropriate response is often the same.

Ways to deal with physical confrontation and aggression

It is very important to minimise the risk of physical confrontation in the first instance, rather than having to take action after the event. Dunckley (1999, p. 16) comments that students who are 'in an agitated state' need 'guidance and direction to increase their sense of security … where possible and appropriate give a choice, time for the student to respond, then, after an appropriate time, follow through with consequences'. It seems sensible for teachers to avoid confrontations with students where these can be avoided and use physical restraint only as a last resort to manage a dangerous situation.

> In a non-statutory advisory document on the use of 'reasonable' force in schools in England (DfE, 2013b, p. 4), school staff are advised that reasonable in this context means 'using no more force than is needed' to control or restrain young people:
>
> - 'Control means either passive physical contact, such as standing between pupils or blocking a pupil's path, or active physical contact such as leading a pupil by the arm out of a classroom.

- 'Restraint means to hold back physically or to bring a pupil under control. It is typically used in more extreme circumstances, for example when two pupils are fighting and refuse to separate without physical intervention.'

School staff are urged always to try not to cause injury, but it is acknowledged that 'in extreme cases it may not always be possible to avoid injuring the pupil.' All members of a school staff have the power to use such 'reasonable' force, and this includes searching pupils for 'prohibited items' such as knives or illegal drugs.

In Northern Ireland the Department of Education has made a 'model policy' available to schools on the use of 'reasonable force' also (DENI, 2002).

Bullying behaviour in schools and colleges

An example of student behaviour which is the focus of teachers' concerns in many schools and colleges is that of bullying. Such behaviour can be explained from a variety of viewpoints.

Views of what constitutes bullying

Rigby (2002) concludes that, from his analysis of work on what constitutes bullying behaviour (for example, Olweus, 1993, 1999; Randall, 1991; Smith & Sharp, 1994; Farrington, 1993), bullying is a combination of the wish to hurt somebody together with hurtful action, an imbalance and unjust use of power, enjoyment on the part of the bully, the victim's feeling of oppression and, often, repetition of the bullying behaviour. Rogers (2003, p. 129) views bullying as forcing others to do, act and feel the very things a bully would never want done to him/her. Government guidance in England (DfE, 2014c) advises that bullying means behaviour by an individual or group, repeated over time, that intentionally hurts another individual or group either physically or emotionally. Bullying can take many forms, including cyber-bullying.

The cycle of bullying

 Reflective activity: Personal experiences of bullying

Think about your own experience of bullying, and consider the following:

- Have you ever been the victim of bullying behaviour, or have you ever been the perpetrator of bullying yourself?
- If so, how did it make you feel?
- Looking back, to what would you attribute this behaviour?

Bullying is often associated with an imbalance of power between victim and per-petrator. Once the victim begins to react to the bullying by showing signs of stress, the bully or bullies may experience great pleasure and enjoyment from their feel-ings of power and dominance. The cycle of bullying may continue and/or grow more intense and continue for a long time. Sometimes the victim may fight back (literally), sometimes she or he may find ways to avoid the bullying by hovering around teachers or staying at home. Do you recognise any of this from your own experience?

Despite the risk of supporting the use of stereotypes, there does seem to be some con-sensus among researchers about the correlates of victimisation. For example, victims of bullying may have low self-worth and self-esteem, be non-assertive and have poor social skills, be introverted, relatively uncooperative and physically less strong than others. They may also be physically shorter than others, be lonely and isolated, and prone to anxiety, depression and suicide (Rigby, 2002, pp. 139–40).

Ways to address bullying behaviour

As with other areas of difficulty that require special or additional provision to meet them, the first step should be to ensure that the school environment predisposes to positive student behaviour and is unsupportive of bullying between peers. If, despite attention to the school environment, individual bullying behaviour continues, the next step may well be action through the assess→plan→do→review cycle.

Action at whole-school/college level

One of the crucial factors in accounting for the degree of severity of bullying in schools is the behaviour of bystanders. Research on bystander behaviour assumed popularity after the murder in 1964 of the New Yorker, Kitty Genovese, which became notorious as a result of the non-intervention of 38 neighbours who heard her screams for help for over 30 minutes but failed to assist her (Atkinson, R. L., Atkinson, R. C., Smith & Bem, 1993). Social psychologists researching what they termed 'bystander apathy' found that the presence of others seems to deter individuals from intervening in diffi-cult or dangerous situations where they could be of assistance to the person in danger or trouble. However, a training programme focusing on raising awareness of bystander apathy can be shown to make a significant difference to the preparedness of bystand-ers to help others in trouble (Beaman et al., 1978).

7.3   Bullies trade in secrecy, not from their peers but from adults. Breaking through this secrecy is crucial in addressing bullying of any kind. There need to be clear, school-wide consequences for bullying, otherwise the bully will continue in the belief that s/he can continue with impunity (Olweus, 1978). Such consequences need to be set out in a formal process for dealing with bullying behaviour in an educational context that emphasises rights-respecting behaviour. These consequences will be:

- known in advance and published in a school-wide policy document;
- explained to all students in relation to what the school means by bullying;
- discussed within classroom meeting time, during the establishment phase of the year, and at times when the school experiences any spate of bullying behaviour. (Rogers, 2003, p. 132)

State schools should have an anti-bullying policy (DfE, 2014c) which sets out the way that bullying should be dealt with in the school. This includes:

- bullying related to race, religion and culture;
- bullying pupils with disabilities or special educational needs;
- sexist bullying and harassment;
- bullying pupils because of their sexuality or perceived sexuality;
- cyberbullying (the use of mobile phones and the internet to bully pupils).

Action at individual student level

Responses to bullying behaviour in schools often fall into one of two categories. There are those that assume bullying is an anti-social act which needs to be reduced through the application of responses from a behaviourist approach, such as various types of punishment contingencies. From this view 'we can best proceed by identifying and punishing behaviour we wish to stop' (Rigby, 2002, p. 463). Typically any violation of rules is treated similarly whether major or minor. Policies may rely completely on 'rules and sanctions and zero tolerance for rule infractions' (Rigby, 2002, p. 238). Other responses focus on establishing respectful behaviour between people so as to minimise bullying through the abuse of power in personal relationships (Rigby, 2002). From this view, 'positive improvement in behaviour between people can be brought about through instruction, persuasion and modelling of respectful behaviour' (ibid., p. 238).

Bullying and the law

Under the Children Act 1989 bullying should be seen as a child protection concern when there is 'reasonable cause to suspect that a child is suffering, or is likely to suffer, significant harm'. If this is the case, staff should report their concerns to their local authority children's social care. Schools may need to draw on a range of external services to support pupils who are being bullied, or to address any underlying issue which has contributed to a child's bullying behaviour (DfE, 2014c).

In England Government guidance advises that schools should discipline pupils who bully, whether inside or outside the school premises. At the same time, the school should look at the reasons for the bullying and whether the bully also needs help.

If the bullying is extremely serious and the bully is over the age of ten, the bully could be prosecuted for a criminal offence, for example, assault or harassment. If the bully is under the age of ten, it may be possible to take legal action for negligence against the school and the local education authority for failure in their duty of care to the pupil.

In England, the guidance (noted above) about bullying for parents, pupils and teachers is available from the Department for Education at: https://www.gov.uk/government/uploads/system/uploads/attachment_data/file/444862/Preventing_and_tackling_bullying_advice.pdf – accessed 03.03.16.

Cyberbullying

The secrecy that supports bullying behaviour in schools and colleges is a major factor in explaining cyberbullying where the anonymity of the bully(ies) is likely to increase the fear or anxiety of the victim and the sense of power of the perpetrator.

Ways to address cyberbullying

Childnet International and the Department for Children, Schools and Families together issued guidance to schools about how to address cyberbullying in schools: *Let's fight it together. What we can all do to prevent cyberbullying* (Childnet International and DCSF, 2007–8) available at http://www.digizen.org/downloads/cyberbullyingOverview.pdf – accessed 15.08.16. Section 4 explains the rationale underpinning this guidance document:

> It is important to equip young people with strategies for getting out of situations involving inappropriate, unwanted or difficult contact online, and to leave them feeling empowered after the session. It is imperative that children and young people are aware of the school policies and strategies for dealing with cyberbullying. For example, it is recommended that all children are made aware of what cyberbullying is, what the sanctions are for cyberbullying, and to whom or where they can report cyberbullying behaviour.

Strategies that should be discussed with students include:

- Respect for others: Be careful what is said online and what images are sent. Ask permission before photographing someone.
- Forethought: Think carefully before posting information on a website. Information could stay online forever. Do not give your mobile phone numbers to others in a public domain.

- Maintain the confidentiality of passwords: Do not disclose these to anyone, and change them regularly.
- Block bullies: Websites and services often allow individuals you to block or report someone who is bullying.
- Do not retaliate or reply to bullies.
- Save the evidence of offending messages, pictures or online conversations.
- Report online bullying. Such bullying may be reported to a trusted adult, the provider of the service, the school or the police, if the cyberbullying is serious.

If pupil safety is compromised it is important not to promise confidentiality to the child. The child will need to know what will happen to the information, and why. The first point of contact following disclosure should be the designated child protection officer within the institution. An accurate account of what the child has disclosed should be recorded as soon as possible. If possible the child should be present when the incident is reported to the designated officer.

Practices and procedures to report and respond to incidents of bullying should already be in place in the school. Most cyberbullying cases can be effectively dealt with within existing systems.

In all cases of bullying, incidents should be properly documented, recorded and investigated, support should be provided for the person being bullied, other staff members and parents and carers should be informed as appropriate, and those found to be bullying should be interviewed and receive appropriate sanctions.

 Reflective activity: Advice about cyberbullying for head teachers and school staff

The Department for Education has issued a publication entitled *Cyberbullying: Advice for headteachers and school staff* (DfE, 2014) which includes sets of links to resources that offer guidance to professionals and families who might be concerned about what to do in cases of suspected cyberbullying. This is available at https://www.gov.uk/government/uploads/system/uploads/attachment_data/file/374850/Cyberbullying_Advice_for_Headteachers_and_School_Staff_121114.pdf

Access this document and the links that are embedded in it.

How useful and practical do you find the advice that is offered here?

Restorative practice

In some schools and local areas, particular programmes have been designed to focus on traditional community values in order to harness the necessary resources to address problems that have resulted in, and are a result of, unacceptable, unsociable behaviours (Schweigert, 1999). One such initiative is based in general terms on the principles of 'restorative justice'. The prime focus in a restorative justice approach is on 'putting things right' between all those involved or affected by wrongdoing. Restorative justice can employ traditional conflict resolution processes and culturally appropriate mechanisms drawn from the external community to address and resolve tension and make justice visible and more productive in communities inside the school (Anderson et al., 1996). In New Zealand, for example, where restorative justice practices are influenced by traditional Maori cultural values and preferred ways of responding to wrongdoing, the emphasis is on the restoration of harmony between the individual, the victim and the collective (tribe or subtribe). In order for restoration to take place, all those involved in the offence 'need to be heard in the process of seeking redress' (Restorative Practices Development Team, 2003, p. 11).

 Reflective activity: An example of a restorative approach

Wearmouth, McKinney and Glynn (2007) describe an example of restorative practice from New Zealand. As you read the text below, consider whether and how this kind of approach might be used in schools and colleges in the United Kingdom.

In this example the teachers, mother and wider family members of 15-year-old 'Wiremu' had become increasingly concerned about his negative, challenging behaviour in school and anti-social activities outside. Things came to a head when he took his mother's car out joyriding and crashed into the neighbour's garden, damaging the gnomes given to the elderly neighbour by his deceased wife. The behaviour support teacher to whom he had been referred organised a meeting at the local rugby club where Wiremu was a keen member, and invited everyone who knew him to attend. When the boy arrived, unaware of the true reason why he was being taken to the club, everyone was given a chance to speak about him, teachers, community elders, friends and relations. Mostly it was in very glowing terms – about his captaincy of a rugby team, his personal qualities, and so on. Then his mother talked about the loss of the car that meant so much to the family, and the neighbour talked about his dead wife and the broken gnomes.

What happened next surprised everybody. Wiremu stood up to speak. He was crying. He turned to the elderly neighbour whose garden he had wrecked and asked to be forgiven. He offered to help mend the fence, to sort out the plants in the garden and to repair the garden gnomes. The [behaviour support] teacher recalled him saying: 'As a child I remember your wife … she used to give my sister flowers to take to mum. She was always smiling and she had a nice face'. Wiremu hugged his mother and apologized over and over again (Wearmouth et al., 2007, p. 43).

Summary

Anti-social or challenging behaviour in classrooms and around the school is sometimes explained as a problem that stems from the student him/herself and his/her family or circumstances. This may be the case with some students. However, student behaviour in schools does not occur in a vacuum. All students' behaviours are situated in a social context and result from interactions between people and their environments or social events. Participation in school activities involves the whole person in its combination of doing, talking, feeling, thinking and belonging. It refers both to taking part in activity and also to the connections with others during this process. Personal identity in schools is constituted in the way in which learners participate in activities with others and, therefore, by definition, non-participation. The implication is that the most important concern should be first to establish effective whole class management and positive classroom learning environments in which individual disruptive behaviour is much less likely to happen. Often individual students are blamed for their own failure and/or disturbing behaviour in schools rather than looking to explanations at the way society is structured to favour some children, or at the level of school structure, organisation, curriculum and classroom management. This has meant that there has been no real pressure to change society's ills or to make schools more responsive to students' needs (Armstrong, 1994, pp. 141–2).

Despite the best efforts of the school to create an inclusive learning environment and to ensure high quality and curriculum support in classrooms, individual student anti-social behaviour may continue to be a barrier to his/her progress and disrupt the education of peers. In this case the barriers to learning resulting from this behaviour should be addressed through the assess→plan→do→review cycle, with a behaviour plan frequently based on behaviourist principles requiring consistency of approach in its implementation.

Chapter 8
Uses of technology to support learning needs

The major questions in this chapter are:

- What are some of the issues relevant to teachers who are interested in the way in which technology applications can serve to address difficulties in accessing the school curriculum that are experienced by students?
- What is the range of technology that is available in schools to support young people's special learning need?

Introduction

The potential effectiveness of particular technological devices and programs in supporting the learning and achievement of many young people who experience difficulties of various kinds, and, in some cases, in enabling greater independence, has been acknowledged for some time. Mitchell (2014, p. 192), for example, notes that, over 20 years ago, the US Congress expressed a view that appropriate technology can enable individuals to:

- have greater control over their own lives;
- participate in and contribute more fully to activities in their home, school and work environments, and in their own communities; and
- interact to a greater extent with non-disabled individuals.

In the current book, the devices and programs under consideration include the use of what might be termed 'assistive technology'. Here, 'assistive technology' refers to items of equipment or products that are used to increase, maintain, or improve functional capabilities of individuals who have disabilities of any kind.

It is easy to be impressed by new initiatives such as the development of technology usage. However, incorporating the use of new resources designed to support young people with special educational needs and disability (SEND) into everyday activities in schools and colleges requires careful planning. Just to take one example, Williams (2015, p. 13), from a study of users of websites with difficulties in learning, recommends 'having a fairly large text size', using a 'horizontally oriented menu list (or at least one that is unlikely to go below screen level if placed vertically)', including 'appropriate images where possible', and also audio. At the same time he notes provisos to these recommendations. Text size that is 'fairly large' is 'hard to quantify, as different screens and browsers display text in various ways'. Images 'do not necessarily aid comprehension' unless the user is thoroughly familiar with what they mean. 'Similarly, a large text size does not necessarily indicate an easier or faster read.'

The ability of the teacher in making decisions about what form(s) of technology are appropriate to address needs is as important as the technology itself. Firstly, there is the issue of ensuring that everything is in place where and when it is needed, and applying it appropriately. Then there is an important question of fairness in making (sometimes) expensive technologies available to some students but not to others. Schools, of course, also need to know the range of technology that has been developed, and which particular program, app or device has the potential to address which learning, physical or sensory need. Further, there are affective considerations to be taken into account. The views and feelings of the student are very important here.

Principles for effective use of technology to support individual learning needs

Developing ways of working with any unfamiliar resource can be challenging to the teacher, but beneficial. Becoming confident with the use of technology is no different. One head teacher described crucial factors in the development of technology provision to meet the special learning needs of young people with multiple and profound difficulties in learning in his special school as

- sheer 'bloody-mindedness';
- keeping the development of technology under control;
- stimulating interest among the staff by focusing on authentic, relevant uses of technology;
- giving staff 'something that will work the first time';
- offering staff training from well informed sources.

(Wearmouth, 2009, p. 178)

Matching technology resources to individual needs

Technology does nothing on its own 'but rather needs to be made to work in practice by the skill and perseverance of the school team' (Florian & Hegarty, 2004, p. 3).

 Reflective activity: How to match technology provision to individual needs

Do you have any experience of using technology to meet individual students' needs? If so, what do you feel are the most important issues to be taken into account when considering whether to make use of such technology?

In an early study, the National Council for Education Technology (NCET) (1995, pp. 8–9) developed a very useful checklist to assist the process of matching technology resources to the educational objectives set out on individual learning plans and on identifying appropriate strategies for support. This checklist maintains its relevance in the context of today's educational institutions. First, we need to think about the reasons for considering using technology rather than current available support, and the purpose this will serve for the individual student. In terms of

- *Context:* Why is the present provision inadequate? What evidence is there to support the need for technology?
- *Purpose:* What are the learner's goals in learning? What else, apart from technology, is needed to meet the learner's needs? Is the technology provision clearly mapped on to the learner's individual learning plan?

Then we should consider the availability of the technology, how compatible it is with the school's setup, and the training needs of both student and support staff:

- *Availability of resourcing:* Is the currently available technology in the school/classroom being fully utilised? Is any proposed equipment compatible with the technology already available in the school? Is the provision appropriate for the learner's age and development?
- *Support:* The tools of technology: word-processing programs, hand-held computers, and assistive devices such as switches and touch-screens, specialist keyboards and voice-activated software designed to overcome barriers to learning resulting from sensory or physical impairments all require the acquisition of skills to use that technology to best effect. Are the learner and any adults working with him/her familiar with any proposed resources? Do staff know where to find help?

- *Expectations:* Have the learner's and family's views been taken into account? What are the class teacher's expectations?
- *Management:* Are all staff committed to supporting a learner with technology provision in the classroom? Who will take responsibility for ensuring that the equipment is functioning correctly?

Finally we have to work out ways to evaluate the success of the provision and how to plan for the future learning needs of the student:

- *Monitoring:* What criteria will be used to monitor the effectiveness of the provision in enabling the student to meet his/her targets? What planning is in place to consider the student's changing needs, both in school and beyond school, and also developments in technology?

The principles in this checklist can be applied to any other form of resource which might be considered appropriate to meet particular learning needs. There is obviously the question of how far the particular resource can facilitate the individual student's access to the curriculum. There is also the issue of the time required for staff development and, crucially, that of budgetary implications.

More recently, Mitchell (2014, p. 195) has outlined guidelines that he suggests are important for those choosing technological devices or programs to be used by young people with a variety of learning or physical needs:

- involve the learner and his or her parents in selecting the device;
- customise it to suit the requirements of the learner and his or her usual environments;
- keep it as simple as possible and as similar as possible to those already in use;
- ensure that it is durable under the anticipated conditions of use;
- ensure that it is aesthetically pleasing, age-appropriate, fashionable and culturally acceptable; and
- give it an evaluation trial.

Issues of fairness

 Reflective activity: Responding to questions about fairness

Whenever there is a question of allocating additional, alternative or 'special' resources to particular students, inevitably the issue of fairness arises. On a number of occasions, when running a learning support department in schools the current author, for example, was asked by both colleagues and students: 'Why should x

(student identified as experiencing some kind of difficulty in learning) be given extra time and resources when other students are just as deserving?'
    How would you answer this question if you were asked this by a colleague?

Differences between equity and equality

To understand the issues of fairness and justice inherent in the paragraph above it is important, first, to be very clear about the difference between equal opportunities and equity in education. Both are concerned with fairness and justice. The concept of equality makes an assumption that all students start in the same place and that fairness therefore means making the same things available to everyone. The concept of equity, on the other hand, assumes that individual students are different and that some experience barriers of various kinds that prevent them from accessing the curriculum in the same way as peers, and achieving what they otherwise might do. Fairness in this case is making special provision available to enable students to overcome these barriers.   🖰 8.1
    There are other factors at play here also. For example:

- The kind of special provision which a student is deemed to 'need' or deserve implies a value that is being attributed to that student (Loxley & Thomas, 2007). This issue is clearly important in relation to the cost or availability of a particular equipment.

- There is often no clear dividing line on the continuum of need between those whose requirements for special provision are, indeed, special, and those whose requirements are lesser.

- The power of parents also has to be taken very seriously by schools in a climate of increasing accountability, recourse to litigation and parental choice of schools to which their children will be sent.

In summary, therefore, it is vital that teachers in classes where students have been allocated additional or special resources are very clear in their procedures and practices which must be open to scrutiny.

Justifying additional resources for some

The equity argument, overcoming barriers to access to the curriculum, is often used as a justification for providing additional or alternative resources for students in schools. The practical implications of putting this principle into practice will vary across schools, depending on

- the context,
- the particular aspect of the curriculum,
- the severity of an individual student's need.

There are schools where many of the students experience very great difficulty in communication with others, in mobility and in being able to control anything at all in their environment. Hence 'access' may imply:

- ways of being able to express a need, want or choice to someone else;
- means by which to move oneself about or to control aspects of the environment, to turn on a light or stimulate a sound.

For some students with the most profound difficulties in communication it is possible to devise sequences of communication systems from single preset greetings activated by a switch through to e-mail messages associated with voice simulation programmes and/or symbols representing individual words or whole concepts. Curriculum access for other students, for example those who experience specific difficulties in literacy, might be facilitated with the use of laptop computers with talking word-processors, spell check facilities and use of a printer.

Range of technology support for individual needs

 Reflective activity: Personal experience of the use of technology for young people who experience difficulties

Think back on any experience you have of using technology to address the needs of young people who experience barriers to their learning of various sorts.
    Did the technology achieve its aims?

At international level, over 20 years ago the Salamanca Statement (UNESCO, 1994, p. viii) stated a very clear principle that the right to an education for all must include children who experienced difficulties in accessing the school or college curriculum of various sorts:

> Every child has a fundamental right to education [...] those with special educational needs must have access to regular school which should accommodate them within a child-centred pedagogy capable of meeting these needs.

If we accept the assumption that 'every child has unique characteristics, interests, abilities and learning needs', and that 'education systems should be designed and educational programmes implemented to take into account the wide diversity of these characteristics and needs' (ibid.), it follows that teaching approaches must be differentiated to develop curricula capable of accommodating all differences. Appropriate use of assistive technology and its applications may certainly play a role in this. In support of this view UNESCO (2006, p. 48) stated that the use of technology

> can build the necessary bridge between the students' functioning and participation in school activities, offering them the possibility to learn. Through facilitating functional abilities, overcoming some impairment, eliminating architectural barriers, supporting the student, AT is the best ally, sometimes the solution, to let children with disabilities take part in the educational process to the full.

A wide range of devices and software has the potential to meet aspects of a wide range of difficulties within and across the four areas of need outlined in Chapter 4, as well as literacy and numeracy difficulties discussed in Chapters 5 and 6, provided its use is very carefully considered and matched to the individual, the curriculum and the learning context.

Addressing physical difficulties through the use of technology

Students with physical impairments may have difficulties in motor control and may experience reduced or no movement; imprecise movement, low speed and muscular strength; fatigue or difficulties in hand–eye coordination. They may experience other difficulties in addition, for example, cognitive, visual, hearing and verbal language difficulties.

Sometimes simple technical adaptations can enable the student to participate fully in school or classroom activities. For example modified grippers attached to the hand and clamped to the pen, enlarged pens that are easier to grasp, weighted pens that reduce tremor and clips or magnets that stick paper to a desk can be useful in supporting the physical act of writing.

The kinds of physical access supported by technology can considerably reduce physical barriers to the learning of students with a greater degree of physical difficulty, using both hardware and software that have been specially designed for the purpose. For example, the standard computer keyboard with the numeric keypad on the right favours right-handed people. It is also sensitive. Strings of letters may appear on the screen if a key is held down too long. Keyboard behaviour can be changed, however, by using some of the features in, for example, Windows (http://windows.microsoft.com/en-nz/windows/make-keyboard-easier-to-use#1TC=windows-7, accessed 29.02.16). The use of 'StickyKeys' can enable one finger to be used to operate shift, control and alt keys. 'FilterKeys' allow adjustment to the length of time a student needs to hold down a key before it appears on the screen. 'MouseKeys' enable the mouse pointer to be moved around with the use of numeric keypad keys. Keyguards can be fitted for use when required. These have holes positioned over each key to make it impossible to press two keys at once but possible to rest hands and arms on the guard without pressing the keys (http://www.bltt.org/quicktips/foakeyguards.htm, accessed 29.02.16). For users with physical, visual or cognitive disabilities, 'IntelliKeys' can be used as a programmable alternative keyboard that plugs into the keyboard or USB port to enable typing, entering of numbers, navigating on-screen displays and carrying out menu commands (http://www.inclusive.co.uk/intellikeys-usb-keyboard-p2392#, accessed 29.02.16).

Different sizes and shapes of keyboards can also replace the standard keyboard, and the position of the keyboard can be changed to accommodate individual needs. Retractable lap trays bolted under the desk can hold the keyboard to enable a lower typing position if needed. Keyboards can be tilted, and switches and pointers can be fixed in specific positions where they can be handled more easily. Alternatively, on-screen keyboards enabling letters to be selected by a mouse or trackball can be used to make the selection. Some on-screen keyboards also have a facility for word prediction to make typing quicker (http://windows.microsoft.com/en-us/windows/type-without-keyboard#type-without-keyboard=windows-7, accessed 29.02.16).

The way the mouse operates, for example the speed, and the amount of time needed for double clicking, can be adjusted. The buttons can be swapped over for left-handed use. Mice also come in different sizes and shapes; and require varying amounts of pressure on buttons. A trackball is like an upturned mouse but it is a static device with the ball on the top which is moved with fingers, thumbs and palms (http://www.trackballmouse.org/, accessed 29.02.16). Larger trackballs can be moved with the feet.

With screen-based devices such as touchscreens and a light pen, which is a light-sensitive stylus wired to a video terminal that is used to draw pictures or choose an option from a menu, selections and movements can be made by pointing at the screen surface. However, where a user is physically or cognitively unable to use any keyboard or pointing device, then a starting point can be to use a switch. This is a button which sends a signal to the computer to control the software. Switches can be operated by any controlled movement of the body.

In recent years some companies specialising in technology in education, in particular in the area of SEND, have produced software for mobile devices that includes switch access. Inclusive Technology, for example, refers to its iPad and Android apps as 'carefully designed to meet a range of special educational needs including switch access for those with physical disabilities'. One of its apps that has been designed to support language acquisition is described as

> [a] simple sequential story activity that helps to develop early language. "It's a nice day for a picnic, let's call a friend. But what happens when it starts to rain?" Simply touch the screen or press a switch to unfold each part of the story to see what happens next. Bold, clear graphics, relevant sound effects and a clear sequence of events make this story suitable for young learners and those with additional needs. (http://www.inclusive.co.uk/apps/mobile-cell-phone – accessed 18.08.16)

Use of apps on mobile devices has the added advantage, in relation to provision for SEND, that these can be shared with others outside the classroom, most notably parents and families.

An example of the use of assistive technology to address physical difficulties

Lilley (2004, pp. 82–4) offers examples of programmes for individual students that have been developed to incorporate the use of technology for students with physical difficulties and/or multiple and profound difficulties in learning. For instance, 13-year-old Samantha had cerebral palsy and was 'functioning academically at her chronological age but has no expressive language and has poor fine and gross motor control'. The school made provision to give her more independent access to the computer:

- 'An ultra-compact keyboard with guard and a gated joystick allows her to move the cursor on the screen.
- A large 'jelly-bean' switch replaces the left-click function on a normal mouse.
- All the above are linked to a Mouser 3. The Mouser links a normal mouse plus a joystick (or other device). It is a device that connects between the mouse and the computer to allow switches to be used instead of the mouse buttons. It can turn off unwanted mouse buttons to avoid unplanned presses bringing up unwanted menus. It allows any or all of the standard mouse buttons to be turned off. It also allows switch access to these buttons for young disabled users.' (Lilley, 2004)

Lilley also describes the use of technology to support curriculum access for 11-year-old Ann who was confined to a wheelchair after a road accident when she lost expressive language. A jelly-bean switch was fixed to a specially adapted tray on her wheelchair, and Ann was encouraged to use a range of software programs designed to help learners understand the principle of cause and effect – a press of the switch causes a reaction on the computer screen.

In terms of software, content-free programs that can be adapted by the teacher can support access to concepts, skills and knowledge by enabling presentation of these in a variety of ways. Students can use computers to drive a robot round an obstacle course on the floor, for example, using the keyboard to direct its movements from, by instructing the robot how far and in which direction to travel.

Addressing visual difficulties

The effect of visual problems on a child's development and progress in a school depends on the severity, type of loss, age at which the condition appears, and overall functioning of the child. When a student's primary disability is visual, his/her visual needs must be carefully evaluated within the educational context so that appropriate technological resources can then be accommodated to him/her.

In mainstream schools, vision is the primary sense through which information is shared. Consequently, students with low vision or those who are legally identified as blind may need help in using their residual vision more efficiently and in using specially designed aids and materials.

A lot of special toys and games exist to support play and development of a visually impaired child. There are also enlarged and tactually labelled playing cards, Braille versions of common board games, dice, and computer games emphasising text and sounds rather than graphics. Both talking watches that can announce the date and time at the touch of a button and Braille watches are available (www.rnib.org.uk – accessed 18.08.16), as well as portable devices that 'read' paper money and voice the denomination.

Graphical User Interfaces (GUI) indicating the relative spatial positions of objects on the screen have been made accessible through the development of screen readers, which, in summary, translate the screen into speech pronounced by a synthesiser. As the American Foundation for the Blind (2016) outlines:

> Screen review software translates on screen information into electronic text. This electronic text is then sent to a speech synthesizer or a refreshable braille display. The user is then able to hear the text spoken or read it tactually with the refreshable braille display. (http://www.afb.org/info/living-with-vision-loss/using-technology/assistive-technology-videos/screen-reading-technology/1235 – accessed 18.08.16)

Hardware and software designed for Braille users can be used together with the software developed for screen reading with speech synthesis. Braille printers are now available that create tactile dots on heavy paper, making written documents accessible to visually impaired students. Current embossing printers can produce a tactile paper representation of the graphical content of a document, while the textual content is translated into Braille. It is now possible to print directly from any application running in the Windows environments, for example.

Screen magnifiers, with or without a speech facility, can support students who experience visual difficulties to access on-screen text, graphics, tool bars, icons through magnification, colour-changing options, speech, Braille output, and so on (Mitchell, 2014). The shape of the mouse pointer is crucial, as to its dimension, colour, borders, tail, and contrast with the background. Some free software is downloadable from the internet giving a wider choice of mouse pointers; see, for example, http://www.bltt.org/accessibility/winxp/mouse_visibility.htm.

Addressing hearing impairments through technology

Hearing impairments can have two major effects on students in schools and colleges: loss of the input of information from direct speech and inability to monitor personal speech output (UNESCO, 2006). The latter can cause significant impairment in oral communication and verbal language acquisition, both receptive and expressive and, consequently, especially for those with severe impairment, difficulties in school learning. In due course logical and problem-solving activities that are mediated by language use can be affected.

Particular technological devices can provide oral communication support for students with a hearing impairment:

- Hearing aids or cochlear implants can help to maximise whatever level of hearing a student has, but in many cases there remains the problem of background noise. Radio aids are used widely in schools and colleges to help address this problem. A radio aid consists of a transmitter, worn, often, by a teacher, and a receiver, worn by the student. The radio aid makes the teacher's voice clearer in relation to background noises.

- Computer-based feedback that represents speech patterns can be either tactile or visual. Tactile feedback (haptics) is based on the skin sensation of human organisms. Currently, for example, a jacket embedding sensors that vibrate in specific patterns to represent words is being developed to enable the profoundly deaf to 'feel' human speech (Kurp-Rice, 2015, http://www.futurity.org/deaf-vest-vibration-senses-893352/ – accessed 18.08.16). Alternatively visual displays in the form of subtitles or translation in the national sign language may be made available on a computer screen.

Other assistive technology is available to help to improve the quality of music and speech by connecting a student's hearing device to audio equipment, such as smartphones, tablets, MP3 players and games consoles. In the United Kingdom, the National Deaf Children's Society has a borrowing service for its members to try out assistive technology used for this purpose (http://www.ndcs.org.uk/family_support/technology_and_products/technology_test_drive_product_loan_service/products_for.html – accessed 18.08.16).

Addressing cognitive difficulties through the use of technology

Most students who experience cognitive difficulties can benefit from educational and assistive technologies. However, the use of such technologies to support those who experience the most severe difficulties must be carefully planned with regard both to accessibility and learning objectives.

A keyboard or a mouse may be difficult to use for students who experience slow and inaccurate hand–eye coordination, problems of response, and/or poor memory. Different access devices or options can be adopted, depending on the student's competence and the individual curriculum plan (see 'Addressing physical difficulties through the use of technology' (ms page 238; to update with page number)). Cognitively, the easiest means of selection is through direct pointing, so a touchscreen is often very useful to enable a direct control on the PC interface by means of a responsive and transparent screen surface.

A complex software interface with multiple types of text, graphics, sounds and feedback, and backgrounds full of illustrations and colours is probably not the most suitable for some students with very complex needs (UNESCO, 2006). Whilst multi-media software may be very attractive, teachers should monitor very carefully a student's understanding of what a program is all about and whether s/he can do what is expected.

In terms of programs, students who experience complex difficulties in learning and/ or require a very high degree of support might benefit from the opportunity to explore simulated or virtual environments in ways that otherwise might not be possible. Exploratory programs can enable students collaboratively to construct knowledge through, for example, simulations and virtual environments, as well as content-free programs. Having said this, however, encouraging students to engage in virtual worlds is no substitute for real life. One might think of a number of instances where using this medium is inappropriate. As an information and communication technology coordinator in a residential school for students with complex physical disabilities commented, for example, it is patronising to suppose that a computer simulation of a bus ride will substitute in every respect for students who find independent movement difficult (Wearmouth, 2009).

Some researchers, for example Fernandez-Lopez, Rodriguez-Fortiz, Rodriguez-Almendros, and Martinez-Segura (2013), have begun to exploit mobile devices to support the construction of learning activities in the 'real world' because they have the potential to provide

> freedom of movement between different locations within the school (classroom, dining room or playground) or outside (house, street, park, etc.). Users can always take out the application to be used when they need it. (Fernandez-Lopez et al., 2013, p. 78)

These particular researchers describe a project where they developed

> a mobile platform (based on iPad and iPod touch devices), called Picaa and designed to cover the main phases of the learning process: preparation, use and evaluation. It includes four kinds of educational activities (Exploration, Association, Puzzle and Sorting), which can be personalized by educators at content and user interface levels through a design mainly centered on student requirements, whose user profiles can also be adapted. (Fernandez-Lopez et al., 2013, p. 78)

In this particular project they showed how use of their mobile applications supported a measured increase in students' skills in the areas of language, mathematics, environmental awareness, autonomy and social.

Addressing language and speech needs through technology

For those with limited or no speech because of severe cognitive difficulties, including students with autistic spectrum disorders and difficulties in understanding language, as already noted in Chapter 4, Augmentative Alternative Communication (AAC) is a useful means of communicating with others. In supporting the development of expressive and receptive language, it can reduce frustration levels. An example of a software program for AAC is the symbol system produced by Widgit Software. Widgit explains this symbol system as follows:

> It is important to understand that symbols are different from pictures. We use the word picture to describe an illustration in a book, or a drawing on the wall. A picture conveys a lot of information at once and its focus may be unclear, while a symbol focuses on a single concept. This means that symbols can be put together to build more precise information.
>
> There are different types of symbols . . .
>
> Symbols are grouped in different sets. The most commonly used across the UK are Widgit Literacy Symbols (previously known as Rebus). (http://www.widgit.com/parents/information/ – accessed 26.02.16)

 =   ABC

Symbols   are   images   used to support   reading   text.

Symbols   help   people   understand   information   or   communicate.

Symbols   are linked to   words   to form   a symbol set.

Design   rules   help   people   understand   symbols.

Figure 8.1 Widgit Symbol Set

Widgit claims that symbols can help to support:

- *communication* – making a symbol communication book can help people make choices.
- *independence and participation* – symbols aid understanding which can increase involvement, choice and confidence.
- *literacy and learning* – symbol software encourage users to 'write' by selecting symbols from a predetermined set in a grid.
- *creativity and self expression* – writing letters and stories and expressing your own opinions.
- *access to information* – all of us need accessible information and this should be presented in such a way that the reader can understand and use.

(https://www.widgit.com/symbols/about_symbols/symbol_
uses.htm – accessed 26.02.16)

Among those students for whom Widgit claims to be able to cater with its symbol-based programs are those with communication, language or learning disabilities (http://www.widgit.com/sectors/education/special.htm, accessed 26.02.16).

 Reflective activity: Using assistive technology to reduce physical barriers to learning

Above we have discussed how a number of assistive devices are available to enable students to communicate, for example, electronic language boards, voice synthesisers and voice recognition software, screen magnifiers, with or without a speech facility, to support students who experience visual difficulties to access on-screen text, graphics, tool bars, icons through magnification, colour-changing options, speech, Braille output, and so on.

You might choose to access the following website: http://www.inclusive.co.uk/product-list?Text=screen%20magnifier – accessed 29.02.16 – and reflect on ways in which the devices described here might assist students' communication.

Addressing specific learning difficulties through technology

Among the most common specific learning difficulties are dyslexia and dyscalculia. Problems with oral expression, listening, written expression, basic reading skills or comprehension, and mathematics can predispose to difficulties in autonomous understanding of complex texts and problem-solving. Effective computer use can reduce problems through school or college, support reading acquisition, and improve spelling and intelligibility of written work.

Reading difficulties

Those who experience reading difficulties may be assisted with audio books that are available in a variety of formats, including CDs and MP3 downloads, optical character recognition (OCR) devices which enable text to be scanned into a computer or handheld unit and the scanned text then read aloud through a speech decoder, and speech synthesisers/screen readers that display and read aloud text on a computer screen, including text that may have been typed by the student (Mitchell, 2014). An example of a program to develop switch-accessible stories and slide shows is 'SwitchIt! Maker 2' (http://www.inclusive.co.uk/switchit-maker-2-p2353 – accessed 29.02.16). Each activity has a sequence of on-screen pages which can have a picture, video or text-based material, music or recorded speech. Pages can be turned by a simple switch, the computer's spacebar, the mouse buttons or IntelliKeys.

Recent developments of apps for mobile devices include those designed to assist reading, for example, 'Speak it!' (https://itunes.apple.com/gb/app/speak-it!-text-to-speech/id308629295?mt=8 – accessed 18.01.16), Webreader available for Android, Smartphones and iPads (http://www.getwebreader.com/ – accessed 18.08.16).

Writing difficulties

Using technology can also facilitate the physical task of writing for some pupils and/or support correct spelling, punctuation, grammar and word usage.

Word-processing can offer

> a means of drafting and re-drafting that is easy, efficient and accessible and so is a great equaliser in presentation ... Pupils can work more quickly and demonstrate different types of writing exercise and have the opportunity to experiment ... and thus demonstrate their true ability. (Lilley, 2004, p. 89)

The use of a word processor can encourage students whose writing or spelling skills do not adequately reflect their higher general level of performance and can produce results which may look as good as that of peers (Wearmouth, 2016a). The word processor may avoid the aversion that is often produced by pen and paper: the computer provides a safe environment for students who can take their time without holding the rest of the class back and make mistakes in private, without fear of humiliation. Some systems have practical features related to grammar and syntax. Using a word processor improves the content and presentation of work; students are therefore more likely to experiment with their writing and to express themselves confidently.

Anecdotal evidence from secondary classrooms suggests that technology may be particularly effective in encouraging older students to complete written coursework:

> L.C.: Please can you run me off another copy (a piece of extended coursework in English Literature)?
> Shirley: Why, L.?
> L.C.: Because I want to take it home to show my Mum. (Never been known before!)
> One of the lads, S.: Look at how much I've done. I've never written ten pages before.
>
> (Wearmouth, 1996, pp. 124–5)

Word processors with speech synthesis can be very powerful. Learners can hear what they have written, either as they are writing, or hear the whole text after they have finished. Sound can be introduced to text by dropping it into a standard text to speech utility or talking word processor. Sound to support reading and writing can be used in many different ways. Voice recognition is an alternative to typing on a keyboard. There can be a difficulty in the use of voice recognition software to support the writing of text, however, where students' words are not sufficiently clear to be encoded into text.

An example of a writing support and multimedia tool for children of all abilities is 'Clicker Writer'(http://www.cricksoft.com/uk/products/clicker/home/writer.aspx, accessed 29.02.16). At the top of the screen is a word processor, at the bottom the 'Clicker Grid'. This has 'cells' containing letters, words or phrases that teachers can click on, to send them into Clicker Writer so that students can write sentences without actually writing or using the keyboard. 'Clicker 7' has now been developed to work with 'eye gaze' software, so that those students who access computers through the use of eye gaze can now access a whole range of Clicker sentence building grids, word bank grids, writing frames, matching activities, talking books and speaking and listening activities (http://www.inclusive.co.uk/clicker-7 – accessed 18.08.16).

 Reflective activity: Awareness of issues relating to the use of spell checkers

Some writers have noted how software support such as spell checkers and word prediction facilitate the growth of the learner's communicative skills (UNESCO, 2006). Spell checkers can prevent students from making a huge number of mistakes in writing words; students can correct their document before printing it, and get advice from the built-in thesaurus. . Another useful tool for those with writing difficulties is the spelling predictor which predicts the word based on the first letter(s) typed. An 'intelligent' predictor will also learn the words commonly used, and put them near the top of each list. Word prediction can correct writing and can accelerate the writing rate.

What issues would you say that teachers should be aware of when encouraging to use spell checking software?

The main difficulty for a spell checker is the writer with faulty auditory perception/ articulation who uses bizarre spellings or has inconsistent errors. Many spell checkers expect the first letter to be typed correctly at least, yet some learners with literacy difficulties do not always do this. Other strategies will be needed by the writer. Even more useful is a spell checker that will speak the words as well, so that a writer does not have to rely solely on the visual medium to pick out the correct spelling. It is unclear, however, how far a facility of this type can be used by older students.

Mathematical difficulties

Students who experience difficulties with organising, aligning and copying down mathematical problems might well benefit from

- electronic mathematics worksheets (software programs that can help users organise, align and work through maths problems on a computer screen)
- talking calculators (calculators with built-in speech synthesisers that read aloud each number, symbol or operation key a user presses), and
- a range of drill and practice software. (Mitchell, 2014, p. 193)

A number of software programs are available that are designed to address many of the difficulties outlined in Chapter 6 which lead students to dislike mathematics, including poor skills in ordering and sequencing, poor short-term memory often associated with limited understanding of number-ness in the first place, and so on.

 Reflective activity: Reflecting on the uses of programs to support mathematics acquisition

An example of a program designed to motivate students and support better mathematics achievement is Numbershark – http://www.wordshark.co.uk/numbershark.aspx – accessed 20.08.16.

The program is advertised as addressing each of the four number operations together with fractions, decimals and simple percentages in small steps and including word problems.

'To help those with dyslexia and dyscalculia many of the games give a visual idea of what is happening when you add, subtract, multiply or divide. Numbers are shown as objects, digits, rods, or on an abacus, a number line, a number pad, a 100 square – to help basic understanding. Fractions and decimals are also shown visually.'   (http://www.wordshark.co.uk/numbershark/numbershark-school-use.aspx#Help)

Look at the website above and reflect on whether, or how, a program such as this might be used to support students' specific difficulties in the area of mathematics.

As with any other initiative it is essential that teachers are familiar with it so that they can match provision to needs.

Individualised tutoring

Some early programs became popular because they seemed to offer a solution to differentiate teaching for individual students who experience difficulties, for example in literacy and numeracy acquisition. In the area of literacy difficulties, for example, in the early days, individual learners were given programs designed to emphasise drill and practice only, for example ongoing drill in individual letter sounds, or simple number bonds with plenty of repetition and reinforcement. Later, more sophisticated design and so-called integrated learning systems (ILS) enabled the integration of:

- presentation of curriculum material, often in the area of literacy or mathematics;
- assessment of students' understanding of the material, typically through multiple-choice or single word answers, and immediate feedback;
- management of decision-making about what the next step should be in the learning process. If the student's answer is wrong, the software is often programmed to present similar questions to check the student's understanding more closely. Where the student continues to make errors, the system will present material to fill the gap in the student's knowledge.

Reflective activity: Reflecting on the uses of integrated learning systems

An example of an ILS is 'Successmaker', marketed in the United Kingdom by Pearson Publishing (http://www.pearsonschool.com/index.cfm?locator=PS2qJ 3&acornRdt=1&DCSext.w_psvaniturl=http%3A%2F%2Fwww.pearsonschool. com%2Fsuccessmaker – accessed 29.02.16). This includes courses in mathematics, writing, spelling and reading from Key Stage 1 to Key Stage 4. It is an online individualised reading and mathematics program with embedded ongoing assessment of a student's progress. The program is advertised as supporting students to work at their own level by providing step-by-step tutorials and interventions.

Look at the website above and reflect on whether, or how, an ILS might be used to support young people's learning needs.

It is really important to stress that teachers using the program are thoroughly acquainted with it so that they can decide whether and why it really is appropriate to their students' mathematical needs.

Use of the internet

Use of the internet appears, at face value, to be a very useful medium for supporting the communication needs of students. However, accessibility requires careful consideration of students' special learning needs (Mitchell, 2014, p. 195). Important issues associated with the use of the internet in relation to meeting students' special learning needs are as Wearmouth (2012) points out:

- 'Real' time access to raw information from the Worldwide Web is unrealistic for many students. This means that teachers will need to find time to save for future use any material that they or students have found interesting or useful.

- Use of e-mail provides purpose for reading and writing skills and is highly motivating to students. An e-mail system which integrates the use of a concept keyboard, symbols, a talking word processor and text, and which automatically deletes headers when messages are received would be useful.

- The creation of the schools' own website functions to advertise the school, publish students' work and, perhaps most importantly, reduce the isolation of a special school context by promoting e-mail links.

- There appears to be the potential for groups of teachers involved in modifying curriculum materials to share those materials in order to reduce time demands.

- There is a serious concern over the issue of equal opportunities where use of the internet has a clear contribution to make to the learning of students with a wide range of needs but many schools do not have the necessary prerequisites for its development: a member of staff who is knowledgeable and highly skilled in technology to act as the catalyst, a computer network, adequate resources, support from senior management, time and resources for staff training.

Mapping these potential barriers against the facilities provided by the software described above shows that recent developments have come a long way in making access a reality for many students with special learning needs.

 Reflective activity: Sensitive issues related to the use of the internet

Use of e-mail and video conferencing, on the face of it, might seem to be a very useful way to enable students with, for example, mobility difficulties to be able to communicate easily with peers. Where students are isolated from peers for whatever reason, for example the location of their home, or difficulties with mobility, it may seem especially appropriate for students to make contact through e-mail or video conferencing with peers elsewhere.

If you decided to introduce this kind of communication to a group of students, what factors do you think you should take into consideration?

The manner in which students are given choice of e-mail and video conferencing partners is very important. This is the kind of consideration that tends to generate very strongly held feelings about who, among the students, is allowed to be put into contact with whom.

Affective considerations

There is evidence that some students prefer working with a computer rather than having intensive tuition from a teacher (UNESCO, 2006). However, any individually devised program for a student must take into account that student's views and wishes as well as the purpose for which the program is designed. Even the most highly developed system will be useless unless the student is motivated enough to engage with it. There may, for example, be a stigma attached to its use, but this may well depend on the norms of the particular classroom or school. It may be seen as a high-status piece of equipment. Technology can motivate learners to acquire specific skills for reading, spelling and writing, as well as giving more general support in the curriculum (Singleton, 1991; 2002). Fear of failure is often thought to prevent some learners from making the effort which is needed for them to succeed (Lawrence, 1996). Part of the attraction of computers is their emotional neutrality. The learner with a history of failure is enabled to avoid situations of public failure and consequent damage to self-esteem. The computer can put learners in control of the learning situation and enable them to pace themselves, unlike the usual teaching situation where the teacher has the power and control.

Computer-based activities can allow learners with poor self-esteem to experience the success needed to boost their confidence, allowing written work to be presented to a high standard (Wearmouth, 2016a).

Summary

Rapid developments in technological devices and software have opened up new challenges for the use of technology for students with SEND in schools and colleges. Most recently, such developments

> have expanded through the ubiquitous access to smartphone technologies, including access to SMS messaging, Twitter and other forms of social networking. As well, exponential advances are currently being made in the development of AAC apps on iPhones, iPods, iPads and Android devices. Rapid developments are likely, too, in wearable technologies, image processing, nanotechnology and artificial intelligence. (Mitchell, 2014, p. 194)

Effective use of technology for students with special educational, or additional support, needs and/or disabilities in classrooms requires a clear understanding of a number of issues. Among these are accountability to students, parents, the school and other stakeholders such as local authorities; the principle of equal opportunities; the nature, availability and function of resources - human, physical and financial; and ways of embedding the use of unfamiliar technology into the curriculum.

Pragmatically, as Wearmouth, (2016a) notes, it is obvious that schools should ensure machines are working and available at the moment they are needed. Computers should be updated regularly so that they can accommodate new software as required. The school should have a licence to enable staff and students access to the relevant software. If machines 'crash', there should be contingency arrangements for ensuring that students' work is not lost. Enough time and specialist staff support should be provided to ensure that machines are set up for every student for whom special technology resources have been provided. Not to do so is to risk contravening the law.

Good practice in classrooms of teachers intending to include students who have been identified as experiencing special learning difficulties of some kind might be summarised as follows:

- Decide whether a computer, or other technological device, is needed to enable effective access to the curriculum by students.
- Determine how students will access the equipment and make the peripherals and furniture that are needed available.
- Ensure the use of technology, including apps on mobile devices, is integral to the curriculum as a whole.

- In classrooms where only one computer is available, make sure that tasks are devised so that a number of students have some access.
- Plan lessons to include students who experience difficulties in learning and those who have disabilities.
- Differentiate the classroom tasks to suit the different levels of students' learning needs.
- Ensure that these tasks are achievable, relevant to the particular stage of the curriculum and meaning to students.
- Avoid putting the computer and/or the classroom assistant at the edge of the group or class so that students identified as experiencing special learning needs are not marginalised.
- Encourage and support all the students in the classroom, ensuring that those who are less confident are not marginalised.
- Organise computer clubs as part of the extracurricular activities of the school. (adapted from Lilley, 2004)

Chapter 9
Professional relationships with others

The major questions in this chapter are:

- What is the range of people who may be involved in support for children who experience some sort of difficulty, and what is their likely role?
- How can we ensure, as far as possible, that additional in-class support, such as that offered by teaching assistants, is effective?
- What constitutes good practice in working with parents and families?
- What might be some of the constraints on multi-agency working, and how might these be addressed?

Introduction

It is highly likely that a student and his/her family will be involved with other agencies in addition to the school if s/he experiences more complex and severe difficulties (as well as some medical conditions associated with learning problems), especially if these have been identified before school age. All young people are different. Without the involvement of others it may not be possible for families or schools either to sort out the complex interaction of factors which result in difficulty in learning, or know how they might begin to address this. For teachers, parents and families, knowing when and how to interact with the range of professionals, inside and outside the school, who may become involved with a particular child is very important to the student's welfare and progress, even though on occasions this may seem confusing and time consuming. This chapter first outlines the roles of the range of people who might have an interest in supporting children who experience some sort of difficulty: the special educational needs co-ordinator, teaching assistants, parents and families, outside agencies, and so on. It then discusses challenges in relation to this kind of partnership work with examples of what might be considered good practice.

The special educational needs co-ordinator (SENCo)

In England, Wales and Northern Ireland the role of the special educational needs co-ordinator (SENCo) developed in response to the introduction of legislation related to the identification of children with SEN and a statutory requirement to meet their needs in schools. In the *Code of Practice* that retains the status of statutory guidance in Wales, for example, the responsibilities in primary and secondary schools (NAW, 2004, 5.32; 6.35) are defined as:

- overseeing the day to day operation of the school's SEN policy
- co-ordinating provision for children with special educational needs
- liaising with and advising fellow teachers
- managing learning support assistants
- overseeing the records of all children with special educational needs
- liaising with parents of children with special educational needs
- contributing to the in-service training of staff
- liaising with external agencies including the LEAs support and educational psychology services, health and social service and voluntary bodies.

Cole (2005) notes how school ethos and the values of individual head teachers have a direct impact on the role, status and, therefore, power of the SENCo to work towards an inclusive culture in the school. Without the support of the senior management team SENCos can face a very heavy workload with vulnerable children who are not particularly popular in schools in competition with each other for position on league tables of pupil outcomes.

In many places the role of the SENCo has developed considerably since the publication of the (DfES, 2001) Code. It may be allocated to members of the school senior management team or class teachers. SENCos may have responsibilities both at the level of the individual child and the whole school. They may take charge of budgeting, resource allocation, timetabling and other managerial and administrative roles. They may also work with individual students, as well as advising, appraising and training staff, and liaising with outside agencies, professionals and parents. The new *SEN and Disability Code of Practice* (DfE, 2015) that operates in England highlights the strategic nature of the role at the level of the senior management team in a school or college:

> The SENCo has an important role to play with the headteacher and governing body, in determining the strategic development of SEN policy and provision in the school. They will be most effective in that role if they are part of the school leadership team. (DfE, 2015, §6.87)

The day-to-day responsibility of the SENCo is outlined as:

> the operation of SEN policy and co-ordination of specific provision made to support individual pupils with SEN, including those who have EHC plans. (DfE, 2015, §6.88)

One of the issues for many SENCos is how to cope with the time demands of the role and, in particular, of the bureaucratic demands of assessment and planning for individual young people, evaluation of progress and the requirement for record-keeping that accompanies this. These days some SENCos have dispensed with individual plans for some children and use group plans instead. Some may rely on 'provision maps' which can be either documents that identify provision for individual children, or whole-school provision with analyses of student outcomes and value for money, or both.

In order to ensure that the SENCo is in a position to carry out this role schools and colleges are advised to

> ensure that the SENCo has sufficient time and resources to carry out these functions. This should include providing the SENCo with sufficient administrative support and time away from teaching to enable them to fulfil their responsibilities in a similar way to other important strategic roles within a school. (DfE, 2015, §6.91)

Support in the classroom

The use of support staff in the classroom to assist students who experience some kind of difficulty in learning or physical disability is common practice in many schools these days. The 'core' team in the classroom is usually the class teacher and one or more teaching assistants (TAs) (who, overwhelmingly, tend to be female). The rapid expansion in numbers of TAs has shifted the focus of TAs' work from simply preparing resources, general assistance, clearing up, student welfare, and so on, to duties much more clearly focused on student learning and achievement (Wearmouth, 2009). Most schools employ assistants in classrooms but their roles vary. They may, or may not, have some formal training.

The responsibility for student–adult interactions in classrooms, together with oversight of support staff's work with individual students, legally belongs to teachers. TAs, for example, cannot, legally, be in loco parentis (in the place of a parent) in the same way as a teacher can. However, as Lorenz (1998) comments, a second adult in the classroom can increase the child/adult ratio, make time to listen to students and their point of view and thus increase the amount of positive attention available to students. S/he can also be responsible for giving regular praise and encouragement to particular students while the class teacher takes responsibility for the learning programme, intervene early where misbehaviour is developing and nip problems in the bud, and give individual children space to calm down without disrupting the class. New TA roles have been introduced, for example 'learning mentors', in some schools.

Most schools employ assistants in classrooms but their roles vary. Infant and primary teachers may well have the help of a Nursery Nurse who may be trained in language and number skills and in social and moral education or qualified classroom assistant, at least for some of the time. Special Support Assistants (SSA)/ Special Attachment Welfare Assistants (SAWA)/Special Individual Teachers (SIT) may be employed in some schools to support children on Statements of SEN, Education, Health and Care (EHC) plans or co-ordinated support plans arising from the relevant Special Needs Code of Practice. SITs are trained teachers allocated to individual children. Special Teacher Assistants (TAs) are trained to work alongside teachers in classrooms, focusing on key curriculum areas such as mathematics and English. In many schools, parents come in to assist teachers in classrooms. Schools should have clear policies for parental involvement and may have a teacher with responsibility for partnership with parents.

Effective use of support staff in classrooms

 Reflective activity: Making best use of support staff

Currently there is a lot of focus on the use of support staff in classrooms, especially teaching assistants. Why do you feel this might be the case?

In your experience, how can teachers ensure the most effective use of support staff?

In the past twenty years there has been a large investment in increasing levels of support staff, and providing training. Between 1997 and 2003 there was a 99 per cent increase in TAs in English schools, for example. Funding in-class support is an expensive option for schools. It was always inevitable, therefore, that the effectiveness of this kind of provision would come under great scrutiny as demands for accountability in education have grown.

Relatively few studies have provided evidence on which to base conclusions about the impact of TAs beyond teacher reports, so it is worth examining some of the evidence that does exist. Effective use of staff and their skills can often depend on how the team is organised. Cremin, Thomas and Vincett (2003) describe 'room management', an approach that emphasises the need for clarity of roles among adults that are defined by looking first at the roles that teachers usually carry out on their own and then determining which of these it is appropriate for others to perform. They also discuss 'zoning', that is, dividing the classroom into learning zones where the teacher takes responsibility for the learning and activities of students in one zone, and the TA for the rest. Findings from a study that used a number of indicators to evaluate the effectiveness of TAs in schools, the Deployment and Impact of Support Staff (DISS) project (Blatchford et al., 2009), concluded that:

- TAs impacted positively on teachers' workloads, job satisfaction and levels of stress. They were able to focus their attention on individual pupils and minimise disruptive behaviour.

- TAs spent the majority of their time working with small groups or 1:1, usually those pupils with SEN or lower attaining, much more rarely with high and middle attaining pupils.

- Teachers tended to spend the majority of their time leading or supervising the whole class. Comparatively little of their time was spent working with groups or individual pupils, and when they did it was rarely with pupils with SEN.

- TAs were often expected to lead interventions which tended to be separate from the whole class teaching and learning environment.

- In general, pupils receiving the greatest support from TAs made less progress than similar pupils who had less TA support. This remained the case even after allowance had been made for influencing factors such as SEN, English as an Additional Language (EAL), Free School Meals (FSM) and prior attainment.

- TAs tended to be focussed on finishing a set task, rather than encouraging independent learning through open questioning and focussed discussion, whereas teachers tended to extend learning through specific feedback and more detailed explanations of new concepts to ensure understanding.

- There was a consistently expressed view that teachers and TAs had little or no designated planning and feedback time. This often leads to TAs feeling insufficiently prepared and dependant on teacher input to gain subject knowledge and task requirements.

- Teachers had very often not received training on deploying and managing TAs.

An important conclusion of the project was that the lack of impact on pupil achievement related to the way in which TAs were poorly prepared for the pedagogical role they were usually deployed to, with a tendency to be reactive rather than proactive when addressing pupil needs, thus creating pupil dependency on them rather than fostering independent learning. Some of the recommendations from this report relate to preparedness, deployment and the practice of support staff:

- Preparedness: more needs to be done to prepare teachers with the necessary skills and preparation to manage support staff and to prepare classroom-based support staff for their role in schools, especially for the pedagogical role with pupils. More time should be available for joint planning and feedback, and for considering how TAs might be deployed effectively.

- Deployment: support staff should not routinely support lower attaining pupils. Instead, pupils in most need should get more teacher time. Teachers should take responsibility for curriculum and pedagogical planning for all pupils in the class.

- Practice: conceptualising the pedagogical role of TAs needs to be built into professional development, school deployment decisions and the management, support and monitoring of support staff.

A further study, the Effective Deployment of Teaching Assistants (EDTA) project (Blatchford, Webster & Russell, 2012; Webster, Russell & Blatchford, 2016), put the recommendations from the Deployment and Impact of Support Staff (DISS) project into effect in ten primary schools over the course of one year. The evaluation showed that the trials conducted by each school improved the way school leaders and teachers thought about and deployed TAs:

- Preparedness: TAs' pre-lesson preparation was improved over the year, as were the quality and clarity of teachers' lesson plans. Teachers made more effort to meet with TAs before lessons, and some schools adjusted TAs' hours of work to create meeting time. The tasks and expectations of TA roles were made explicit in planning.

- Deployment: TAs worked more often with middle and high attaining pupils, spent less time in a passive role and withdrew pupils as little as possible from the classroom to help maintain contact with the mainstream curriculum, and teachers spent more time with low attaining pupils and those with SEN. There was a greater emphasis on peer support, collaborative group work and self-help strategies in the classroom.

- In terms of practice, there was a growing focus on changing the nature of TA/pupil talk and giving pupils longer time to respond, on open, rather than closed, questioning, on enhancing pupil understanding rather than task completion, and on encouraging autonomy in learning rather than adult dependency.

- Teachers also became more aware of the significance of the role of the TA, and TAs felt more valued and appreciated, enabling them to carry out their tasks with greater confidence.

Engaging with parents' or carers' perspectives

In a number of different countries across the world there is a formal acceptance that parents and carers have the right to know about decisions taken in schools in relation to their children, and that they themselves are, potentially, an important source of additional support in addressing difficulties in learning and/or behaviour experienced by young people. The right of parents and/or carers to be consulted at every stage of decision-making about their children is enshrined in law across the United Kingdom (Special Educational Needs and Disability [Northern Ireland] Order, 2005; Children and Families Act, 2014 in England; 1996 Education Act, Part 1V in Wales; Education [Additional Support for Learning] [Scotland] Acts, 2004 and 2009). A number of guides for parents and carers have been issued to support families to understand their entitlements also, for example *The parents' guide to additional support for learning* (Enquire, 2014) that is funded by the Scottish government and the *Special Educational*

Needs and Disability (SEND) – A guide for parents and carers (DfE, 2014d) published in England. Parents' and families' entitlements are made very clear in these *Guides*. For example the *Guide* in England (DfE, 2014d) makes very clear the basic principles that parents and families (p. 11):

> should have a real say in decisions that affect their children, should have access to impartial information, advice and support and know how to challenge decisions they disagree with.

Regular assessments of the progress of all students should take place, with gathering of information that should include discussion early on with both student and parents so that all can be clear about the pupil's areas of strength and difficulty, any concerns the parent(s) might have, the outcomes agreed for the child and the next steps. Parents and families are advised in the *Guide* (pp. 8–9):

> If you think your child has SEN, you should talk to your child's early education setting, school, college or other provider. They will discuss any concerns you have, tell you what they think and explain to you what will happen next

However, entitlement in law in not always synonymous with experience in practice. Families were entitled to be involved with decision-making regarding special or additional provision for their children prior to the most recent legislation. In 2009, the Lamb Enquiry into special educational needs and parental confidence in the system concluded that 'Failure to comply with statutory obligations speaks of an underlying culture where parents and carers of children with SEN can too readily be seen as the problem and as a result parents lose confidence in schools and professionals.' Lamb went on to say: 'As the system stands it often creates "warrior parents" at odds with the school and feeling they have to fight for what should be their children's by right; conflict in place of trust' (Lamb, 2009, 1.1). The recommendations in this report suggested a new framework for the provision of SEN and disability information that 'puts the relationship between parent and school back at the heart of the process' and 'trades adherence to a "laundry list" of rules for clear principles to guide that relationship' (Lamb, 2009, 1.4). Clearly these recommendations informed the terms of the Children and Families Act (2014) in England.

 Reflective activity: Effective working relationships with parents and families

Schools and colleges have a lot of power to affect the lives of children and their families and carers through the kind of consultation arrangements, assessment and provision that they make. Embedded within the particular discourses, approaches and strategies of schools are a variety of preconceptions about the ability and right of parents, families and/or communities, from a diversity of backgrounds and cultures, to support the learning and development of their children.

Recently a group of SENCos listed a series of principles for ensuring that families know that schools/colleges will take their contributions seriously during meetings to review their children's progress (Wearmouth, unpublished):

- Building trust and rapport;
- Keeping parents/families up to date;
- Transparency – under promise and over deliver;
- Communication with all involved that enables everyone to be heard;
- Remember differences between primary and secondary;
- Mutual respect – ground rules;
- Listening without talking;
- Establish understanding of the 3-way partnership, students, families and schools/ colleges;
- The meeting must be 'going somewhere'.

To what extent do you recognise these principles as important in contexts with which you are familiar?
Are there any other principles you would add to this list?

Issues in inter-agency collaboration

The concept of 'special educational', or 'additional support' needs covers a wide area that may go well beyond school and the conventional realm of 'education' into, sometimes, health and welfare. Multi-agency collaborative working practices have been encouraged by various governments as paramount for the safety of children since the 1980s, with subsequent recommendations about training in joint working practices for health professionals, social workers, teachers and others (Dunhill, 2009). In the past it has often been quite difficult for schools to work closely with outside agencies to protect the welfare of individual students seen by teachers as at risk of injury or abuse. In terms of child welfare, there is a long history of problems in inter-agency work in, for example, the exchange of information between agencies and of disputes over responsibility for offering particular services, sometimes with duplication of interventions by different agencies working on the same case (Roaf & Lloyd, 1995). The three primary care agencies, Education, Health and Social Services, have tended to operate to different legislative frameworks with different priorities and definitions of what constitutes a need. Lack of a clear structure to determine responsibilities in inter-agency working could also generate considerable tension, especially when resources were under pressure. The loser has been the client and his or her parents or carer.

Ofsted inspectors (2010) found poor evaluation by a wide range of public agencies of the quality of the additional support provided for children and young people. Too often, the agencies focused simply on whether a service was or was not being provided rather than whether it was effective. In particular, it was not enough for pupils to have a statement of special educational needs. The statement itself did not mean that their current needs were being met, but merely that they were likely to receive the service prescribed by their original statement.

System failures is illustrated, most notably, in recent years, in the case of the tragic death of Victoria Climbié, a child known to be at risk by both educational and social services. In 2003, alongside the formal response to the report into the death, the Government published a Green Paper, *Every Child Matters* (H. M. Treasury, 2003), followed by the Children Act (2004) that gave legal force to five interdependent outcomes (DfES, 2004). The clear failure in the system restated the need for closer co-operation between agencies which exist to support children in difficulties and their families or carers. The 'Every Child Matters' agenda (DfES, 2004) has sought to resolve these difficulties by unifying the range of children's services. All local education authorities combined with other services to become local authorities (LAs). One important implication for all teachers, particularly classroom teachers, is to listen carefully to what students say and how they behave, and work closely with, and under the guidance of, the teacher(s) designated to oversee the safety and well-being of the students in the school.

As part of this agenda a Common Assessment Framework (CAF) for use across the children's workforce has been developed to provide a shared framework for enabling decisions 'about how best to meet [children's] needs, in terms of both what the family can do and also what services could be provided (CWDC, 2009, par 1.11). As a result of the common assessment discussion, concerns about the child might be resolved, or particular actions for the professional undertaking the CAF and his/her service might be agreed with a date for review and monitoring progress. Alternatively, actions might be identified for other agencies. This involves sharing the assessment with these agencies (subject to the appropriate consent of the child or young person/ family); and forming a team around the child (TAC) to support the child or young person. The actions needed would be agreed with the other agencies and a plan and responsibilities for delivering the actions recorded on the CAF form (CWDC, 2009).

Clearly, in the attempt to ensure the 'joined-up thinking' that is required by the 2004 Children Act and the ECM agenda, in schools there is a potential overlap between assessment associated with provision for special educational needs and that carried out for the CAF. However, the CAF is not intended to replace other statutory assessments, but to complement or be integrated with them. The CAF is also not intended for assessment of a child where there is any suggestion of harm. Guidance given by the CWDC (2009, par. 1.4) states, 'The CAF is not for a child or young person about whom you have concerns that they might be suffering, or may be at risk of suffering, harm. In such instances, you should follow your Local Safeguarding Children Board (LSCB) safeguarding procedures without delay'.

In 2009, Laming confirmed that significant problems remained in the 'day-to-day reality of working across organisational boundaries and cultures, sharing information to protect children' (Laming, 2009, par. 1.6). There were training issues still to be resolved and data systems to be improved (par. 1.5). Ultimately children's safety depends on individual staff having the time and the skill 'to understand the child or young person and their family circumstances'. Laming also felt that 'Staff across front-line services … need to be able to notice signs of distress in children of all ages, but particularly amongst very young children who are not able to voice concerns and for whom bedwetting, head-banging and other signs may well be a cry for help' (par. 3.1).

Inter-agency collaboration and statutory assessment of individual support needs

Across the United Kingdom statutory assessment of children and young people's special educational needs and disabilities and/or additional support needs requires effective inter-agency collaboration in order to ensure that they are supported with the special/additional provision that they need to engage with the school or college curriculum and make good progress. In Scotland the individual plan that results from statutory assessment is termed 'a co-ordinated support plan':

> a number of children and young people have additional support needs arising from complex or multiple factors which require a high degree of co-ordination of support from education authorities and other agencies in order that their needs can be met. This support is co-ordinated through the provision of a co- ordinated support plan under the Act. (Scottish Government, 2010, p. 74, §1)

To achieve the level of effective inter-agency collaboration that is required the *Code* in Scotland (2010, p. 30, §8) reads:

> Education authorities need to play their part in ensuring that there is effective communication, collaboration and integrated assessment, planning, action and review when other agencies are involved.

In England the new Education, Health and Care plans introduced by the Children and Families Act, 2014, by definition also require a similar degree of collaboration, however problematic the history of such collaboration may have been in previous years. In England also there is the issue of the continuation of the CAF process that, in some ways, appears to duplicate the EHC assessment process. The relationship between the CAF process and that of EHCs does not seem to be entirely clear at the time of writing (March, 2016).

Essential factors in multi-agency partnerships

 Reflective activity: Good practice in multi-agency working

Do you have any experience of multi-agency partnerships? If so, what were the facilitators and inhibitors of good practice?

In your view, what are the hallmarks of effective multi-agency working?

Recently a group of SENCos on a professional development course listed a series of principles for successful practices in multi-agency working, and factors that they felt inhibit effectiveness.

To what extent do you recognise these principles as important in contexts with which you are familiar?

Are there any other principles, or inhibiting factors, you would add to this list?

Principles for effective practice:

- Liking the person/people
- Having the necessary information (everybody!) in advance of the meeting (organisation)
- Good communication regardless of allocated time – colleagues being available when needed
- Reliable follow up
- Availability of useful, appropriate resources
- Getting to know colleagues as people
- Reciprocal respect for everyone involved
- Sense of equality between colleagues irrespective of role/status
- Trust in colleagues' judgment
- Enough time to talk and get things sorted
- Appreciation for what everyone in the multi-agency team does
- A sense of team effort – everyone working together
- Consistency of staff
- Genuine interest in what everyone is saying
- Knowing that external colleagues like and know children
- Having a common goal and clear vision for what is being discussed.

Unsuccessful practices:

- Unnecessary use of unfamiliar jargon
- Paperwork for paperwork's sake
- Writing '!' on emails
- Not keeping all the stakeholders in the loop
- Unrealistic promises by various agencies about what they will do
- Defensiveness
- Meeting outcomes that are a waste of time and do not achieve what is needed
- Not asking all colleagues their opinion
- No contact between the school and some specialists.

If multi-agency partnerships are to be effective in developing, resourcing and maintaining statutory assessment and provision for special, or additional, educational needs, then it is patently obvious that what constitutes good practice in such relationships should be developed and maintained.

It is clear that where cultures and core professional beliefs conflict multi-agency working is likely to be inhibited (Nethercott, 2015). Key to effective multi-agency working (Atkinson, Jones & Lamont, 2007) is the establishment of clear and realistic aims and objectives that are understood by everyone, with a shared vision and culture and strategic management commitment and drive.

Co-location and improved lines of communication that can result from this (Atkinson *et al.*, 2007) can enhance common values and the development of a shared vision. Having said this, however, there is some evidence (Collins & McCray, 2012) that professionally qualified workers from education, health, and social care backgrounds may be less willing to include practitioners from voluntary organisations with a lower, vocational, level of qualifications, possibly as a result of concerns about issues of confidentiality. Collins and McCray concluded (ibid.) that the inclusive, co-operative process that has been envisaged in policy is not yet reflected in practice, hence casting doubt on whether professionals yet have the capability to deliver services within a multi-agency environment.

As Nethercott (2015) notes, reports from many child protection reviews within the United Kingdom over the past twenty years (Brandon et al., 2008, 2009; Laming, 2003; Reder & Duncan 2003; RBSCB, 2012) have concluded that a lack of communication between agencies, has contributed to the death or serious abuse of a child. Communication difficulties may include the problems created by the use of differing terminologies (Taylor & Daniel, 1999) as well as the unwillingness at times to become involved in difficult situations, including those relating to child protection (Corby, 2006).

Challenges in developing Education, Health and Care plans

A number of 'Key challenges and enabling factors' were identified during the piloting of EHC plans in England (DfE, 2014f, p. 14). In some cases these issues were interpreted as 'fundamental to the new process' (ibid.). The first identified challenge was 'ensuring sufficiency and consistency of multi-agency working' that might be addressed by:

- increased levels of strategic and operational commitment to contribute to the new process;
- provision of clear guidance to all professionals detailing expectations of how, when and why they should be involved;

- creation of 'champions' or 'spearheads' for individual agencies (and services within these) to act as the point of contact for the EHC planning process.
- Introduction of proportionate approaches to multi-agency working, e.g., use of multi-media to enable capacity constrained professionals to input to meetings.

The second was 'resourcing the delivery of a more family-centred process' to be addressed by:

- creation of dedicated EHC co-ordinators that have sufficient time to undertake the required family-facing elements of the process, which in turn will mean limiting their caseload;
- adoption of proportionate approaches to key working and family engagement based on the complexity of the child or young person's needs.

Next was 'meeting the reduced 20 week statutory timeframe', potentially to be addressed by:

- alignment of early years and school paper work to enable efficient translation of pre-referral information into the EHC planning process;
- creating efficiencies between agencies through sharing of assessments and reports;
- introduction of proportionate approaches to multi-agency working, e.g., use of multi-media to enable capacity constrained professionals to input to meetings
- development of integrated resourcing and funding mechanisms.

Fourth was the 'sharing of information between agencies and with families' that might be achieved by (p. 15):

- having the family as the holder of all information and paperwork and relying on them to give permission and transfer it from place to place;
- development of an integrated technology system that enables all relevant professionals and families to access the 'live' EHC plan and grants differing levels of permissions for distinct parties to edit the plan.

Fifth was 'increased paperwork' that might need:

- providing EHC plan co-ordinators with sufficient time to draft the summary assessment;
- training for EHC plan co-ordinators in interpreting assessments and drafting in plain English.

Next was 'ensuring all families have the capacity to engage' (p. 17) that might mean:

- time needs to be allocated to EHC plan co-ordinators to allow them to be flexible to family needs;

- EHC plan co-ordinators also need training in communicating expectations and flexibilities to families, and in negotiating time with them;
- providing independent advice and support for families.

Finally (p. 17) there was 'negotiating between family members when conflicts arise' that could involve the following:

- clarity in the Code of Practice about whose views take precedence when there is a difference of opinion between young people and their parents;
- key workers, independent supporters and EHC plan co-ordinators need to be sure to identify any differences at an early stage, perhaps through taking separate soundings from each member of the family;
- they also need to have good negotiation and mediation skills to enable them to conclude an agreed plan.

Summary

In schools, clearly the major role in supporting young people with special educational, or additional support, needs falls to the co-ordinator of whatever provision is made. The most recent legislation across the United Kingdom has strengthened the rights of parents and families to have their views heard about the kind of provision that is made. It is essential therefore that the lines of communication between the co-ordinator and families are clear, and that the relationship between schools and colleges is positive.

Of the support staff in class, teaching assistants form the largest group. A recent survey of 210 school leaders by Unison (2013) generated overwhelming support for the role and impact of TAs. Recruitment, deployment, management and training were reported as often inconsistent, but, when systematic, TA impact on raising attainment is deemed to be effective. Interestingly, nearly all respondents stated that they employed TAs to work with individual pupils, small groups and those with SEN, adding weight to the possibility that teachers are delegating their teaching responsibility for lower attaining pupils to, predominantly, less well-qualified TAs. However, when there is a deliberate focus on teacher and TA preparedness for in-class support work, a principled approach taken to TA deployment and consideration of the pedagogical role of TAs is built into teacher professional development, TA effectiveness can be considerably enhanced.

The essentials of effective multi-agency practice to ensure the needs of young people are assessed may be summed up from the findings of a systematic literature review 'Multi-agency working and its implications for practice' (Atkinson, Jones, & Lamont, 2007) which are as follows:

- clarifying roles and responsibilities;
- securing commitment at all levels [...] engendering trust and mutual respect;

- fostering understanding between agencies (e.g. through joint training and recognition of individual expertise);

- developing effective multi-agency processes: ensuring effective communication and information sharing;

- securing the necessary resources for multi-agency work and [...] securing adequate and sustained funding (e.g. through pooled budgets [...]

- ensuring continuity of staffing [...] and an adequate time allocation;

- ensuring effective leadership [...] although also dependent on effective governance and management arrangements [...] and an effective performance management system;

- providing sufficient time for the development of multi-agency working;

- the provision of joint training;

- agreement of joint aims and objectives.

Chapter 10
Including young people: Moving forward

Introduction

Education systems across the world face the common challenge of finding ways to provide for the whole diversity of their student populations. Categories associated with difference from the norm have to be understood within the discourses associated with the political and historical context of their time. Over the years in many countries there has been a variety of provision for students who experience difficulties in learning of various sorts. In the United Kingdom, for example, these students may have been described at one time as 'feeble-minded', 'idiots', 'imbeciles' – or worse – and consigned to special institutions such as the Earlswood Asylum for Idiots whose establishment in 1847 at Highgate was thought to be philanthropic. Children in inner cities with very poor health problems such as tuberculosis might have been categorised as 'delicate' and sent to an open air school in the years leading up to the Second World War when living conditions for the poor were often dire, but very seldom after the National Health Service was introduced and the nation's health improved overall. Or, following Marjorie Boxall's work in London in the 1960s, young children whose behaviour was seen as anti-social might have been seen as in need of nurturing and included in a nurture group in a mainstream school in order to build trusting relationships with adults and learn how to socialise positively with other pupils. In many schools in London this was no longer possible, following the disbanding of the Inner London Education Authority in 1989 and the fact that the new Inner London Boroughs did not include nurture groups in their special education plans (Nurture Group network, 2016 – https://nurturegroups.org/about-us/history, accessed 04.03.16). As discussed in Chapter 2, the differences between interpretations of need across countries in the United Kingdom, against which the appropriateness of response can be judged, seem to be growing. It seems unlikely that the definition of 'special educational need' will alter in the foreseeable future in England, given that the Children and Families Act was passed in 2014. In England, those with Education, Health and Care plans are now entitled to a 'Rolls Royce' level of excellence, with a view to helping them 'achieve the best possible educational and other outcomes' (Part 3 of the Children and Families Act 2014, para 19, (d)). At the time of writing there are, however, proposals to amend the law in both Wales and Northern Ireland. All in all, therefore, as we saw in chapters 1 and 2, there is nothing natural or fixed about labels in the area of special educational, or additional support, needs. It is more an issue of equity: how to ensure that students receive the resources they need to access the curriculum.

Issues of human rights

In the United Kingdom, all students have a legal right to education under legislation related to human rights to which the UK government is a signatory. Human rights themselves relate to the rights and freedoms that belong to every person in the world. These are based on principles such as dignity, fairness, equality, respect and autonomy. It was the 1998 Human Rights Act that brought human rights into UK law. One of these is 'Everybody has the right to an effective education' (Equality and Human Rights Commission, 2016 – http://www.equalityhumanrights.com/your-rights/human-rights/what-are-human-rights%3F/the-human-rights-act/right-to-education – accessed 04.03.16). Under the UN Convention on the Rights of People with Disabilities, ratified by the United Kingdom in 2009, the UK government agreed to work to ensure that the education system at all levels is inclusive and geared towards supporting disabled people to achieve their full potential and participate equally in society (UN, 2007, Annex 1).

The practice in recent years of requiring mainstream schools to accept and respond to a wider range of educational needs (particularly from a human rights perspective) and the needs of society therefore necessitated those schools becoming more 'inclusive'. This does not necessarily imply mainstream, however. Warnock and Norwich (2005), for example, rejected the interpretation of inclusion as all students in the same location and expressed a preference for the concept of inclusion as all students being included in a common enterprise of learning in the location where they learn best. In the view of the current author, one might add the importance of a sense of belonging combined with access to a broad, balanced curriculum and an expectation that they will achieve at the highest level. We may well concur with the National Association of Head Teachers' view that:

> Inclusion is a process that maximises the entitlement of all pupils to a broad, relevant and stimulating curriculum, which is delivered in the environment that will have the greatest impact on their learning. All schools, whether special or mainstream, should reflect a culture in which the institution adapts to meet the needs of its pupils and is provided with the resources to enable this to happen. [...] Inclusive schooling [...] involves having an education service that ensures that provision and funding is there to enable pupils to be educated in the most

appropriate setting. This will be the one in which they can be most fully included in the like of their school community and which gives them a sense both of belonging and achieving. (NAHT, 2003, p. 1)

Conforming to legal requirements

Legal entitlement is not necessarily reflected in practice, of course, as we saw in relation to the 2009 Lamb Enquiry. Only time will tell whether the vision for children with special educational needs and disability of the Parliamentary Under-Secretary of State for Health and the Parliamentary Under-Secretary of State for Children and Families as set out in the Foreword to the 2015 *Code of Practice* in England will eventuate in practice:

> Our vision for children with special educational needs and disabilities is the same as for all children and young people – that they achieve well in their early years, at school and in college, and lead happy and fulfilled lives. [...]. For children and young people this means that their experiences will be of a system which is less confrontational and more efficient. Their special educational needs and disabilities will be picked up at the earliest point with support routinely put in place quickly, and their parents will know what services they can reasonably expect to be provided. Children and young people and their parents or carers will be fully involved in decisions about their support and what they want to achieve. Importantly, the aspirations for children and young people will be raised through an increased focus on life outcomes, including employment and greater independence.

Creation of an inclusive environment in a competitive climate encouraged currently by central government's intent on target setting and narrowly conceived achievement is a challenging task. In 2001 Sally Tomlinson wrote:

> In my view, it seems clear that creating competitive markets in education based on parental 'choice' of schools and fuelled by league tables and competition for resources, is totally incompatible with developing an inclusive education system. In England there is now a divided and divisive school system, with middle-class and aspirant parents avoiding schools catering for children with special educational needs, and some schools finding ways of rejecting socially and educationally vulnerable children. (Tomlinson, 2001, pp. 192)

With further expansion of the private-within-the-state system of education in the past 14 years it seems that the competitive climate has increased even further. The challenge to mainstream schools is to respond to real individual differences within existing measures of school effectiveness which are based on average attainment and take too little account of the fact that schools produce a range of individual students.

Inclusion in practice

One might very well ask, then, what might constitute an inclusive school, and what might be the attributes of a teacher with inclusive practice.

Inclusive schools

Over the years there have been some very good examples of what an inclusive school can 'look like' in practice even within a national context of growing competitiveness. Corbett (2001) reported on a case study researching the characteristics of successful pedagogy to support inclusion in a primary school in the London Borough of Tower Hamlets. Her conclusions indicate that the school's system was permeated by a sense that all learners and the entire staff were included in curriculum decision-making:

> There is a real effort made to involve the learners, to create situations in which they can meet with success and to build on their existing level of knowledge. Learning Support Assistants (LSAs) are well briefed by teachers and work co-operatively to ensure that there are no individuals who are isolated from the group and not participating in any meaningful way. So many skilful strategies have been learnt and adapted by the teaching team that it is hard to say where mainstream teaching ends and specialist teaching begins. I felt that they had skilled themselves up to be able to accommodate the needs of children with Asperger's syndrome, autism, Down's syndrome, Williams syndrome and Attention Deficit Hyperactivity Disorder, who were included within their school population. There is a will to learn and a capacity to be highly flexible. (Corbett, 2001, p. 58)

School culture was characterised by co-operation across the school.

> Every morning, the staff team meet before school starts in order to go through the key events of the day and to share any particular issues or problems. There is no stigma attached to being unable to cope with a child who is behaving in a way which is disruptive to the class. As the headteacher says 'We have informal support structures where everybody knows that a difficult child is not your fault. You don't have to take on the guilt for that. We have very good communication with our educational psychologist who will always come up with strategies if we ask her. Our SENCo has regular meetings for all children at any stage of the *Code of Practice* and we share our IEPs and our different ways of doing them. Teachers feel less threatened when they share problems. It's always been a culture of this school that you don't take on someone's behaviour as our problem. It's a whole school problem and the whole school has to work at it ... In most cases, we have very good relationships with parents. Teachers go to their homes. They seem very willing to come to school to discuss things.'

... There is a culture of reasoned dialogue, rather than confrontation. Children are listened to with respect. This overtly child-centred approach does not make this an anarchic school but one which feels safe, comfortable and confident.

The provision of informal support structures for teachers facing disruptive students, the emphasis on people and relationships and the commitment to reasoned dialogue all pointed to a school that would be culturally safe for students from different backgrounds.

School policy for inclusion focused on the use of funding for personnel, and the use of specialist support staff:

nearly all the school's disposable income is put into *people* – learning support assistants, primary helpers, *not* including LEA-funded LSAs. This really helps if you are trying to meet individual needs.

Among the adult resources the school has access to are specialists in specific learning difficulties and autism and a counsellor, who works in the school three days a week. This greatly assists children experiencing emotional difficulties and their teachers and support staff . . .

Differentiation in classrooms was widely practised.

. . . differentiation means using many teaching styles and sharing specialist skills. There is a real commitment to including all learners which involves using diverse strategies and working at many different levels on whole-class tasks. [. . .] Individual achievement is the goal. As the SENCo says: 'This means ensuring that children are all working on something at which they can gain success and move forward at their own level so that they can take the next step.'

(Corbett, 2001, pp. 56–7)

Inclusive teaching practices

One factor that is often missing from much of the debate around inclusion is any acknowledgement of the situated nature of difficulties in learning and behaviour in schools. Curricular experiences offer students ways of knowing the world. Within an institution, educators and students are defined by that institution's social practices. The individual teacher's understanding of the student whose behaviour is seen as challenging, or learning seen as problematic, is part of that social practice. If both learning and behaviour are reconceptualised as situated, dynamic and interactive between students and the learning environment, and learning as occurring through engagement in a social context, pedagogy therefore needs to be interactive and 'intersubjective' to take account of individual meaning-making.

Schools play a critical part in shaping students' beliefs in their sense of self-efficacy, that is, their ability, responsibility and skill in initiating and completing actions and tasks. As we have already stressed in a number of places, it is really important to listen to the students themselves and highlight strengths on which interventions might draw.

There is no golden formula for addressing the special learning needs of all students who experience difficulties in schools. There are some general principles, however. Every student is different and every situation is different. Addressing difficulties is a question of problem-solving. Firstly, find out about the learner and the difficulties s/he experiences. Then think about the requirements of the particular curriculum area and barriers to learning in the classroom environment and in the particular curriculum area. Finally, reflect on and implement what will best address those barriers to help the learner achieve in the classroom.

Final word

Substantive educational opportunity is not guaranteed for children with disabilities either by access to similar educational resources or by participation in a common and universal curriculum, the very conditions which created special education. The way schools mediate success and failure are crucial to the development of a sense of personal agency (Bruner, 1996). Teachers should therefore reflect continuously on the impact of school processes and practices on young people's sense of agency and ability. Student learning in schools takes place within an educational community. The sense of belonging to, or marginalisation from, that community affects every aspect of participation and, therefore, learning within it, and necessarily affects a student's behaviour and self-perception. 'Inclusion', therefore, can be interpreted as the extent to which students are able to participate in the school community. Students who experience difficulties of any sort in schools have the same basic needs as any other individual. Failing to support the development of students' understanding and ability to act in a social context risks marginalising and alienating young people and limiting their autonomy. We might agree with Gerber (2004) that, if schools changed to respond to individual differences, then they would be effective when their poorest performing students demonstrate significant achievement gains.

The current marketisation of education fuelled by league tables in some areas and competition and accountability for resources makes the creation of inclusive climates in schools problematic without a really determined whole-school and whole-staff effort. Pragmatically, therefore, we leave the last word to a group of experienced special educational co-ordinators committed to achieving the very best educational provision for young people experiencing special or additional needs, as well as all other students, despite the context of competition and high-stakes assessment. When asked the question: 'What, in your experience, are important features of 'inclusion' in schools and colleges?' (Wearmouth, 2016a, pp. 7–8) they made the following observations:

- All children have equal opportunities to participate in all areas of broad balanced curriculum and feel valued, which implies:
    - removing barriers to learning so everyone can access curriculum and make progress regardless of any circumstance – health, finance, behaviour etc;

- treating young people differently according to various needs and adopting a holistic approach to support a tailored, individual approach to the curriculum;
- differentiation in classrooms and awareness of how the learning context supports inclusion or excludes some children;
- acceptance of diversity without negative comments or notice, with care taken regarding the language used about others;
- a sense of belonging, taking account of the individual's feelings;
- all young people know they have a voice;
- young people with needs have access to appropriate provision (internal and external) to meet those needs, irrespective of location;
- deliberate consideration of strategies, procedures, resources and people to make it happen.

- Schools getting to know families really well, understand their backgrounds and engage positively with parents/guardians to ensure they are actively involved with all decision making/communication, so they are confident that they:
  - know they are listened to by the school;
  - can support their children and feel a part of the community;
  - understand their responsibility and that of the school.

- Supporting pupils and staff to create a safe environment for learning for everyone where everybody has a positive attitude towards everyone else and there is mutual respect.

- Schools having high expectations, enabling a high level of achievement for all, which implies:
  - progress data are taken often and analysed by department/leadership teams and used to inform staff/parents/students and put appropriate, thoughtful interventions in place where progress is not at the level expected of individual pupils;
  - progress towards self-directed learning to be functioning members of society.

References

Adams, C. & Lloyd, J. (2007) The effects of speech and language therapy intervention on children with pragmatic language impairments in mainstream school, *British Journal of Special Education*, 34(4), pp. 226–33.

Adams, M. J. (1994) *Beginning to read: Thinking and learning about print*, Cambridge, MA: MIT Press.

Adult Literacy and Basic Skills Unit (1992) *The ALBSU standards for basic skills students and trainees*, London: Adult Literacy and Basic Skills Unit.

Aitken, S. (2000) Understanding deafblindness, in S. Aitken, M. Buultjens, C. Clark, J. T. Eyre & L. Pease (eds), *Teaching children who are deafblind*, London: David Fulton Publishers.

Alborz, A., Pearson, D., Farrell, P. & Howes, A. (2009) *The impact of adult support staff on pupils and mainstream schools: A systematic review of evidence*, London: Institute of Education, EPPI Centre.

Alexander, R. J. (2004) Excellence, enjoyment and personalised learning: A true foundation for choice? *Education Review*, 18(1), pp. 15–33.

Alton-Lee, A. (2003) *Quality teaching for diverse students in schooling: Best evidence synthesis*, Wellington: Ministry of Education.

American Psychiatric Association (1994) *Diagnostic and Statistical Manual of Mental Disorders (DSM-IV)*, Arlington, VA: American Psychiatric Association.

American Psychiatric Association (2013) *Diagnostic and Statistical Manual of Mental Disorders (DSM-5)*, Arlington, VA: American Psychiatric Association.

Anderson, C., Gendler, G., Riestenberg, N., Anfang, C. C., Ellison, M. & Yates, B. (1996) *Restorative measures: Respecting everyone's ability to resolve problems*, St Paul, MN: Minnesota Department of Children, Families and Learning: Office of Community Services.

Angier, C. & Povey, H. (1999) One teacher and a class of school students: Their perception of the culture of their mathematics classroom and its construction, *Educational Review*, 51(2), pp. 147–60.

Anthony, G. & Walshaw, M. (2007) *Effective pedagogy in mathematics/Pàngarau: Best evidence synthesis Iteration*, Wellington, New Zealand: Ministry of Education.

Apel, K. & Masterton, J. (1998) Assessment and treatment of narrative skills: What's the story? in *RTN Learning Book*, Rockville, MD: American Speech-Language-Hearing Association.

Armstrong, D. (1994) *Power and partnership in education: Parents, children and special educational needs*, London: Routledge.

Askew, M., Brown, M., Rhodes, V., Johnson, D. & Wiliam, D. (1997) *Effective teachers of numeracy*, London: Kings College.

Asperger, H. (1991) *Autism and Asperger syndrome*. U. Frith (trans. and ed.). Cambridge, New York: Cambridge University Press (Original work published 1944), pp. 37–92.

Assessment Reform Group (1999) *Assessment for learning: Beyond the black box*, Cambridge: University of Cambridge School of Education.

Atkinson, M., Jones, M. & Lamont, E. (2007) *Multi-agency working and its implications for practice: A review of the literature*, Slough, Berkshire: CfBT Education Trust.

Atkinson, R. L., Atkinson, R. C., Smith, E. E. & Bem, D. J. (1993, 11th edn) *Introduction to psychology*, Fortworth, TX: Harcourt Brace College Publishers.

Audit Commission (1992) *Getting in on the act: Provision for pupils with special educational needs*, London: HMSO.

Baer, D. M., Wolf, M. M. & Risley, T. R. (1968) Some current dimensions of applied behavior analysis, *Journal of Applied Behavior Analysis*, (1), pp. 91–7.

Ball, D. L. & Bass, H. (2000) Interweaving content and pedagogy in teaching and learning to teach: Knowing and using mathematics, in J. Boaler (ed.), *Multiple perspectives on the teaching and learning of mathematics*, pp. 83–104, Westport, CT: Ablex.

Balshaw, M. (1991) *Help in the classroom*, London: David Fulton.

Bandura, A. (1969) *Principles of behavior modification*, New York: Holt, Rinehart & Winston.

Bartholomew, H. (2003) Ability grouping and the construction of different types of learner in mathematics classrooms, in L. Bragg, C. Campbell, G. Herbert & J. Mousley (eds), *Mathematics education research: Innovation, networking, opportunity* (Proceedings of the 26th annual conference of the Mathematics Education Research Group of Australasia, Vol. 1, pp. 128–35), Sydney: MERGA.

Barton, D. (1995) *Literacy: An introduction to the ecology of written language*, Oxford: Blackwell.

Beattie, R. (2006) The oral methods and spoken language acquisition, in P. Spencer & M. Marshark (eds), *Advances in the spoken language development of deaf and hard-of-hearing children*, New York: Oxford University Press.

Bell, D. (Ed.) (1967) *An experiment in education: The history of Worcester College for the blind, 1866–1966*, London: Hutchinson.

Benn, C. & Chitty, C. (1996) *Thirty years on: Is comprehensive education alive and well or struggling to survive*. London: David Fulton.

Bennathan, M. (2000) Children at risk of failure in primary schools, in M. Bennathan & M. Boxall (eds.), *Effective Intervention in Primary Schools: Nurture groups* (2nd edn), pp. 1–18, London: David Fulton.

Bennett, R. (1992) Discipline in schools: The report of the Committee of Enquiry chaired by Lord Elton, in K. Wheldall (ed.), *Discipline in Schools: Psychological perspectives on the Elton Report*, London: Routledge.

Bentley, D. (2002) Teaching spelling: Some questions answered, in J. Wearmouth, J. Soler & G. Reid (eds), *Addressing difficulties in literacy development: Responses at family, school, pupil and teacher levels*, pp. 340–53, London: RoutledgeFalmer.

Berryman, M. & Glynn, T. (2001) *Hei Awhina Matua: Strategies for bicultural partnership in overcoming behavioural and learning difficulties*, Wellington: Specialist Education Service.

Bird, G. & Thomas, S. (2002) Providing effective speech and language therapy for children with Down syndrome in mainstream settings: A case example, *Down Syndrome News and Update*, 2(1), pp. 30–1.

Bishop, A. J. (1983) Space and geometry, in R. Lesh & M. Landau (eds), *Acquisition of mathematical concepts and processes*, London: Academic Press.

Bishop, D. V. M. & Norbury, C. F. (2002) Exploring the borderlands of autistic disorder and specific language impairment: A study using standardised diagnostic instruments, *Journal of Child Psychology and Psychiatry*, 43(7), pp. 917–29.

Bishop, R., Berryman, M. & Wearmouth, J. (2014) *Te Kotahitanga: Towards effective education reform for indigenous and other minoritised students*, Wellington, New Zealand: NZCER.

Black, D. (1998) Coping with loss: Bereavement in childhood, *British Medical Journal*, 316 (7135), pp. 931–6.

Black, P. & Wiliam, D. (1998) Assessment and classroom learning, *Assessment in Education*, 5(1), pp. 7–74.

Blackledge, A. (2000) *Literacy, power and social justice*. Stoke on Trent, Staffordshire: Trentham.

Blatchford, P., Bassett, P., Brown, P., Martin, C., Russell, A. & Webster, R. (2004) *Deployment and impact of support staff project*, London: Institute of Education.

Blatchford, P., Russell, A., Bassett, P., Brown, P. & Martin, C. (2004) *The role and effects of teaching assistants in English primary schools (Years 4 to 6) 2000–2003: Results from the Class Size and Pupil-Adult Ratios (CSPAR) KS2 Project*, Nottingham: DfES.

Blatchford, P., Webster, R. & Russell, A. (2012) *Challenging the role and deployment of teaching assistants in mainstream schools: The impact on schools*, London: Institute of Education. Available at: http://maximisingtas.co.uk/assets/content/edtareport-2.pdf (09.03 2016).

Bliss, J., Askew, M. & Macrae, S. (1996) Effective teaching and learning: Scaffolding revisited, *Oxford Review of Education*, 22(1), pp. 37–61.

Boaler, J., Wiliam, D. & Brown, M. (2000) Students' experiences of ability grouping: Disaffection, polarisation and the construction of failure? *British Educational Research Journal*, 26(5), pp. 631–48.

Bond, G. L. & Dykstra, R. (1967) The co-operative research program in first-grade reading instruction, *Reading Research Quarterly*, 2, pp. 5–142.

Borthwick, A. & Harcourt-Heath, M. (2007) Calculation strategies used by Year 5 children, *Proceedings of the British Society for Research into Learning Mathematics*, 27(1), pp 12–23.

Bowers, T. (1996) Putting back the 'E' in EBD, *Emotional and Behavioural Difficulties*, 3(1), pp. 37–43.

Bowlby, J. (1944) Forty-four juvenile thieves: Their character and home life, *International Journal of Psychoanalysis*, 25, pp. 19–52.

Bowlby, J. (1952) A two-year-old goes to hospital, *Proceedings of the Royal Society of Medicine*, 46, pp. 425–7.

Boxall, M. (2002) *Nurture groups in school: Principles and practice*, London: Paul Chapman.

Bradley, L. (1981) The organisation of motor patterns for spelling: An effective remedial strategy for backward readers, *Developmental Medicine and Child Neurology*, 23, pp. 83–91.

Bradley, L. & Bryant, P. E. (1983) Categorising sounds and learning to read: A causal connection. *Nature*, 301, pp. 419–21.

Brandon, M., Bailey, S., Belderson, P., Gardner, R., Sidebotham, P., Dodsworth, J., Warren, C. & Black, J. (2009) *Understanding serious case reviews and their impact: A biennial analysis of serious case reviews 2005–07*, London: Department for Children, Schools and Families.

Brandon, M., Belderson, P., Warren, C., Gardner, R., Howe, D., Dodsworth, J. & Black, J. (2008) The preoccupation with thresholds in cases of child death or serious injury through abuse and neglect, *Child Abuse Review*, 17(5), pp. 313–30.

British Psychological Society (BPS) (1996) *Attention Deficit Hyperactivity Disorder (ADHD): A psychological response to an evolving concept*, Leicester: BPS.

British Psychological Society (BPS) (1999) *Dyslexia, literacy and psychological assessment*, Leicester: BPS.

Broadfoot, P. (2011) *Assessment, schools and society*, London: Routledge.

Bruner, J. (1966) *Toward a theory of instruction*, Cambridge, MA: Harvard University Press.

Bruner, J. (1996) *The culture of education*, Boston, MA: Harvard University Press.

Buhler, C. (1935) *From birth to maturity: An outline of the psychological development of the child*, London: Routledge & Kegan Paul.

Buhler, C. (1967) Human life goals in the humanistic perspective, *Journal of Humanistic Psychology*, 7(1), pp. 36–52.

Buikema, J. L. & Graves, M. F. (1993) Teaching students to use context cues to infer word meaning, *Journal of Reading*, 33, pp. 504–8.

Burman, D., Nunes, T. & Evans, D. (2006) Writing profiles of deaf children taught through British Sign Language, *Deafness and Education International*, 9, pp. 2–23.

Buzan, T. (2000) *The mind map book*, London: Penguin.

Cambourne, B. (2003) Taking a naturalistic viewpoint in early childhood literacy research, in N. Hall, J. Larson & J. Marsh (eds), *Handbook of early childhood literacy*, ch. 33, pp. 411–23, London: Sage.

Cameron, L. & Murphy, J. (2002) Enabling young people with a learning disability to make choices at a time of transition, *British Journal of Learning Disabilities*, 30, 105–12.

Center, Y., Freeman, L. & Robertson, G. (2001) A longitudinal evaluation of the Schoolwide Early Language and Literacy Program (SWELL), in R. E. Slavin & N. A. Madden (eds), *Success for all: Research and reform in elementary education*, pp. 111–48, Mahwah, NJ: Lawrence Erlbaum.

Central Advisory Council for Education (1963) *Half our future* (The 'Newsom Report'), London: HMSO.

Central Advisory Council for Education (1967) *Children and their primary schools* (The 'Plowden Report'), London: HMSO.

Chazan, M., Laing, A. & Davies, D. (1994) *Emotional and behavioural difficulties in middle childhood*, London: Falmer Press.

Childnet International & Department for Children, Schools and Families (DCSF) (2007/8) *Let's fight it together: What we can all do to prevent cyberbullying*, London: Childnet International & DCSF.

Children's Workforce Development Council (CWDC) (2009) *The Common Assessment Framework for children and young people*, A guide for practitioners, London: CWDC.

Chinn, S. (2012) *The trouble with maths: A practical guide to helping learners with numeracy difficulties* (2nd edn), London: Routledge.

Chitty, C. & Dunford, J. E. (1999) *State schools: New Labour and the Conservative legacy*, London: Woburn Press.

Choat, E. (1974) Johnnie is disadvantaged; Johnnie is backward. What hope for Johnnie? *Mathematics Teaching*, 69, pp. 9–13.

Chomsky, C. (1978) When you still can't read in third grade after decoding, what? in S. J. Samuels (ed.), *What research has to say about reading instruction*, pp. 13–30, Newark, DE: International Reading Association.

Clark, C., Dyson, A., Millward, A. & Skidmore, D. (1997) *New directions in special needs*, London: Cassell.

Clay, E. & Silverman, J. (2009) Reclaiming lost opportunities: The role of the teacher in online asynchronous collaboration in mathematics teacher education, in I. Gibson, R. Weber, K. McFerrin, R. Carlsen & D. Willis (eds), *Proceedings of Society for Information Technology & Teacher Education International Conference 2009*, pp. 519–26, Chesapeake, VA: Association for the Advancement of Computing in Education.

Clay , M. M. (1979) *Reading: The patterning of complex behaviour*, Auckland: Heinemann.

Clay, M. M. (1991) *Becoming literate: The construction of inner control*, Auckland: Heinemann.

Clay, M. M. (1993) *Reading recovery*, Auckland, New Zealand: Heinemann.

Clay, M. M. (1998) *An observation survey of early literacy achievement*, Auckland, New Zealand: Heinemann.

Cobb, P. & Hodge, L. L. (2002) A relational perspective on issues of cultural diversity and equity as they play out in the mathematics classroom, *Mathematical Thinking and Learning*, 4(2&3), pp. 249–84.

Cockroft, W. H. (1982) *Mathematics counts: Report of the Committee of Inquiry into the teaching of mathematics in schools. (The Cockcroft Report)*, London: Her Majesty's Stationery Office.

Cole, B. A. (2005) Mission impossible? Special educational needs, inclusion and the re-conceptualization of the role of the SENCO in England and Wales, *European Journal of Special Needs Education*, 20(3), pp. 287–307.

Cole, T. (1989) *Apart or a part? Integration and the growth of British special education*, Milton Keynes: Open University Press.

Cole, T. (1990) The history of special education: Social control of humanitarian progress? *British Journal of Special Education*, 17(3), pp. 101–7.

Collins, F. & McCray, J. (2012) Partnership working in services for children: Use of the common assessment framework, *Journal of Interprofessional Care*, 26(2), pp.134–40.

Cooper, J. O., Heron, T. E. & Heward, W. E. (1987) *Applied behavior analysis*, Columbus: Merrill Publishing Company.

Cooper, P. (1990) Respite, relationships and re-signification: The effects of residential schooling on pupils with emotional and behavioural difficulties, with particular reference to the pupils' perspective, Unpublished PhD thesis, University of Birmingham.

Cooper, P. (1999) Changing perceptions of EBD: Maladjustment, EBD and beyond, *Emotional and Behavioural Difficulties*, 4(1), pp. 3–11.

Corbett, J. (1996) *Bad mouthing: The language of special needs*, London: Falmer Press.

Corbett, J. (2001) Teaching approaches which support inclusive education: A connective pedagogy, *British Journal of Special Education*, 28(2), pp. 55–9.

Corby, B. (2006) The role of child care social work in supporting families with children in need and providing protective services – past, present and future, *Child Abuse Review*, 15(3), pp.159–77.

Cornwall, J. (2000) Might is right? A discussion of the ethics and practicalities of control and restraint in education, *Emotional and Behavioural Difficulties*, 5(4), pp. 19–25.

Cornwall, J. (2004) Pressure, stress and children's behaviour at school, in J. Wearmouth, R. C. Richmond, T. Glynn & M. Berryman (eds), *Understanding pupil behaviour in schools: A diversity of approaches*, ch. 20, pp. 307–21, London: Fulton.

Council of Europe (1966) *European Convention on Human Rights (Rome, 1950) and its five protocols*, Strasbourg, Council of Europe.

Cowling, K. & Cowling, H. (1993) *Toe by Toe*, Baildon: Toe by Toe.

Cremin, H., Thomas, G. & Vincett, K. (2003) Learning zones: An evaluation of three models for improving learning through teacher/teaching assistant teamwork, *Support for Learning*, 18(4), pp. 154–61.

Crombie, M. (2000) *Hickey multisensory language course*, London: Whurr.

Cruse Bereavement Care (2016) http://www.cruse.org.uk/, accessed 9 March 2016.

Cummins, J. (2009) Multilingualism in the English-language classroom: Pedagogical considerations, *TESOL Quarterly*, 43(2), pp. 317–21.

Davey, R. & Parkhill, F. (2012) Raising adolescent reading achievement: The use of sub-titled popular movies and high interest literacy activities, *English in Aotearoa*, 78(Oct.), pp. 61–71.

Davis, P. (2003) *Including children with a visual impairment in mainstream schools: A practical guide*, London: Fulton.

de Lemos, M. (2002) *Closing the gap between research and practice: Foundations for the acquisition of literacy*, Camberwell, Victoria: Australian Council for Educational Research.

de Shazer, S. (1985) *Keys to solution in brief therapy*, New York: W. W. Norton.

de Shazer, S. (1988) *Investigating solutions in brief therapy*, New York: W. W. Norton.

de Shazer, S., Dolan, Y., Korman, H., McCollum, E., Trepper, T. & Berg, I. K. (2007) *More than Miracles: The state of the art of solutions-focused brief therapy*, New York: Haworth.

Department for Education (2014a) *Special Educational Needs and Disability (SEND) – a guide for parents and carers*, London: DfE.

Department for Education (DfE) (1994) *The Code of Practice for the identification and assessment of special educational needs*, London: DfE.

Department for Education (DfE) (2011) *Review of best practice in parental engagement*, London: Institute of Education.

Department for Education (DfE) (2013a) *The national curriculum in England, Key stages 1 and 2 framework document*, London: DfE.

Department for Education (DfE) (2013b) *Use of reasonable force: Advice for headteachers, staff and governing bodies*, London: DfE.

Department for Education (DfE) (2014a) *Behaviour and discipline in schools: Advice for head teachers and school staff*, London: DfE.

Department for Education (DfE) (2014b) *National Curriculum for England inclusion statement*, London: DfE.

Department for Education (DfE) (2014c) *Preventing and tackling bullying: Advice for head teachers, staff and governing boards*, London: DfE.

Department for Education (DfE) (2014d) *Special Educational Needs and Disability (SEND) – a guide for parents and carers*, London: DfE.

Department for Education (DfE) (2014e) *Supporting pupils at school with medical conditions: Statutory guidance for governing bodies of maintained schools and proprietors of academies in England*, London: DfE.

Department for Education (DfE) (2014f) *Special educational needs and disability pathfinder*, London: DfE

Department for Education (DfE) (2015) *Special educational needs and disability code of practice: 0 to 25 years*, London: DfE.

Department for Education and Skills (DfES) (2001) *Special educational needs code of practice*, London: DfES.

Department for Education and Skills (DfES) (2003) *Excellence and enjoyment: A strategy for primary schools*, London: DfES.

Department for Education and Skills (DfES) (2004) *Every child matters: Change for children*, London: DfES.

Department for Education and Skills (DfES) (2005) *Learning behaviour: The Report of the Practitioners' Group on School Behaviour and Discipline ('Steer Report')*, Nottingham: DfES.

Department for Education and Skills (DfES) (2006) *Primary framework for literacy and mathematics*, Norwich: DfES.

Department of Children, Families and Schools (DCSF) Primary National Strategy (PNS) (2005) *Speaking listening learning: Working with children who have special educational needs (Ref 1235/2005)*, London: QCA.

Department of Education and Science (DES) (1978) *Warnock Report. The Special Educational Needs: Report of the Committee of Enquiry into the Education of Handicapped Children and Young People, Cmnd. 7212*, London: HMSO.

Department of Education and Science (DES) (1989) *Discipline in schools: Report of the Committee of Enquiry chaired by Lord Elton* (Elton Report), London: HMSO.

Department of Education and Skills (DES) (2001) *Special educational needs code of practice*, London: DES.

Department of Education, Northern Ireland (DENI) (1998) *Code of practice on the identification and assessment of special educational needs*, Bangor: DENI.

Department of Education, Northern Ireland (DENI) (2002) *Towards a model policy in schools on the use of reasonable force*, Bangor: DENI.

Department of Education, Northern Ireland (DENI) (2005) *Supplement to the Code of Practice on the identification and assessment of special educational needs*, Bangor: DENI.

Dockrell, J. & McShane, J. (1993) *Children's learning difficulties: A cognitive approach*, Oxford, Blackwell.

Donaldson, M. (1984) *Children's minds*, London: Fontana.

Doolittle, P. E., Hicks, D., Triplett, C. F., Nichols, W. D. & Young, C. A. (2006) Reciprocal teaching for reading comprehension in higher education: A strategy for fostering the deeper understanding of texts, *International Journal of Teaching and Learning in Higher Education*, 17(2), pp. 106–18.

Douglas, G. & McLinden, M. (2005) Visual impairment in B. Norwich & A. Lewis (eds), *Special teaching for special children? Pedagogies for inclusion*, ch. 3, Maidenhead, UK: Open University Press.

Douglas, J. W. B. (1967) *The home and the school*, St Albans: Panther.

Down, J. L. H. (1866) Observations on an ethnic classification of idiots, *Clinical lecture reports*, London Hospital 3: 259–62. http://www.neonatology.org/classics/down.html.

Dunckley, I. (1999) *Managing extreme behaviour in schools*, Wellington, New Zealand: Specialist Education Services.

Dunhill, A. (2009) *What is communication? The process of transferring information*, Exeter, UK: Learning Matters Ltd.

Dunn, L., Parry, S. & Morgan, C. (2002) Seeking quality in criterion referenced assessment, Learning Communities and Assessment Cultures Conference, University of Northumbria, 28–30 August 2002.

Dwivedi, K. & Gupta, A. (2000) 'Keeping cool': Anger management through group work, *Support for Learning*, 15(2), pp. 76–81.

Dykens, E. M. & Kasari, C. (1997) Maladaptive behavior in children with Prader-Willi syndrome, Down syndrome, and nonspecific mental retardation, *American Journal on Mental Retardation*, 102(3), pp. 228–37.

Eden, G. F., Van Meter, J. W., Rumsey, J. M., Maisog, J. M., Woods, R. P. & Zeffrio, T. A. (1996) Abnormal processing of visual motion in dyslexia revealed by functional brain imaging, *Nature*, 382, pp. 66–9.

Education Department (1898) *Report of the Departmental Committee on Defective and Epileptic Children (Sharpe Report)*, London: HMSO.

Ehri, L. C. (2002) Reading processes, acquisition and instructional implications In G. Reid and J. Wearmouth (eds), *Dyslexia and literacy: Research and practice*, Chichester: Wiley.

Eldridge, R. G., Jr. (1995) The possibility of knowledge and reality without science', In B. Hayes & K. Camperell (eds), *Linking literacy: The past, present and future*, Logan, UT: American Reading Forum.

El-Naggar, O. (1996) *Specific learning difficulties in mathematics – a classroom approach*, Tamworth: NASEN.

El-Naggar, O. (2001) *Specific learning difficulties in mathematics– a classroom approach.* Tamworth: NASEN.

Englert, C. & Raphael, T. (1988) Constructing well-formed prose: Process, structure and metacognition in the instruction of expository writing, *Exceptional Children*, 54, pp. 513–20.

Enquire (2014) *The parents' guide to additional support for learning*, Edinburgh: Enquire.

Equality and Human Rights Commission (2016) *Private and public sector guidance: Reasonable adjustments.* http://www.equalityhumanrights.com/private-and-public-sector-guidance, accessed 9 March 2016.

Everatt, J. (2002) Visual processes, in G. Reid & J. Wearmouth (eds), *Dyslexia and literacy: Research and practice*, Chichester: Wiley.

Farrington, D. P. (1993) Understanding and preventing bullying, in M. Tonry (ed.), *Crime and justice: A review of research*, Chicago: University of Chicago Press.

Fernandez-Lopez, A., Rodriguez-Fortiz, M. J., Rodriguez-Almendros, M. L. & Martinez-Segura, M. J. (2013) Mobile learning technology based on iOS devices to support students with special educational needs, *Computers and Education*, 61, pp. 77–90.

Field, E. M. (1999) *Bully Busting*, Lane Cove, NSW: Finch Publishing.

Fisch, H., Hyun, G., Golden, R., Hensle, T. W., Olsson, C. A. & Liberson, G. L. (2003) The influence of paternal age on Down syndrome, *Journal of Urology*, 169(6), pp. 2275–8.

Fisher, G., Richmond, R. & Wearmouth, J. (2004) *E804 managing behaviour in schools: Study guide part 4*, Milton Keynes: Open University Press.

Florian, L. & Hegarty, J. (eds) (2004) *ICT and special educational needs: A tool for inclusion*, Maidenhead: Open University Press.

Ford, J., Mongon, D. & Whelan, M. (1982) *Special education and social control*, London: Routledge.

Ford, T. (2015) Connecting with Māori whānau and community, in M. Berryman, A., Nevin, S. SooHoo & T. Ford (eds), *Relational and responsive inclusion*, ch. 10, pp. 183–202. New York: Peter Lang.

Fraivillig, J., Murphy, L. & Fuson, K. (1999) Advancing children's mathematical thinking in everyday mathematics classrooms, *Journal for Research in Mathematics Education*, 30(2), 148–70.

Freeman, S. B., Taft, L. F., Dooley, K. J., Allran, K., Sherman, S. L., Hassold, T. J., Khoury, M. J. & Saker, D. M. (1998) Population-based study of congenital heart defects in Down syndrome, *American Journal of Medical Genetics*, 80(3), pp. 213–17.

Fulcher, G. (1989) *Disabling policies: A comparative approach to educational policy and disabilities*, London: Falmer Press.

Furlong, V. J. (1985) *The deviant pupil: Sociological perspectives*, Milton Keynes: OU Press.

Galloway, D. M. & Armstrong, D. & Tomlinson, S. (1994) *The assessment of special educational needs: Whose problem?* Harlow: Longman.

Galloway, D. M. & Goodwin, C. (1987) *The education of disturbing children: Pupils with learning and adjustment difficulties*, London: Longman.Gamlin, R. (1935) *Modern School Hygiene*, James Nisbet: London.

Gay, G. (2010) *Culturally responsive teaching: Theory, research and practice.* New York: Teachers' College Press.

Gee, J. (2000) New people in new worlds: Networks, the new capitalism and schools, in B. Cope and M. Kalantzis (eds), *Multiliteracies: Literacy learning and the design of social futures*, London: Routledge.

Gerber, M. (2004) Reforming special education beyond inclusion, in J. Wearmouth, T. Glynn, R. C. Richmond & M. Berryman (eds), *Inclusion and behaviour management in schools: Issues and challenges*, pp. 341–60, London: Fulton.

Gersch, I. (1995) Involving the child, in P. Stobbs, T. Mackey, B. Norwich, N. Peacey & P. Stephenson (eds), *Schools' Special Educational Needs Policies Pack*, London: National Children's Bureau.

Glynn, T. (1982) Antecedent control of behaviour in educational contexts, *Educational Psychology*, 2, pp. 215–29.

Glynn, T. & Bishop, R. (1995) Cultural issues in educational research: A New Zealand perspective, *He Pūkengo Kōrero*, 1(1), pp. 37–43.

Glynn, T. & McNaughton, S. (1985) The Mangere home and school remedial reading procedures, *New Zealand Journal of Psychology*, 15(2), pp. 66–77.

Glynn, T., Wearmouth, J. & Berryman, M. (2006) *Supporting students with literacy difficulties: A responsive approach*, Maidenhead: Open University Press.

Goldberg, L. R. & Richberg, C. M. (2004) Minimal hearing impairment: Major myths with more than minimal implications, *Communication Disorders Quarterly*, 24, pp. 152–60.

Goodman, K. S. (1996) *On reading*, Portsmouth, NJ: Heinemann.

Gordon, A. (1961) Mongolism (Correspondence), *The Lancet*, 277(7180): 775.

Graham, S. & Harris, K. R. (1993) Teaching writing strategies to students with learning disabilities: Issues and recommendations, in L. J. Meltzer (ed.), *Strategy assessment and instruction for students with learning disabilities*, Austin, TX: Pro-Ed MacArthur and Graham.

Grandin, T. (1996) *Emergence: Labelled autistic*, New York: Warner Books.

Grauberg, E. (2002) *Elementary mathematics and language difficulties*, London: Whurr.

Graves, A., Montague, M. & Wong, Y. (1990) *The effects of procedural facilitation on story composition of learning disabled students.* Paper presented at Annual Meeting of the American Educational Research Association, San Francisco.

Graves, D. (1983) *Writing: Teachers and children at work*, Exeter: NH: Heinemann.

Graves, M. & Watts-Taffe, S. M. (2002) The place of word-consciousness in a research-based vocabulary programme, in A. Farstrup & S. J. Samuels (eds), *What research has to say about reading*, Newark, NJ: International Reading Association.

Gray, P., Miller, A. & Noakes, J. (1996) *Challenging behaviour in schools*, London: Routledge.

Greaney, K. T., Tunmer, W. E. & Chapman, J. (1997) The development of onset-rime sensitivity and analogical transfer in normal and poor readers, *Journal of Educational Psychology*, 89, pp. 645–51.

Greeno, J. G. (1998) The situativity of knowing, learning, and research, *American Psychologist*, 53(1), pp. 5–26.

Gregory, E. (1996) *Making sense of a new world*, London: Paul Chapman.

H. M. Treasury (2003) *Every child matters*, London: HMSO.

Hage, C. & Leybaert, J. (2006) The effect of cued speech on the development of spoken language, in P. Spencer & M. Marshark (eds), *Advances in the spoken language development of deaf and hard-of-hearing children*, New York: Oxford University Press.

Hall, J. (2008) Mental deficiency – changing the outlook, *The Psychologist*, 21(11), pp. 1006–7.

Hanko, G. (1994) Discouraged children: When praise does not help, *British Journal of Special Education*, 21(4), pp. 166–8.

Hannell, G. (2003) *Dyslexia*, London: David Fulton.

Hargreaves, D. H. (1967) *Social relations in a secondary school*, London: Routledge.

Harris, M. & Moreno, C. (2006) Speech reading and learning to read: A comparison of 8-year-old profoundly deaf children with good and poor reading ability, *Journal of Deaf Studies and Deaf Education*, 11, pp. 189–201.

Harris-Hendriks, J. & Figueroa, J. (1995) *Black in white: The Caribbean child in the UK*, London: Pitman.

Harrison, C. (1994) *Literature review: Methods of teaching reading*, Edinburgh: SOED.

Hatcher, J. & Snowling, M. (2002) The phonological representations hypothesis of dyslexia, in G. Reid & J. Wearmouth (eds), *Dyslexia and literacy: Research and practice*. Chichester: Wiley.

Hatcher, P. J. (2000) *Sound linkage*, London: Pearson.

Hattie, J. (2002) What are the attributes of excellent teachers? in B. Webber (ed.), *Teachers make a difference: What is the research evidence?* Proceedings of the New Zealand Association of Research in Education Conference, pp. 3–26, Wellington, New Zealand: NZARE.

Hayes, J. R. & Flower, L. S. (1986) Writing research and the writer, *American Psychologist*, 41(10), pp. 1106–13.

Helme, S. & Clarke, D. (2001) Identifying cognitive engagement in the mathematics classroom, *Mathematics Education Research Journal*, 13(2), 133–53.

Henderson, A. (1998) *Maths for the dyslexic: A practical guide*, London: David Fulton Publishers.

Hiebert, J., Carpenter, T., Fennema, E., Fuson, K. C., Wearne, D., Murray, H., Olivier, A. & Human, P. (1997) *Making sense: Teaching and learning mathematics with understanding*. Portsmouth, NH: Heinemann.

Hill, H., Rowan, B. & Ball, D. (2005) Effects of teachers' mathematical knowledge for teaching on student achievement, *American Educational Research Journal*, 42(2), 371–406.

Hobby, R. & Smith, F. (2002) *A national development agenda: What does it feel like to learn in our schools?* London: The Hay Group.

Holmes, J. (1993) *John Bowlby and attachment theory*, London: Routledge.

Howard-Jones, N. (1979) On the diagnostic term 'Down's disease', *Medical History* 23(1), pp. 102–4.

Hughes, M. (1986) *Children and number*, Oxford: Blackwell.

Irlen, H. (1991) *Reading by the colors*, New York: Avery.

Joffe, L. S. (1983) School mathematics and dyslexia: A matter of verbal labelling, generalisation, horses and carts, *Cambridge Journal of Education*, 13, pp. 22–7.

Joint Council for Qualifications (JCQ) (2014) *Adjustments for candidates with disabilities and learning difficulties*, London: JCQ.

Jordan, R. (1999) *Autistic spectrum disorders: An Introductory Handbook for Practitioners*, London: David Fulton.

Kanner, L. (1943) Autistic disturbances of affective contact, *Nervous Child*, 2, pp. 217–50.

Kilpatrick, J., Swafford, J. & Findell, B. (eds) (2001) *Adding it up: Helping children learn mathematics*, Washington, DC: National Academy Press.

Kirby, A. H. P. (1914) *Legislation for the feeble-minded*, London: John Bale, Sons & Danielsson.

Klin, A., Sparrow, S., Marans, W. D., Carter, A. & Volkmar, F. R. (2000) Assessment issues in children and adolescents with Asperger syndrome, in A. Klin, F. R. Volkmar & S. Sparrow (eds), *Asperger Syndrome*, New York: Guilford Press.

Korat, O. (2009) The effect of maternal teaching talk on children's emergent literacy as a function of type of activity and maternal education level, *Journal of Applied Developmental Psychology*, 30(1), pp. 34–42.

Kozulin, A. (2003) Psychological tools and mediated learning, in A. Kozulin, B. Gindis, V. S. Ageyev & S. M. Miller, *Vygotsky's educational theory in cultural context*, ch. 1, pp. 15–38, Cambridge: Cambridge University Press.

Krutetskii. V. A. (1976) *The psychology of mathematical abilities in school children* (trans. J. Kilpatric & I. Wirszup), Chicago: University of Chicago Press.

Kurp-Rice, P. (2015) Vibrating vest to let deaf people 'feel' sound, available at http://www.futurity.org/deaf-vest-vibration-senses-893352/

Lamb, B. (2009) *Report to the Secretary of State on the Lamb Inquiry Review of SEN and Disability Information*, London: DCSF.

Laming, Lord (2003) *The Victoria Climbié Inquiry. Report of an Inquiry by Lord Laming*, London: Crown.

Laming, Lord (2009) *The protection of children in England: A progress report*, London: HMSO.

Lampert, M. (1990) When the problem is not the question and the solution is not the answer: Mathematical knowing and teaching, *American Educational Research Journal*, 27(1), pp. 29–63.

Lave, J. (1993) The practice of learning, in S. Chaiklin & J. Lave (eds), *Understanding practice: Perspectives on activity and context*, Cambridge: Cambridge University Press.

LaVigna, G. W. & Donnellan, A. M. (1986) *Alternative to punishment: Solving behavior problems with non-aversive strategies*, New York: Irvington.

Lawrence, D. (1996) *Enhancing Self Esteem in the Classroom*, London: Paul Chapman.

Le Couteur, A., Lord, C. & Rutter, M. (2003) *Autism Diagnostic Interview-Revised (ADI-R)*, Los Angeles: Western Psychological Services.

Le Fevre, D., Moore, D. & Wilkinson, I. (2003) Tape-assisted reciprocal teaching: Cognitive bootstrapping for poor decoders, *British Journal of Educational Psychology*, 73(1), pp. 37–58.

Leadbetter, J. & Leadbetter, P. (1993) *Special Children: Meeting the challenge in the primary school*, London, Cassell.

Leinonen, E., Letts, C. & Smith, R. (2000) *Children's pragmatic communication difficulties*, London: Whurr.

Lennox, D. (1991) *See me after school*, London: David Fulton.

Lever, M. (2003) *Number activities for children with mathematical learning difficulties*, London: David Fulton.

Lewis, A. (2002) Accessing through research interviews the views of children with difficulties in learning, *Support for Learning*, 17(3), pp. 110–16.

Lewis, S. (1996) The reading achievement of a group of severely and profoundly hearing-impaired school leavers educated within a natural aural approach, *Journal of the British Association of Teachers of the Deaf*, 20, pp. 1–7.

Lifton, R. J. (2000) *The Nazi doctors: Medical killing and the psychology of genocide*, New York: Basic Books.

Lilley, C. (2004) A whole-school approach to ICT for children with physical disabilities, in L. Florian & J. Hegarty (eds), *ICT and special educational needs: A tool for inclusion*, Maidenhead: Open University Press.

Littleton, K. & Mercer, N. (2013) *Interthinking: Putting talk to work*, London: Routledge.

Lorenz, S. (1998) *Effective in-class support*, London: David Fulton.

Lowe, R. (1867) *Primary and classical education, an address delivered before the Philosophical Institution of Edinburgh, on Friday, November 1, 1867*, Edinburgh: Edmonston and Douglas.

Loxley, A. & Thomas, G. (2007) *Deconstructing special education and constructing inclusion*, Maidenhead: Open University Press.

MacArthur, C. & Graham, S. (1987) Learning disabled students' composing under three methods of text production: Handwriting, word processing, and dictation, *Journal of Special Education*, 21, pp. 22–42.

Macfarlane, A. (1997) The Hikairo rationale: Teaching students with emotional and behavioural difficulties: A bicultural approach, *Waikato Journal of Education*, 3, pp. 135–68.

Macfarlane, A. (2000a) Māori perspectives on development, in L. Bird & W. Drewery (eds), *Human development in Aotearoa: A journey through life*, Auckland: McGraw-Hill.

Macfarlane, A. (2000b) The value of Māori ecologies in special education, in D. Fraser, R. Moltzen& K. Ryba (eds), *Learners with special needs in Aotearoa New Zealand* (2nd edn), Palmerston North, New Zealand: Dunmore Press.

Maslow, A. (1943) A theory of human motivation, *Psychological Review*, 50(4), pp. 370–96.

Mason, H. (2001) *Visual impairment*, Tamworth: NASEN.

Mason, H., McCall, S., Arter, C., McLinden, M. & Stone, J. (1997) *Visual impairment: Access to education for children and young people*, London: Fulton.

McLeod, J. (1998) *An introduction to counselling* (2nd edn), Buckingham: Open University Press.

McNaughton, S. (2002) *Meeting of minds*, Wellington: Learning Media.

McNaughton, S., Glynn, T. & Robinson, V. (1987) *Pause, prompt and praise: Effective tutoring of remedial reading*, Birmingham: Positive Products.

Meichenbaum, D. & Turk, D. (1976) The cognitive-behavioural management of anxiety, anger and pain, in P. O. Davidson (ed.), *The behavioural management of anxiety, anger and pain*, New York, Brunner/Mazel.

Mencap (n.d.) *About profound and multiple learning disabilities*, London: Mencap.

Mencap (n.d.) *Communicating with People with Profound and Multiple Learning Disabilities*. http://www.jpaget.nhs.uk/media/186401/Communicating_with_people_with_PMLD__a_ guide__1_.pdf).

Merrett, F. (1985) *Encouragement works better than punishment*, Birmingham: Positive Products.

Mesibov, G. B., Shea, V. & Schopler, E. (2004) *The TEACCH approach to autism spectrum disorders*, London: Springer.

Miles, T. R. & Miles, E. (2004) *Dyslexia and mathematics* (2nd edn), London: Routledge.

Milgram, S. (1974) *Obedience to authority: An experimental view*, New York: Harper and Row.

Millar, S. V. & Nisbet, P. D. (1993) *Accelerated writing for people with disabilities*, Edinburgh: CALL Centre, University of Edinburgh.

Miller, O. & Ockleford, A. (2005) *Visual Needs*. London: Continuum.

Ministry of Education (1946) *Special educational treatment*, Ministry of Education Pamphlet No. 5, London: HMSO.

Ministry of Education (2005) *Effective literacy practice*, Wellington: Learning Media.

Ministry of Education (MoE) (1945) *The nation's schools*, London: MoE.

Ministry of Education (2006) *Effective literacy practice in years 5–8*, Wellington: Learning Media.

Mitchell, D. (2014) *What really works in special and inclusive education*, London: Routledge.

Moeller, M. P., Tomblin, J. B., Yoshinaga-Itano, C., Connor, C. & Jerger, S. (2007) Current state of knowledge: Language and literacy of children with hearing impairment, *Ear and Hearing*, 28, pp. 740–53.

Montgomery, J. K. & Kahn, N. L. (2003) You are going to be an author: Adolescent narratives as intervention, *Communication Disorders Quarterly*, 24(3), pp. 143–52.

Moore, D. (2004) Behaviour in context: Functional assessment of disruptive behaviour in classrooms, in J. Wearmouth, R. Richmond & T. Glynn (eds), *Addressing pupil behaviour: Responses at district, school and individual levels*, London: David Fulton.

Moores, D. (2001) *Educating the deaf*, Boston: Houghton Mifflin.

Moores, D. (2008) Research in Bi-Bi instruction, *American Annals of the Deaf*, 153, pp. 3–4.

Morris, J. K., Wald, N. J., Mutton, D. E. & Alberman, E. (2003) Comparison of models of maternal age-specific risk for Down syndrome live births, *Prenatal Diagnosis*, 23(3), pp. 252–8.

Mosley, J. (1996) *Quality circle time in the primary classroom: Your essential guide to enhancing self-esteem, self-discipline and positive relationships*, Cambridge: LDA.

Murphy, S. (2002) Literacy assessment and the politics of identity, in J. Soler, J. Wearmouth & G. Reid (eds), *Contextualising difficulties in literacy development: Exploring politics, culture, ethnicity and ethics*, ch. 7, pp. 87–101, London: Routledge.

Myhill, D. & Warren, P. (2005) Scaffolds or straitjackets: Critical moments in classroom discourse, *Educational Review*, 57(1), pp. 55–69.

Nash, R. & Harker, R. (2002) How are school composition effects and peer group mechanisms related? A theoretical and methodological discussion from the Progress at School Project, *New Zealand Journal of Educational Studies*, 37(2), pp. 171–90.

National Assembly of Wales (NAW) (2004) *Special Educational Needs Code of Practice*, Cardiff: NAW.

National Association of Head Teachers (2003) *Policy paper on special schools*, London: NAHT.

National Autistic Society (2016) About autism. http://www.autism.org.uk/about/diagnosis. aspx, accessed 9 March 2016.

National Autistic Society (2016) What is Asperger Syndrome? http://www.autism.org.uk/ about/what-is/asperger.aspx, accessed 9 March 2016.

National Council for Educational Technology (NCET) (1992) *Competencies in information technology*, Coventry: NCET.

National Council for Educational Technology (NCET) (1995) *Access technology: Making the right choice*, Coventry: NCET.

National Deaf Children's Society (NDCS) (2008) *Acoustics toolkit*, London: NDCS.

National Deaf Children's Society (NDCS) (2010) *Communicating with your deaf child*, London: NDCS.

National Health Service (NHS) (2015) Hearing loss – diagnosis. http://www.nhs.uk/ Conditions/Hearing-impairment/Pages/Diagnosis.aspx, accessed 9 March 2016.

National Institute for Health and Care Excellence (NICE) (2011) *Autism in under 19s: Recognition, referral and diagnosis*, London: NICE.

National Institute of Child Health and Human Development (2000) *Report of the National Reading Panel. Teaching children to read: An evidence-based assessment of the scientific research literature on reading and its implications for reading instruction* (NIH Publication No. 00-4769), Washington, DC: US Government Printing Office.

National Institute of Neurological Disorders and Stroke (NINDS) (2005) *Tourette syndrome fact sheet*, Bethesda, MD: NINDS.

Neale, M. D. (1999) *The Neale Analysis of reading ability* (3rd edn), London: GL Assessment.

Nethercott, K. (2015) Understanding the use of the Common Assessment Framework exploring the implications for frontline professionals, unpublished PhD thesis, Luton: University of Bedfordshire.

Newell, A. F. & Beattie, L. (1991) The use of lexical and spelling aids with dyslexics, in C. H. Singleton (ed.), *Computers and Literacy Skills*, Hull: Dyslexia Computer Resource Centre, University of Hull.

Nicholson, T. (2000) *Reading and writing on the wall: Debates, challenges and opportunities in the teaching of reading*, Palmerston North: Dunmore Press.

Nicholson, T. & Tan, A. (1997) Flashcards revisited: Training poor readers to read words faster improves their comprehension of text, *Journal of Educational Psychology*, 89, pp. 276–88.

Noddings, N. (1995), *Philosophy of education*, Oxford: Westview Press.

Norbury, C. F. & Bishop, D. V. M. (2003), Narrative skills in children with communication impairments, *International Journal of Language and Communication Impairments*, (38), pp. 287–313.

Norwich, B., Cooper, P. & Maras, P. (2002) Attentional and activity difficulties: Findings from a national study, *Support for Learning*, 17(4), pp. 182–6.

Norwich, B. & Lewis, A. (2001) Mapping a pedagogy for special educational needs, *British Educational Research Journal*, 27(3), pp. 313–29.

Nunes, T., Bryant, P. & Bindman, M. (1997) Morphological spelling strategies: Developmental stages and processes, *Developmental Psychology*, 33, pp. 637–49.

Nurture Group Network (2016) *History*, https://nurturegroups.org/about-us/history, accessed 9 March 2016.

O'Connor, M. C. (1998) Language socialisation in the mathematics classroom: Discourse practices and mathematical thinking, in M. Lampert & M. Blunk (eds), *Talking mathematics in school: Studies of teaching and learning*, pp. 17–55, Cambridge: Cambridge University Press.

Office for Standards in Education (Ofsted) (2001), *Improving attendance and behaviour in secondary schools*, London: Ofsted.

Office for Standards in Education (Ofsted) (2010) *The special educational needs and disability review*, London: Ofsted.

Office for Standards in Education (Ofsted) (2011) *Safeguarding in schools: Best practice*, London: Ofsted.

Office for Standards in Education (Ofsted) (2015) *School inspection handbook*, Manchester: Ofsted.

Oliphant, J. (2006) Empowerment and debilitation in the educational experience of the blind in nineteenth-century England and Scotland, *History of Education*, 35(1), pp. 47–68.

Olweus, D. (1978) *Aggression in the schools: Bullies and whipping boys*, New York: Wiley.

Olweus, D. (1993) *Bullying at school: What we know and what we can do*, Oxford: Blackwell.

Olweus, D. (1999) Sweden, in P. K. Smith, Y. Morita, J. Junger-Tas, D. Olweus, R. Catalano & P. Slee (eds), *The nature of school bullying: A cross-national perspective*, London: Routledge.

Open University (2000) Audio interview in *E831 professional development for special educational needs co-ordinators*, Milton Keynes: Open University.

Open University (2002) Audio interview in *E801 difficulties in literacy development*, Milton Keynes: Open University.

Padden, C. & Gunsals, D. (2003) How the alphabet came to be used in a sign language, *Sign Language Studies*, 4, pp. 1–13.

Palincsar, A. S. (1998) Social constructivist perspectives on teaching and learning, *Annual Review of Psychology* (49), pp. 345–75.

Palincsar, A. S. & Brown, A. L. (1984) Reciprocal teaching of comprehension – fostering- and comprehension-monitoring activities, *Cognition and Instruction*, 1(2), pp. 117–75.

Park, K. (1997) How do objects become objects of reference? *British Journal of Special Education*, 24(3), pp. 108–14.

Paveley, S. (2002) Inclusion and the Web: Strategies to improve access, in C. Abbott (ed.), *Special educational needs and the Internet: Issues for the inclusive classroom*, London: RoutledgeFalmer.

Peacey, N. & Wearmouth, J. (2007) *A guide to special educational needs for trainee teachers*, London: TDA.

Pearson, P. D., Roehler, L. R., Doel, J. A. & Duffy, G. G. (1992) Developing expertise in reading comprehension, in S. Samuels & A. Farstrup (eds), *What research has to say about reading instruction* (2nd edn), pp. 145–99, Newark, DE: International Reading Association.

Peeters, T. & Gilberg, C. (1999), in I. Roth (2002) The autistic spectrum: From theory to practice, in N. Brace and H. Westcott (eds), *Applying Psychology*, pp. 243–315, Milton Keynes: Open University.

Perso, T. (2003) School mathematics and its impact on cultural diversity, *Australian Mathematics Teacher*, 59(2), pp. 10–16.

Piacentini, J., Woods, D. W., Scahill, L., Wilhelm, S., Peterson, A. L., Chang, S., Ginsburg, G. S., Deckersbach, T., Dziura, J., Levi-Pearl, S. & Walkup, J. (2010) Behavior therapy for children with Tourette disorder, *Journal of the American Medical Association*, 303(19), pp. 1929–37.

Piaget, J. (1954) *Construction of reality in the child*, New York: Basic Books.

Piaget, J. (1964) Cognitive development in children, *Journal of Research in Science Teaching*, 2(3), pp. 176–86.

Piaget, J. (1969) *The child's conception of time*, London: RKP.

Piaget, J. & Inhelder, B. (2016) *Memory and intelligence*, London: Psychology Press.

Pickles, P (2001) Therapeutic provision in mainstream curricula, in J. Wearmouth (ed.), *Special educational provision in the context of inclusion: Policy & practice in schools*, ch. 16, pp. 291–304, London: Fulton.

Pitchford, M. (2004) An introduction to multi-element planning for primary aged children, in J. Wearmouth, R. C. Richmond & T. Glynn (eds), *Addressing pupils' behaviour: Responses at district, school and individual levels*, ch. 19, pp. 310–27, London: Fulton.

Pohlschmidt, M. & Meadowcroft, R. (2010) *Muscle disease: The impact – incidence and prevalence of neuromuscular conditions in the UK*, London: Muscular Dystrophy Campaign.

Pollard, A. (2002) *Reflective teaching: Effective and evidence-informed professional practice*, London: Continuum.

Porter, J., Ouvry, C., Morgan, M. & Downs, C. (2001) Interpreting the communication of people with profound and multiple learning difficulties, *British Journal of Learning Disabilities*, 29(1), pp. 12–16.

Poulou, M. & Norwich, B. (2002) Cognitive, emotional and behavioural responses to students with emotional and behavioural difficulties: A model of decision-making, *British Educational Research Journal*, 28(1), pp. 111–38.

Preece, D. (2002), Consultation with children with autistic spectrum disorders about their experience of short-term residential care, *British Journal of Learning Disabilities*, 30 (3), pp. 97–104.

Pressley, M. (2002) Comprehension strategies instruction: A turn-of-the-century status report, in C. C. Block & M. Pressley (eds), *Comprehension instruction: Research-based best practices*, pp. 11–27, New York: Guilford.

Randall, P. E. (1991) *The prevention of school-based bullying*, Hull: University of Hull.

Rapin, I. & Allen, D. A. (1998) The semantic-pragmatic deficit disorder: Classification issues, *International Journal of Language & Communication Disorders*, 33(1), pp. 82–7.

Reason, R. & Boote, R. (1994) *Helping children with reading and spelling*, London: Routledge.

Reder, P. & Duncan, S. (2003) Understanding communication in child protection networks, *Child Abuse Review*, 12(2), pp. 82–100.

Restorative Practices Development Team (2003) *Restorative practices for schools*, Hamilton, New Zealand: University of Waikato.

Richmond, W. K. (1978) *Education in Britain since 1944*, London: Routledge.

Riddick, B. (1996) *Living with Dyslexia*, London and New York: Routledge.

Riddick, B., Wolfe, J. & Lumsdon, D. (2002) *Dyslexia: A practical guide for teachers and parents*, London: David Fulton.

Rigby, K. (1997) What children tell us about bullying in schools, *Children Australia*, 22(2), pp. 28–34.

Rigby, K. (2002) *New Perspectives on Bullying*, London, Jessica Kingsley.

Roaf, C. & Lloyd, C. (1995) Multi-agency work with young people in difficulty, *Social Care Research Findings* No. 68, June 1995, York: Joseph Rowntree Foundation.

Rochdale Borough Safeguarding Children Board (RBSCB) (2012) *Review of multi-agency responses to the sexual exploitation of children*, Rochdale: The Rochdale Borough Safeguarding Children Board.

Rogers, B. (1994) Teaching positive behaviour in behaviourally disordered students in primary schools, *Support for Learning*, 9(4), pp. 166–70.

Rogers, B. (2003) *Behaviour recovery*, Melbourne, Victoria: ACER Press.

Rogers, B. (2013) Communicating with children in the classroom, in T. Cole, H. Daniels & J. Visser (eds), *The Routledge international companion to emotional and behavioural difficulties*, ch. 26, pp. 237–45, London: Routledge.

Rogers, C. R. (1942) *Counselling and psychotherapy*, Boston: Houghton Mifflin.

Rogers, C. R. (1992) The necessary and sufficient conditions of therapeutic personality change, *Journal of Consulting and Clinical Psychology*, 60(6), pp. 827–32.

Rogers, J. (2007) Cardinal number and its representation: Skills, concepts and contexts, *Early Childhood Education and Care*, 178(2), pp. 211–25.

Rogers, W. (1994a) Behaviour recovery: A whole school approach for behaviourally disordered children, Melbourne: Australian Council for Educational Research.

Rogers, W. (1994b) *The language of discipline*, Plymouth: Northcote House.

Rogoff, B. (1990) *Apprenticeship in thinking: Cognitive development in social context*, New York: Oxford University Press.

Rose, J. (2009) *Identifying and teaching children and young people with dyslexia and literacy difficulties*, London: DCFS.

Rosenthal, R. & Jacobson, L. (1968) *Pygmalion in the classroom*, New York: Holt, Rinehart and Winston.

Royal College of Psychiatrists (2016) *Mental health and growing up factsheet: Cognitive behavioural therapy (CBT). Information for young people*, London: Royal College of Psychiatrists.

Royal National Institute for the Blind (RNIB) (2008) *See it right checklist*, London: RNIB.

Royal National Institute for the Deaf (RNID) (2004) *Inclusion strategies*, London: RNID.

Ruthven, K. (2002) Assessment in mathematics education, in L. Haggarty (ed.), *Teaching mathematics in secondary schools*, pp. 176–91, London: RoutledgeFalmer.

Rutter, M. (1966) *Children of sick parents*, Oxford: Oxford University Press.

Rutter, M., Maughan, B., Mortimore, P. & Ouston, J. (1979) *Fifteen thousand hours: Secondary schools and their effects on children*, London, Open Books.

Rutter, M., Le Couteur, A. & Lord, C. (2003) *ADI-R: The Autism Diagnostic Interview-Revised*, Los Angeles, CA: Western Psychological Services.

Rutter, M., Tizard, J. & Whitmore, K. (1970) *Education, health and behaviour*, London: Longman.

Samuels, S. J. (2002) Reading fluency: Its development and assessment, in S. Samuels & A. Farstrup (eds), *What research has to say about reading instruction*, Newark, DE: International Reading Association.

Sarbin, T. (1986) *Narrative psychology: The storied nature of human conduct*, New York: Praeger.

Schön, D. (1983) *The reflective practitioner: How professionals think in action*, New York: Basic Books.

Schön, D. (1987) *Educating the reflective practitioner*, London: Jossey-Bass.

Schweigert, F. J. (1999) Moral behaviour in victim offender conferencing, *Criminal Justice Ethics*, Summer/Fall 1999, pp. 29–40.

Scottish Executive Education Department (SEED) (2004) *Curriculum for excellence*, Edinburgh: Scottish Executive.

Scottish Government (2010) *Supporting children's learning code of practice* (revised), Edinburgh: Scottish Government.

Scottish Government (2014) *Planning improvements for disabled pupils' access to education*, Edinburgh: Scottish Government.

Seligman, M. E. P. (1975) *Helplessness: On depression, development, and death*, San Francisco: W. H. Freeman.

Selikowitz, M. (2008) *Down syndrome*, Oxford: Oxford University Press.

Selinger, M., Littleton, K., Kirkwood, A., Wearmouth, J. et al. (1998) *Educational Internet service providers project: Final evaluation report*. Final report to NCET.

Shapiro, S. & Cole, L. (1994) *Behaviour change in the classroom: Self-management interventions*, New York, Gulliford Press.

Sharron, H. (1995) Behaviour drugs – headteachers speak out, *Special Children*, April, pp. 10–13.

Sheehy, K. (2004) Approaches to autism, in J. Wearmouth, R. C. Richmond & T. Glynn (eds), *Addressing pupils' behaviour: Responses at district, school and individual levels*, pp. 338–56. London: Fulton.

Shuayb, M. & O'Donnell, S. (2008) *Primary Review Research Survey 1/2 Aims and Values in Primary Education: England and other countries*, Cambridge: Cambridge University Primary Review.

Shulman, L. & Shulman, J. (2004) How and what teachers learn: A shifting perspective, *Journal of Curriculum Studies*, 36(2), pp. 257–71.

Simon, B. (1974) *The two nations and the educational structure 1780–1870*, London: Lawrence and Wishart.

Singleton, C. (1991) *Computers and literacy skills*, Hull: BDA.

Singleton, C. (2002) Cognitive factors and implications for literacy, in G. Reid & J. Wearmouth (eds), *Dyslexia and literacy: Research and practice*, Chichester: Wiley.

Singleton, C. & Simmons, F. (2001) Evaluation of 'Wordshark', *British Journal of Educational Technology*, 32(3), pp. 317–30.

Skinner, B. F. (1938) *The behavior of organisms*, New York: Appleton Century Crofts.

Skinner, B. F. (1953) *Science and human behaviour*, New York: Macmillan.

Skinner, E. A. & Belmont, M. J. (1993) Motivation in the classroom: Reciprocal effects of teacher behavior and student engagement across the school year, *Journal of Educational Psychology*, 85(4), pp. 571–81.

Slee, P. T. (1995) Peer victimization and its relationship to depression among Australian primary school students, *Personality and Individual Differences*, 18(1), pp. 57–62.

Sleeter, C. (2011) *Professional development for culturally responsive and relationship-based pedagogy*, New York: Peter Lang.

Smith, J. & Elley, W. (1997) *How children learn to write*, New Zealand: Longman.

Smith, P. K. & Sharp, S. (1994) *School bullying: Insights and perspectives*, London: Routledge.

Snowling, M. J. (2000) *Dyslexia* (2nd edn), Oxford: Blackwell.

Spencer, P. E. & Marschark, M. (eds) (2006) *Advances in the spoken language development of deaf and hard-of-hearing children*, New York: Oxford University Press.

Spencer, P. E. & Marschark, M. (2010) *Evidence-based practice in educating deaf and hard-of-hearing students*, Oxford: Oxford University Press.

Spörer, N., Brunstein, J. C. & Kieschke, U. L. F. (2009) Improving students' reading comprehension skills: Effects of strategy instruction and reciprocal teaching, *Learning and Instruction*, 19, pp. 272–86.

Sproson, B. (2004) Some do and some don't: Teacher effectiveness in managing behaviour, in J. Wearmouth, T. Glynn, R. C. Richmond & M. Berryman (eds), *Inclusion and behaviour management in schools*, ch. 17, London: David Fulton.

Stahl, S. (1998) Saying the 'p' word: Guidelines for exemplary phonics instruction, in R. Allington (ed.), *Teaching struggling readers: Articles from The Reading Teacher*, Newark: International Reading Association.

Stanovich, K. (2000) *Progress in understanding reading: Scientific foundations and new frontiers*, London: The Guilford Press.

Stipek, D., Salmon, J. M., Givvin, K. B., Kazemi, E., Saxe, G. & MacGyvers, V. L. (1998) The value (and convergence) of practices suggested by motivation research and promoted by mathematics education reformers, *Journal for Research in Mathematics Education*, 29, pp. 465–88.

Strouse Watt, W. (2003) *How visual acuity is measured*, http://www.mdsupport.org/library/acuity.html, accessed 28 February 2016.

Sullivan, P., Mousley, J. & Zevenbergen, R. (2003) The context of mathematics tasks and the context of the classroom: Are we including all students? *Mathematics Education Research Journal*, 15(2), pp. 107–21.

Summerfield, A./Department for Education and Science (DES) (1968) *Psychologists in the education services: Report of the working party (the Summerfield Report)*, London: HMSO.

Tate, R., Smeeth, L., Evans, J. & Fletcher, A. (2008) *The prevalence of visual impairment in the UK: A review of the literature*, http://www.vision2020uk.org.uk/the-prevalence-of-visual-impairment-in-the-uk-a-review-of-the-literature/, accessed 28 February 2016.

Taylor, J. & Daniel, B. (1999) Interagency practice in children with non-organic failure to thrive: Is there a gap between health and social care? *Child Abuse Review*, 8(5), pp. 325–8.

Taylor, K. (2007) The participation of children with multi-sensory impairment in person-centred planning, *British Journal of Special Education*, 34(4), pp. 204–11.

Thomson, M. (1998) *The problem of mental deficiency: Eugenics, democracy and social policy in Britain, c.1870–1959*, Oxford: Clarendon Press.

Tomlinson, S. (1988) Why Johnny can't read: Critical theory and special education, *European Journal of Special Needs Education*, 3(1), pp. 45–58.

Tomlinson, S. (2001) Sociological perspectives on special and inclusive education, *Support for Learning*, 16(4), pp. 191–2.

Topping, K. (1995) *Paired reading, spelling and writing: The handbook for teachers and parents*, London: Cassell.

Topping, K. (1996) Tutoring systems for family literacy, in S. Wolfendale & K. Topping (eds), *Family involvement in literacy*, London: Cassell.

Topping, K. (2001) *Thinking, reading, writing*, London: Continuum.

Topping, K., Duran, D. & Van Keer, H. (2015) *Using peer tutoring to improve reading skills*, London: Routledge.

Tribble, C. (1996) *Writing*, Oxford: Oxford University Press.

Underwood, J. E. A. (1955) *Report of the Committee on Maladjusted Children*, London: HMSO.

Unison (2013) *The evident value of teaching assistants*, https://www.unison.org.uk/content/uploads/2013/06/Briefings-and-CircularsEVIDENT-VALUE-OF-TEACHING-ASSISTANTS-Autosaved3.pdf, accessed 28 February 2016.

United Nations (2007) 61/106 *Convention on the rights of persons with disabilities*, Geneva: UN.

United Nations Educational, Scientific and Cultural Organization (UNESCO, 2006) *ICTs in education for people with special needs*, Moscow: UNESCO Institute for Information Technologies in Education.

Vygotsky, L. S. (1962) *Thought and language*, Cambridge, MA: MIT Press.

Vygotsky, L. S. (1978) *Mind in society: The development of higher psychological processes*, Cambridge, MA: Harvard University Press.

Vygotsky, L. S. (1981) The genesis of higher mental functions, in J. W. Wertsch (ed.), *The concept of activity in Soviet psychology*, pp. 144–88, Armonk, NY: Sharpe.

Walshaw, M. (2004) The pedagogical encounter in postmodern times: Learning from Lacan, in M. Walshaw (ed.), *Mathematics education within the postmodern*, pp. 121–40, Greenwich, CT: Information Age.

Warfield, J. (2001) Where mathematics content knowledge matters, in T. Wood, B. Scott-Nelson & J. Warfield (eds), *Beyond classical pedagogy: Teaching elementary school mathematics*, pp. 135–55, Mahwah, NJ: Lawrence Erlbaum Associates.

Warnock Report, The (1978) *Special educational needs, Report of the Committee of Enquiry into the education of handicapped children and young people*, Cmnd. 7212. Department of Education and Science, London: HMSO.

Waterland, L. (1985) *Read with me*, Strand, UK: Thimble Press.

Watkins, C. & Wagner, P. (1995) School behaviour and special educational needs – what's the link? in *National Children's Bureau, Discussion Papers 1: Schools' special educational needs policies pack*, London: NCB.

Watkins, C. & Wagner, P. (2000) *Improving school behaviour*, London: Paul Chapman.

Watson, A. & de Geest, E. (2005) Principled teaching for deep progress: Improving mathematical learning beyond methods and materials, *Educational Studies in Mathematics*, 58, pp. 209–34.

Wearmouth, J. (1986) Unpublished Masters thesis, Institute of Education, London University.

Wearmouth, J. (1996) Registering special needs – for what purpose? *Support for Learning*, 11 (3), pp. 118–23.

Wearmouth, J. (2000) *Co-ordinating special educational provision: Meeting the challenges in schools*, London: Hodder.

Wearmouth, J. (2004) Talking Stones: An interview technique for disaffected young people, *Journal of Pastoral Care in Education*, 22(2), pp. 7–13.

Wearmouth, J. (2008) Testing, assessment and literacy: A view from England, *Curriculum Perspectives*, 28(3), pp. 77–81.

Wearmouth, J. (2009) *A beginning teacher's guide to special educational needs*, Buckingham: Open University Press.

Wearmouth, J. (2004) Learning from 'James': Lessons about policy and practice for literacy difficulties in schools' special educational provision, *British Journal of Special Education*, 31(2), pp. 60–7.

Wearmouth, J. (2012) *Special educational needs: The basics*, London: RoutledgeFalmer.

Wearmouth, J. (2015) Unit Guide, *Addressing difficulties in literacy and dyslexia*, Bedford: University of Bedfordshire.

Wearmouth, J. (2016a) *Effective SENCo: Meeting the challenge*, Maidenhead: McGraw Hill.

Wearmouth, J. (2016b) *Special educational needs and disability: The basics*, London: Routledge.

Wearmouth, J. & Berryman, M. (2011) Family and community support for addressing difficulties in literacy, in C. Wyatt-Smith, J. Elkins & E. Gunn (eds), *Multiple perspectives on difficulties in learning literacy and numeracy*, London: Springer.

Wearmouth, J., Glynn, T. & Berryman, M. (2005) *Perspectives on student behaviour in schools: Exploring theory and developing practice*, London: Routledge.

Wearmouth, J., McKinney, R. & Glynn, T. (2007) Restorative justice: Two examples from New Zealand schools, *British Journal of Special Education*, 34(4), pp. 196–203.

Weavers, J. (2003) Dyslexia and mathematics, in M. Thomson (ed.), *Dyslexia included*, pp 33–45, London: Fulton.

Webster, R., Russell, A. & Blatchford, P. (2016) *Maximising the impact of teaching assistants: Guidance for school leaders and teachers* (2nd edn), Oxon: Routledge.

Wenger, E. (1998) *Communities of practice: Learning, meaning and identity*, New York: Cambridge University Press.

Westby, C. (1991) Learning to talk – talking to learn: Oral-literate language difference, in C. S. Simon (ed.), *Communication skills and classroom success*, pp.181–218, San Diego: College Hill.

Wheatley, C. L. & Wheatley, G. H. (1979) Developing spatial ability, *Mathematics in school*, 8, pp. 10–11.

Whitehead, D. (1993) *Factual writing think sheets*, Hamilton, New Zealand: Seaforth Education.

Wiliam, D. (1999) Formative assessment in mathematics part 2: Feedback. *Equals*, 5(3), pp. 8–11.

Wilkins, A. J., Evans, B. J. W., Brown, J. A., Busby, A. E., Wingfield, A. E., Jeanes, R. L. & Bald, J. (1994) Double-masked placebo-controlled trial of precision spectral filters in children who use coloured overlays, *Ophthalmic and Physiological Optics*, 14, pp. 365–70.

Wilkins, M. & Ertmer, D. J. (2002) Introducing young children who are deaf or hard of hearing to spoken language, *Language, Speech and Hearing Services in Schools*, 33, pp. 196–204.

Wilkinson, E. (1947) *The new secondary education*, London: HMSO.

Williams, H. & Birmingham City Council Education Department (2004) A three-level approach to intervention for individual behaviour difficulties, in J. Wearmouth, R. C. Richmond & T. Glynn (eds), *Addressing pupils' behaviour: Responses at district, school and individual levels*, ch. 17, pp. 268–86, London: Fulton.

Williams, H. & Birmingham City Council Education Department (1998) *Behaviour in schools: Framework for intervention*, Birmingham: Birmingham City Council Education Department.

Williams, P. (2015) Eliciting web site preferences of people with learning disabilities, *Journal of Research in Special Educational Needs*, doi:10.1111/1471–3802.12099.

Wilson, A. & Charlton, K. (1997) *Making partnerships work: A practical guide for the public, private, voluntary and community sectors*, York: Joseph Rowntree Foundation.

Wing, L. (1996) *The autistic spectrum: A guide for parent and professionals*, London: Constable.

Wing, L. & Gould, J. (1979) Severe impairments of social interaction and associated abnormalities in children: Epidemiology and classification, *Journal of Autism and Developmental Disorders*, 9, pp. 11–29.

Wood, D., Bruner, J. & Ross, G. (1976) The role of tutoring in problem solving, *Journal of Child Psychology and Psychiatry*, 17, pp. 89–100.

Wood, K. C., Smith, H. & Grossniklaus, D. (2001) Piaget's stages of cognitive development, in M. Orey (ed.), *Emerging perspectives on learning, teaching, and technology*, GA: University of Georgia.

Woodhouse, J. (1982) Eugenics and the feeble-minded: The Parliamentary debates of 1912–14, *History of Education*, 11(2), pp. 13.

World Health Organization (WHO) (1994) *The International Statistical Classification of Diseases – ICD-10*, Geneva: WHO.

Wragg, E. C., Wragg, C. M., Haynes, G. S. & Chamberlain, R. P. (1998) *Improving literacy in the primary school*, London: Routledge.

Wray, D. (2002) Metacognition and literacy, in G. Reid & J. Wearmouth (eds), *Dyslexia and literacy: Research and practice*, Chichester: Wiley.

Wright, D. & Digby, A. (1996) *From idiocy to mental deficiency*, London: Routledge.

Yoshinaga-Itano, C. (2003) From screening to early identification and intervention: Discovering predictors to successful outcomes for children with significant hearing loss, *Journal of Deaf Studies and Deaf Education*, 8, pp. 11–30.

Ysseldyke, J. E. & Christenson, S. L. (1987) *The instructional environment scale (TIES)*, Austin, TX: Pro-Ed.

Ysseldyke, J. E. & Christenson, S. L. (1993) *TIES-II: The instructional environment system – II*, Longmont, CO: Sopris West.

Yurdakul, N. S., Ugurlu, S. & Maden, A. (2006) Strabismus in Down syndrome, *Journal of Pediatric Ophthalmology and Strabismus*, 43(1), pp. 27–30.

Zevenbergen, R., Mousley, J. & Sullivan, P. (2004) Making the pedagogic relay inclusive for indigenous Australian students in mathematics classrooms, *International Journal of Inclusive Education*, 8(4), pp. 391–405.

Index